Perennials for the

Western Garden

The Amateur Gardener's Fieldbook for the Growing of Perennials, Biennials and Bulbs

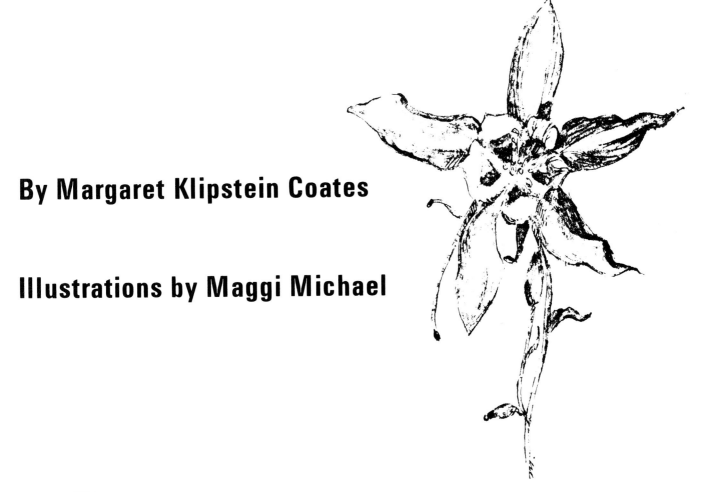

By Margaret Klipstein Coates

Illustrations by Maggi Michael

PRUETT **P** PUBLISHING COMPANY

Library of Congress Cataloging in Publication Data

Coates, Margaret Klipstein, 1919-
    Perennials for the western garden.

    Bibliography: p.
    Includes index.
    1. Perennials — The West. 2. Wild flower gardening — The West. 3. Biennials (Plants) — The West. 4. Bulbs — The West. I. Title.

SB434.C6   635.9'32   76-14356
ISBN 0-87108-088-5

First Edition
1 2 3 4 5 6 7 8 9

Printed in the United States of America

To my sister Kathryn
with love

Preface

Little acknowledgment is given in gardening journals and texts to that poor soul who loves a garden, yet lives in that area of the American continent euphemistically designated as the intermountain region. High plateau and mountain valley. Thin soils. Wind. And it never rains when you need it.

So with friends and fellow idiots in mind, I herein present the notes and culture data compiled during the past twenty years or more (I hate to think of the "more") of bucking the odds on a cattle ranch in Wyoming, 5,800 feet elevation, on a mountain slope. Rainfall, 12 inches (the Chamber of Commerce exaggerates). Wind velocity (yes!). I have concentrated on perennials because (1) they are hardy and able to withstand our perverse weather; and (2) I am basically lazy, and when I put all that effort into raising a plant to maturity, I want it to stick around for a while.

There are certain truths we must face in our highlands if we want more in the way of landscaping than a lawn and a few trees and shrubs. Our gardens will be quite rigidly controled — a microenvironment. so to speak. We must protect it from the wind, add humus to the thin soil, and always, always irrigate. There is no other way. And it all adds up to a lot of work.

Not all of the perennials listed will succeed for all of my fellow highlanders; however, by knowing what they individually require, many will. I have tried all of the genera listed but not all of the species or varieties. It is very possible all of them grow more luxuriantly and bloom more profusely elsewhere, but surely, are never more appreciated.

The growing season may be more accurately predicted in time and length by the rise in elevation than the time of year, and a high country gardener takes that into consideration in his choice of material. Plants that flower in fall will usually freeze before coming into full bloom. Only the earliest of chrysanthemums will make a show year after year for me; the later blooming ones I seldom see. (Some day I shall harden my heart, close my eyes, and yank them out.) Gardeners in towns and those living at lower elevations often enjoy a longer season, and so one cannot make a blanket dictum. The last word will rest with you, the home gardener. Unfortunately, there are few nurseries in the intermountain region that raise their own plant material, and so gardeners from that area who want something out of the usual will have to collect and grow their own.

It is said — and justly so — that plants that will grow in Wyoming, will grow anywhere. With that negative wit in mind and acting upon the advice of friends who have made horticulture their profession, I would like to commend my hard won research on gardening in the highlands to those who make up the larger audience which resides in northern climes. All of the perennials I have tried will "make themselves to home" wherever you live, for perennials are like that — very adaptable. There's only one difference (and oh, what a big one); you won't have to work as hard as I do — watering, watering.

I have included data on the collection and growing of many of our native wild flowers which may seem at variance to the well-meant admonitions of native plants in their habitat. However, looking around you, and tell me — is this not a late hour, indeed, for that sort of advice? How much preservation is accomplished when the earth-moving machines move in?

When I see what is happening all around me — the displacement, the unthinking, uncaring disregard for the earth's surface and all that grows upon it — yes, even Wyoming is not sacrosanct — truly, I despair.

Perhaps in some small way, this manual may be some help. It is a working fieldbook; meant to be used in as practical a manner and with the common sense with which one uses a cookbook. Take it with you into the garden, into the greenhouse, or on that field trip. Use it — and good luck!

Margaret Klipstein Coates
Field Creek Ranch
Casper, Wyoming

Contents

I
Propagation
of
Perennials

Propagation by Seed

All gardeners, sooner or later, gather equipment for starting seeds. Some of the more necessary items which I have collected and used over the years (and would be hard put to do without) are as follows:

Jiffy seed flats: they come in varying sizes—I find the 7½ x 5½ x 2¼ inches size to be the handiest. They are made of a red fiber and are easily sterilized in the oven.

Pano-drench: a 1-ounce bottle goes a long way. Measuring is simpler if an eye-dropper cap is substituted for the regular cap (it fits). This is a soil drench (safe to use) that controls damp-off fungi. The fungi are always present in the soil, and they cause the emerging seedlings to rot off at the soil line. The proportions recommended are 2 teaspoons to 3 gallons of water. The soil may be used immediately after treatment. I use this solution for the initial watering of the seed flats.

Arasan: this is a powdered fungicide. Put the tiniest pinch of this powder in the seed packet, shake so the seed is well coated, and then sow.

Electric heating cable: a 6-foot cable heats 3 square feet and is adequate for most needs. I also have one 24-foot cable which heats about 8 square feet of greenhouse bench. The latter is used as much for warding off disaster from an unpredicted cold snap as an aid to germination. The cables have a built-in thermostat with a fixed temperature setting of 70 degrees. It is usually used as an aid to germinating seeds requiring temperatures of 65 to 70 degrees. Place the seed flat directly on top of the cable, making sure there is only one strand of cable under each container and lengthwise of it. (More than one cable would be too much heat.) I use it even in summer, plugging it in late in the evening, for our nights are always cool.

Rubber hand sprinkler: a squeeze bulb with a fine spray head is excellent for watering the seed flats. The spray will not disturb the surface unduly.

Peat pots: I prefer the 2¼-inch square pot. It holds enough soil in case setting out in spring is delayed, and the square shape takes up less room in a flat or on the bench. Into these are transplanted the seedlings when the plants are large enough to remove from the flats. They are also used to sow directly into, for some plants do not take kindly to being disturbed at any time in their lives.

Egg carton: These are excellent for starting seeds and transplanting seedlings into. Cut the cover off, place the cupped portion into the cover, and you have a waterproof tray. Be sure to poke a hole in each little cup for drainage. These are just the right width to fit on a window sill. Gently pry out the massed ball of roots when setting out the plants; the containers will not disintegrate in the soil as the peat pots do.

Seedling Mix and Method

I use an 18 x 24-inch redwood flat for mixing. It is large enough, sturdy, and the sides prevent the soil mix from spilling (before I acquired a greenhouse, the kitchen table was my potting bench, and my largest metal mixing bowl was pressed into service for blending).

This first method is one I use most frequently: put into the flat the following proportions (using a 1- or 2-quart coffee can as a measure).

> 1 part garden soil
> 1 part sphagnum moss
> ½ part perlite
> ½ part vermiculite

Moisten with a sprinkling can and mix well, eliminating lumps. There are mixes (and you will find many included farther on in the text) which are completely sterile and do not include soil. I do, because I'm lazy. There is enough soil in this mixture to start the seedlings and keep them growing well until it is time to transplant. If you did not use soil, but only the sterile soil conditioners, you would have to fertilize with a soluble fertilizer on a very regimented schedule.

Fill the flats to about ½ inch from the rim and bake in the oven ½ hour at 180 degrees —of course, prior to dumping the seed mix into the flat, plug up the drainage holes with pebbles or pieces of broken crockery (this action merely insures that the mix does not leak out all over the oven). If a flat is used which cannot be put into the oven, the soil will have to be sterilized separately (see directions given for Potting Soil Mixes).

Remove flats from oven and cool before using.

The simplest method of wetting the soil flat is to place it in a flat, shallow container of water (like an old rectangular cake tin) and allow the soil mix to become saturated from the bottom. Remove when the surface shows moisture. Drain.

Dust the surface of the flat with dry sphagnum and sow the seed. For seed which doesn't germinate within a month, or is expensive or difficult to obtain, I advise putting a pinch of Arasan in the seed packet and shake so the seed is well coated. If the seed is very fine, do not cover with additional moss, however, the rule of the thumb is to cover the seed to twice its diameter. For large seed, indent holes in the soil, using the erasure end of a pencil, so the moss cover does not have to be more than ¼ inch thick (the moss is difficult to moisten). The germinating seed will often lift portions of the moss like a cap from the soil surface; merely syringe it back in place as you water or gently push down with a pencil point.

Water the flat again with a fine spray using the bulb sprayer, having added a drop or two of Pano-drench to the water in the sprayer (the bulb holds about 2 cups). Set aside again to drain.

Label your flat. Purchased plastic labels are very inex-

3

pensive. The bits of plastic that fasten bread wrappers may also be used. A waterproof pencil is a necessity. Either enclose the flat in a plastic bag or cover with Saran Wrap. The object is to keep the soil moist. It is rarely necessary to moisten again before germination takes place. As soon as growth is apparent, remove the plastic.

Cover the newly prepared flats with grocer's brown paper. Most seed germinates better with the absence of light. There are, however, a few exceptions as you will note in the plant catalog. Don't place these in the bright sun, though. The average light of a well-lighted room will do.

If germinating temperatures of 65 to 70 degrees are recommended, use a soil cable; otherwise, the average room temperature of the house will do, but germination will be slower.

Where 45 degrees is advised, the cool conditions of early spring are necessary and germination must take place out-of-doors in the cold frame or in a cool greenhouse. (The mean temperature will be about 45 degrees.) I never sow directly in the garden bed; the seed is too expensive and our climatic conditions too severe, not to mention the mice and birds which hover in the background waiting to take advantage of your kind generosity.

If freezing temperatures are needed, either sow in fall and winter over in the cold frame or stratify the seed and sow in spring.

Seed Stratification

Place a small quantity of moistened peat moss in a small plastic bag. Dust the seed with Arasan (put a pinch in the seed packet and shake) and mix it with the moss. If a fungicide is not used, the seed is very likely to develop mold and rot. Fasten the bag with a little wire "twistem" and place in the refrigerator or freezer (some species require actual freezing, in which case, alternate between freezer and refrigerator). What you are trying to do is duplicate the normal conditions of winter to which the seed would normally have been exposed if it had been sown outdoors in fall. Do not forget to enclose your identifying label in the bag.

It is not necessary to separate the seed from the moss when sowing. The stratified seed usually germinates at 45 to 50 degrees.

If you are stratifying more than one kind of seed, place the individual sacks in one container. I use either a large plastic bag, coffee can with plastic top or refrigerator storage bowl with a tightly fitting top. Use what you have. The kitchen is a store house of equipment useful also in gardening—all you need is imagination.

Recipes for Various Seed Mixes

(1) Sphagnum moss. ("Nodampoff" is finely milled specifically for the starting of seeds.) It is sterile and requires the use of a liquid fertilizer after germination occurs.

(2) Vermiculite. Another sterile conditioner. If this is used alone, liquid fertilizer must also be applied to it. Do not use over and over again, as it becomes water-logged. Put used mixes into the garden beds.

(3) Sand and peat in equal parts. Spread about 1 inch over the top of pasteurized soil.

(4) North Platte mix. This is a sterile mix and nutrients must be added.
    1 part fine sphagnum
    2 parts perlite
    2 parts vermiculite

(5) Equal parts pasteurized soil, peat and sand.

(6) John Innes mix. Named after its originator, an Englishman; it is much used in Britain.
    2 parts soil, pasteurtzed
    1 part peat moss
    1 part sand
    to each bushel, add 1½ ounces superphosphate and ¾ ounce hydrated (builders) lime

(7) Cornell University mix.
    4 quarts vermiculite (No. 2 Terralite)
    4 quarts shredded peat moss

1 tablespoon superphosphate (20%)
2½ tablespoons ground limestone
plus either 1½ tablespoons 33% ammonium nitrate or 4 tablespoons 5-10-5 fertilizer

The proportions of the Cornell mix will make one peck. If used for plants which will occupy the container for a longer period than a seedling flat, additional feeding with a water soluble fertilizer will be required. This mix may be purchased from commercial sources, all ready made up, under the trade name "Redi-Earth." Other retail mixes very like this are "Jiffy Mix" and Parks "Sure-Fire" mix. I have used Jiffy Mix and have been very satisfied with its performance; the only drawback is the cost—if your gardening is on a large scale and budget small.

You will be aware of an annoying condition in the seed flats where you have used the light-weight seedling mixes and the seed does not germinate the first season— the surface cakes like a hard frosting. This may be alleviated by sifting fairly fine sand over the surface. The sand will prevent the caking and excessive drying out of the mix.

Bacteria Inoculant for Seeds of Legumes

An aid to the germination of legumes, this inoculant encourages the formation of nodules on the roots of the plants. (Nitrogen is stored in the nodules and used when needed.) Since all soils do not have this bacteria present (mine seems to be lacking), I would advise taking this precaution before sowing seeds of the pea family.

Orchid Mixes

Every gardener has his own idea about these mixes which are used for growing germinated seeds or for purchased plants (in some cases, they may have been collected in the field).

(1) Sand—with bark, peat moss, and leaf mold added.

(2) Peat, sphagnum, garden loam, and osmunda or shredded bark (soak the bark overnight).

(3) 2 parts peat
1 part sphagnum
½ part loam
½ part crushed pot chips

A clay container seems to afford a healthier environment for orchids. Fill ⅓ of the pot with drainage material. Although I have stated elsewhere that this is a wet root plant, do not over-water at this stage, until the roots have taken hold—which is also the reason for using the clay pot, as there is less danger of drowning a plant in clay than in plastic, a material which does not allow oxygen to penetrate.

Fertilize the terrestrial orchid with a fish emulsion.

At some time or other, nearly every true gardener will try his hand at propagating ferns (it is not easy). Here are a few methods of procedure which may be of some use:

(1) Dust spores on pasteurized soil. Cover with glass. Keep in the shade at 65 degrees. Water only with water that has been boiled and cooled. Germination is erratic.

(2) Spread a mixture of sand and peat on the surface of an ordinary brick. Place it in the oven for ½ hour at 250 degrees. Place the brick in a container having 1 to 2 inches of sterile water in it (boiled). When the soil is moist (the brick absorbs water), sow the spores. These may be purchased or if you have some ferns in the garden, cut off a leaf and shake it over the soil. The difficulty here is knowing when the spores (the black dots on the underside of the leaf) are ripe. One way to be sure is to place the frond (leaf) in a paper sack for about 3 weeks to mature.

Germinate at 65 degrees, out of the sunlight. Water as needed only with sterile water.

(3) The third and final method is set forth by the English seed house, Thompson & Morgan. Sterilize a lump of turfy loam. Fill a shallow pan with sterile water and in it place a shallow clay pot (the water must be able to seep through it). Place the lump of sod in the pot, sprinkle the spores over, and cover all with a glass jar, plastic dome, or whatever is available. The object is to keep the air warm and humid and the soil constantly moist. Needless to say, replenish the water level from time to time as it evaporates.

With perseverance and luck, after a few weeks, the surface should look a bit green. These are the plants. Allow to continue growing until just large enough to lift out with a pointed stick. Transplant into small pots (5 or 6 to a pot). An excellent mix for ferns is:
1 part good garden soil
1 part screened woods earth or peat
⅓ part sand

Continue to maintain the warm, humid environment. Pot up into individual pots when plants are large enough. Do not set out into their permanent places in the garden until the following spring.

Transplanting Seedlings and Potting On

First of all, a few basics should be understood concerning plants. If one remembers these, when moving plants, or when providing any care they may need, the chances for their health and survival are greatly enhanced. As soon as the true leaves appear, the plant begins to function as a mature plant. It is now, so to speak, on its own. The primary function of the leaves is to manufacture sugars and other carbohydrates (when in the presence of sunlight, the leaves change carbon dioxide and water into carbohydrates and oxygen, a process called photosynthesis). As you can see, this all comes to a halt completely in winter for deciduous plants which have lost their leaves; in this category would be included most of our perennials. However, where in evergreens, the process is slowed down considerably, but not entirely, and the need for water is greatly reduced.

Secondly, all plants have two kinds of roots, each having its own function. The large structural or tap root primarily holds the plant in an upright position. It takes rather rough treatment and pruning. The thin, fibrous roots are very fragile and delicate. These sustain the plant, and their loss or drying out can cause the plant to die. If it is necessary at any time to expose the plant's roots to the air, *keep them moist.*

When the seedlings have developed a set of true leaves (the first leaves you observe are the cotyledons which are usually round with smooth margins; these are followed by the true leaves which will be the shape of the plant's normal foliage), prick out the seedling with pointed stick or (I use) a table fork, and transplant either to a larger flat, leaving room for development, or to peat pots. I usually use peat pots which allow subsequent moving to the garden with no real setback to the roots. Merely dig a hole and set the plant in, pot and all. Nothing could be simpler, except (and this is important!) be sure the peat pot is sopping wet and the garden soil is moist, or the moisture is drawn out of the soil ball around the roots with dire results.

Another method of removing the seedlings from the seed flat is to place your hand over the flat (soil should be moist), turn the flat upside down, and the soil mass will drop out, remove the flat to one side and carefully place the seedlings (right side up, of course) in one corner of the bench near the potting soil. I find them easier to separate this way. Gently work the young plants apart, using the fork and your fingers, planting as you go.

It is advisable to sort them out a bit as you transplant. I put the largest in individual peat pots and the smallest in a flat, spacing 1½ to 2 inches apart. Always transplant to the same depth they were growing originally. Shade

them the first day and then according to the species requirements.

Continue to grow on at house temperature of 60 to 70 degrees for 2 to 3 weeks and then put out in the cold frame if the weather allows. The cooler temperatures (should be from 45 to 50 degrees) will produce sturdier plants even though this will slow down their growth. This hardening off process is always necessary. If you don't have a frame, set them outdoors in a protected spot for a few hours at a time, gradually lengthening the time until they may be safely set out in the garden. Even then, I often put "Hotkaps" over the delicate sorts for a week or more.

In the case of tender or house plants which will never go outdoors, or those I intend to retain in containers of some kind, I transplant the seedling directly into a small pot of either clay or plastic. My preference is the clay pot, as I believe the plants do better in them. There is less danger of overwatering than when using plastic. However, the plastic pot takes up less room to store, and it is lighter in weight and therefore easier to handle. My budget usually dictates my choice, and I use what I have on hand.

Start out with a small size and as the roots fill the container, pot up to the next size. It is very simple to knock a plant out of its pot; just be sure the soil is moist so it does not fall away from the roots. Place your hand over the top of the pot (your fingers will bridge the soil and go around the stem of the plant), turn it upside down and give the rim

of the pot a sharp rap on the edge of table or bench. The plant, soil ball and all, will slip out; by holding it upside down, you can see at a glance whether the roots have filled the pot and it needs more room—a larger pot.

A clever gimmick that works for plants you wish to maintain in the same size pot for an indefinite time (this will also have the effect of dwarfing the plant) is to knock the plant out of its pot, and with pointed tool of some sort, remove about ½ to 1 inch of soil from around the perimeter of the soil ball, then with a sharp scissors prune away the roots exposed by this operation. Repot with fresh soil.

Potting Soil Mixes

The mix I often use is quite similar to the mix recipe I offered for seed propagation, except that I use more soil, peat moss is substituted for sphagnum, and fertilizer is added.

2 parts garden soil, pasteurized
1 part peat moss
1 part perlite and vermiculite combined
2 tablespoons superphosphate
1 tablespoon dried blood

The soil should be sterilized, if for no other reason than to eliminate the wildlife. A worm in the container will be of no benefit to the plant, believe me. I use the oven method; it is clean, effective, and

simple—and the average gardener has no need of great amounts. I fill a roasting pan with garden soil (moist), cover with foil, and bake 1 hour at 200 degrees. (I specified 30 minutes for the seed flats because of the difference in depth.)

Using a 1-quart coffee can as a measure, the above mix (which is about as large an amount that is easily combined at one time) will be about ½ peck in quantity. Moisten as you mix with hand sprinkler or sprinkling can.

Other Potting Soil Mixes

(1) 3 quarts fibrous loam
3 quarts leaf mold or peat
2 quarts coarse sand or perlite
½ cup superphosphate or bone meal

(2) 2 quarts loam
4 quarts peat (half sphagnum)
4 quarts perlite
1 quart coarse sand
add to this mix
¼ cup bone meal
¼ cup superphosphate
⅓ cup ground limestone
1 tablespoon Fertell
or
1 tablespoon superphosphate
1 tablespoon ground limestone
1 teaspoon Uramite
1 teaspoon muriate of potash

(3) 4 quarts vermiculite or perlite
4 quarts shredded peat
1 tablespoon 5-10-5 fertilizer
1 tablespoon ground limestone

(4) A popular mix in England for perennials is:

    2 parts soil
    1 part peat
    1 part sand
    and add 1½ ounce
    superphosphate per
    bushel

(5) 2 parts soil
    1 part sand
    1 part peat moss
    1 part well-rotted manure
        add a 3-inch pot of
        superphosphate to
        each bushel

(6) 2 to 3 parts soil
    2 parts peat moss
    1 part sand

(7) Acid potting mix for plants which require a more acidic soil.

    6 quarts peat
    4 quarts perlite or perlite
        and sand mixed
    1 quart fibrous loam

or equal parts soil, peat moss and perlite/vermiculite in combination with superphosphate added. A rule of thumb to follow is, the more acid the plant requires, the larger in proportion will be the peat-moss additive.

Fertilizing

A plant confined in a container, of a necessity, requires a regular schedule of fertilizing. I prefer Ra-pid-gro (formula 23-21-17), but any of the water-soluble fertilizers will do. The seedlings which you have raised to go into the garden beds should not require fertilizing prior to their being planted outdoors. However, once they are moved outdoors, it is helpful to soak the soil around newly set

transplants with a soluble fertilizer.

For the Ra-pid-gro solution, I use 1 teaspoon to 1 quart of water. This may also be applied with a sprayer or sprinkling can. Wet down all of the plant; the food is utilized immediately.

As it happens, my home is a cattle ranch where, needless to say, animal manure is a by-product; therefore, because it is plentiful and costs nothing, manure is the primary fertilizer used in my garden beds. I hate the weed problem that one incurs using manure, but nothing can quite take its place as a soil conditioner in these arid lands, where the thin, humus-poor soils bake and crack like cement in the dry summers.

Every spring we also add ammonium nitrate to the lawn, windbreaks, and old established plantings. Hopefully, it is put on between storms so that the moisture will carry it down to the roots. If there is no natural moisture in the offing, it must be irrigated in or else it will burn the emerging vegetation. It should also be noted that the nitrogen has a short life and must be used immediately by the plants.

Superphosphate is cultivated into the surface soil in the perennial beds in spring. Moisture is also necessary for this to be effective. The phosphates last quite a long time.

I often mix a small quantity of bonemeal to the soil in each hole when setting out flowering bulbs, or to the whole bed if a large area is dug.

Fluorescent Lighting

The practice of growing plants under lights is comparatively new, but gardeners are already using them under very ingenious setups, ranging from a simple foil tray with an overhanging fluorescent fixture to quite expensive plant stands. B.G. (or Before Greenhouse) days, I invested in a 3-tray plant stand; each tray except the top had its own 2-tube, 20-watt fluorescent fixture, and I was most pleased with it. The stand was far superior to windowsills as a place to start plants for the garden. There are stands which may be used the year around; for this purpose, the tube lights, Gro-lux, should be used, as they are specifically designed for growing plants indoors; however, the plain fluorescent tubes are sufficient for starting plants.

Whether by raising and lowering the light fixture or raising the seed flats with bricks or blocks of wood, the flats should be 4 inches below the light source. Expose seed flats to the light 24 hours a day until sprouting begins for seeds requiring a germination temperature of 65 to 70 degrees. This indoor method will not be so successful for perennials requiring quite cool germinating temperatures (unless you have an old-fashioned cold basement).

As the plants grow, increase the height of the lamp above the plants' tip to 5 or 6 inches and maintain this difference. Leave the light on 12 to 15

hours a day. Allow the house temperature to drop to 60 to 65 degrees at night for sturdier growth.

Pots

Clay or plastic—that is the question. Whichever you choose, they must be clean and for a very good reason. The water and soils of our region lean toward the saline or alkaline and these salts or soluble minerals will have built up on the walls of the pot through evaporation. Besides being unsightly, these will injure plants' roots.

On the plus side, the clay pots are porous and allow aeration of the plants' roots. A negative aspect is that they require frequent watering especially on those hot, dry, windy days (with which we are all familiar, aren't we?).

Scrub the pots to free them of the salts and green algae that always build up sooner or later on all pots, then dip the pots in a solution of a new product called "Algicide", and the pot will stay free of the slime for about 6 months. I use 1 part Algicide to 9 parts water.

Clay pots may also be sterilized by boiling them in water for at least 15 minutes. It may be unorthodox, but I have found the dishwasher an indispensable ally in sterilizing pots; first scrub them free of soil or you are likely to clog the plumbing.

The only real objection to the plastic pot is that it is an impervious substance and unforgiving of mistakes such as overwatering, especially in winter, and the plants will drown like any air-breathing form of life. It is very difficult to judge how water-logged the soil may be without actually knocking the soil ball out of the pot (tapping on the pot, as some advise, is about as effective as rapping on a watermelon). To disinfect a plastic pot, soak it in a solution of 1 part Clorox to 20 parts water.

Winter Hardiness

The hardy perennial requires a period of cold, a time of dormancy. I have tried carrying some of them through the winter in the greenhouse, but they don't do well at all or utterly succumb. Although it seems contrary to reason, the hardy perennial *must* have that period of *rest*.

There really is no need to mulch a perennial bed, but in any region having dry, windy winters with extremes of mild and frigid temperatures, some effort should be made to prevent the plants being heaved out of the ground by the constant freezing and thawing of the soil. The purpose of the mulch is to keep the ground frozen. (This is not too important if there is a good snow cover; however, where I live, you cannot be sure of that.)

Mulches of hay or straw encourage mice. Leaves blow off. The mulch I have found to be ideal is evergreen boughs (a good use for discarded Christmas trees) and wood chips.

Wilt-pruf

I must mention this product which is so helpful in our dry air. It is a plastic spray that forms a film on the plant, thereby reducing the loss of water through transpiration. It is used for spraying evergreens for the winter or when transplanting, when collecting plants or cuttings in the field, spraying on tree wounds, and as a dip for tubers, corms, and bulbs before storing for the winter (it protects them from drying out). The plastic spray is also added to fungicides, insecticides, and weed killers to make them stick (on some foliage, sprays just form globules and roll off; some ingredient is needed to make the spray stick). As a sticker, use 1 ounce to 6 gallons of water. For all purpose spraying, use 1 part Wilt-pruf to 5 parts water. The air temperature must be 40 degrees or above when using this product.

Vegetative Propagation

While no two plants grown from seed are ever exactly identical, plants grown using vegetative propagative methods are usually exact copies of their parents.

Three requirements must be met when using these methods, indirect light, humidity, and a rooting medium that maintains constant moisture and is well aerated. (These are also conditions which encourage the growth of fungus; to control this nuisance, sprinkle surfaces beforehand with powdered Captan, Fermate, or sulphur.)

Division

This is the easiest and quickest method of increasing plants. I have found early spring, just as new growth starts, preferable to the fall for dividing plants; our season is too short for plants to root properly when disturbed late in the year.

Some plants are easily pulled apart; on others, you may have to resort to a sharp knife or scissors (I have even, in desperation, used a hand axe). If a portion comes away without roots, treat it as a cutting. In all events, dig the clump, lay it on its side and shake or wash off the soil with a hose so that you can clearly see that tangle of roots before hacking away.

Plants that are very valuable, impossible to replace, or that for any reason lead me to believe they may not take hold if simply replanted in the garden, I treat as I would cuttings. I put them in the cold frame, either planting directly into the sand media of the frame or individually potted. I leave them there for several weeks or as long as it takes to be sure they will survive.

Stem Cuttings

It is well to understand the theory of stem cuttings before starting the practice of it. The plant's adventitious buds are formed from embryonic tissue in the roots, stems, or leaves, and upon stimulation, form (depending on their location) roots or sprouts. (In theory, any living cell of a plant may be stimulated to form a new plant. Personally, I have not found it to be all that simple.)

We are mainly concerned here with herbaceous plants. Take your cuttings early in the season, before the dry, hot weather. It is better when possible to use basal shoots (near the base of the plant) than those from the flowering top. Select medium-soft stems (they should snap when bent). Using a sharp knife or razor blade, cut stems 4 to 6 inches long, ¼ inch below a node (place where the leaf grows out of the stem), and remove all but 3 or 4 of the topmost leaves (some are necessary for photosynthesis to take place). Very large leaves may be cut in half to save space and reduce evaporation. Do not pull the leaves off; use fine, pointed scissors. When gathering cuttings in the field, place them in a plastic bag to prevent wilting.

A rooting hormone is optional; it contains a fungicide to prevent rotting. If you use a hormone, dip the base of the cutting in the compound, shake off the excess, and insert 1½ inches deep in a hole made with a blunt-ended stick or pencil. Firm the rooting media against the stem. There are varying strengths of these rooting hormones; be sure you use the one made up for perennials.

Rooting Media

All rooting media should be sterile. Sand mixes alone may be sterilized by pouring boiling water through them. Sand and peat combinations (for acid-loving plants) will have to be pasteurized in the oven as was suggested for soil potting mixes. Vermiculite or perlite, either alone or in combination, are sterile materials and may be used as is. The rooting media should be at least 4 inches deep.

Containers

Any container will do in which to root cuttings, from flower pot to vegetable crisper. There are many plastic boxes with lids on the market, such as those intended for shoe or garment storage, and these are excellent. The principle to be kept in mind is to maintain warmth, light, and moisture. For just a few cuttings, root in a pot and cover with a plastic sack to maintain humidity. Flats may also be used if a tent of sorts is made of clothes hangers with plastic stretched over all.

If rooting only one cutting of one species, simply insert the base of the cutting in a moist ball of sphagnum moss, place the ball in a piece of plastic and bring the plastic up around the moss and tie closely around the stem. Put in good light but not direct sun (which is true of all cuttings).

Rooting temperatures of 60 to 70 degrees may have to be maintained by setting the container on a soil cable. Pot up the cuttings as they root. Often faster rooting is accomplished by dipping the whole cutting in a Rapid-gro solution (1 ounce to 6 quarts of water) before inserting in the rooting media.

Pot-in-Pot Method

Any gardener, however modest his ambitions, may use this simple rooting method. Using a 10-inch clay bulb pan (these are wider than high), fill with rooting medium. In the center, bury a small 3-inch clay pot (plug the drain hole with a cork or wad of clay). Insert the cuttings in the media as usual. Initially moisten it all down well and from then on keep the small pot filled with water which will filter through the porous clay, keeping the rooting media constantly moist. A plastic covering or large jar over all will aid in maintaining the proper humidity.

Root Cuttings

Bud growth from roots is always adventitious and starts from internal tissue (contrariwise, stem buds are formed on the surface).

Suckers are a form of root growth that everyone has some knowledge of. They are formed when an adventitious bud develops from the internal tissue and grows into a stem. They are produced naturally, quite close to the parent, and new plants are obtained by merely cutting the connecting roots. Suckers may be induced by partially girdling or partly severing a root of the plant. (I have induced, not on purpose, any number of saplings by rototilling over the shallow root of a huge old cottonwood tree.)

As a rule, root cuttings should be taken in fall. However, they may also be started in the greenhouse in winter or taken in early spring before top growth begins. Sometimes it may be necessary to dig up the whole plant to obtain cuttings, usually you may easily get a few by thrusting a sharp shovel down beside the plant and prying outward. Cut into lengths 2 to 4 inches long; cut the upper end (the section closest to the crown) square but the lower end slanted. There is a rule to follow on all root cuttings: the finer the root, the longer in length it should be. Dust the cut part of large roots with sulphur to prevent decay.

Fill a flat about three-fourths full of rooting mix (about 2 inches deep). Place the cuttings horizontally, 3 inches apart. Cover with ½ inch of sand and water well. Set out in the cold frame for the winter.

After things have frozen down well for the winter, mulch the cutting flats with about 6 inches of leaves or straw and close your frame. In spring it should be possible to transplant your new plants into the garden, or if they need further growing under pampered conditions, in a nursery bed.

Root cuttings may also be rooted in pots, in which case it is usually advisable to insert them upright, with the upper end (the portion that was closer to the crown of the plant) just at the surface. Spread ½ inch of sand over all and water well.

Root Forms

All serve the purpose of storing food, thereby allowing the plant to survive under less than desirable conditions.

Stolons or runners: these are slender shoots, usually starting away at the base of the plant and drooping or trailing in habit. They root wherever they come in contact with the ground and at the tips (examples: strawberry and ajuga).

Sucker: this is a shoot that starts underground from the roots or underground stem.

Bulb: it is a thick, fleshy bud, usually underground, which has specialized parts for storing food. Fleshy, scale-like leaves are attached to a small basal plate of solid tissue. They may be increased by bulbils (tiny bulbs that form on some lily stems), bulblets (small bulbs that are formed underground), and in other instances by removing the thick outer scales which are then planted in pot or flat after flowering or in late fall.

Many of the amaryllids and hyacinths may be increased by making a cut or scooping out a portion of the base of the bulb, placing the bulb in the cutting media, and giving it bottom heat; new bulblets should form at the cuts (examples of bulbs: lily, tulip, and narcissus).

Corm: this is not a true bulb; instead it is a thick underground stem that looks like a bulb. It is composed of solid tissue. Small buds or new corms form on top of the mature corm as it gradually dries up at the end of the growing season. (examples: gladiolus, crocus).

Tuber: it is a fleshy, swollen root. The sprout is at the neck end. The root serves as a storage house for food until a new root system is formed (example: dahlia).

Rhizome: it usually is a thick, horizontal shoot that grows underground or just on the surface. Finer roots form on the undersides, and leaves or shoots sprout from the aboveground side (examples: bearded iris and Solomon's seal).

Offsets: they are very like runners but much shorter (example: Sempervivum).

II

Field Collecting
Plants and Seed

Recognizing the innate beauty of wild flowers and making them a part of our personal environment is, I believe, the best means we have of conserving and saving them. I do not advocate indiscriminate collection. Nonetheless, in the vast spaces that make up the Rockies, a caring gardener, equipped with adequate knowledge on how to collect specimens, will (in years to come) be doing all of us a vital service. He is selecting and adapting that plant life to cultivation and by doing so (who knows?), something very special may be created for gardeners everywhere. After all, at one time, all flowers were wild.

A wild flower garden, if created artificially, need not necessarily be confined to plants indigenous to one's own region. Although the Rocky Mountain area is a treasure house of material, most plants from the cool temperate regions of the world will flourish here. As you browse through the catalog of perennials found in the second part of this volume, you will find many old friends —there are also many that should be better known.

I would suggest that on your fishing, hunting, hiking, and rock-hound excursions into the wilderness, you take many photos of the landscape and from the ideas gained from this very personal portfolio, create a wild garden setting in a corner of the garden, in the windbreak, or any area not too remote from the house where it can be enjoyed, yet does not have to compete with the cultivated garden for attention. With imagination and ingenuity, a large number

of habitats may be created. Wild flower seeds are available from seed companies and often from botanic gardens. There are some nurseries that handle wild flowers and sell them as plant material. Also a list of dealers that offer seeds of wild flowers may be obtained by writing to the U.S. National Arboretum, Washington, D.C. 20000.

A few general rules to follow in adapting wild flowers to your own scene are as follows: (1) plants of alpine, subalpine, montane (means an area habited mainly by evergreens), and some areas in the foothills, usually require a more acidic soil, as they are in a higher rainfall zone. (2) Plants found on the drier plains and high plateau lean toward the alkaline or neutral conditions where rainfall is less than one dares hope for. At any rate, try to duplicate the environment in which you find the plant.

Seed Collection

Whenever possible, collect your seeds from the field; then you know how fresh they are. Some seeds lose their viability very shortly after maturing. There is usually about a month's time between flowering and the seeds ripening. If you are in any doubt as to the longevity of the seed, sow as soon as possible after gathering.

Use envelopes (one for each kind) in which to put the seeds. If in doubt as to identity, also add a few leaves and

stem so that you may look it up when you get home. Note on the outside of the envelope: (1) place and date found; and (2) soil type, dry or moist site, and sun or shade.

Collect seed pods when they are mature or slightly green (if when mashed, the insides are milky or gelatin-like, they are not ready for collecting). The chances are that podded seeds scatter on the wind when mature, and so it is well to pick the wind-blown kinds when they are slightly green. Handle them with care and place them head down in an envelope or small paper sack when you get home. Store in a warm, dry place until mature.

Empty medicine bottles are ideal containers in which to store seeds. Be sure the seeds are kept in a dry, cool place until used.

Fleshy coated seeds (berries) are handled quite a bit differently. Soak in water (mashing as much as possible) for several days. Pour into a fine sieve and mash and rinse under the faucet; for a persistent pulp, you may need to use a stiff brush as well. These may then be sown immediately or spread out on blotters or paper plates to dry. They must be completely dry before storing or they will mold.

Sowing Wild Flower Seed

Sowing wild flower seed outdoors in fall in the Rocky Mountain area is a waste of time and seed, because most

of us cannot count on a protective snow cover in winter. Seeds of wild flowers from temperate climates usually require one winter in the ground to germinate. If the right conditions are not met, germination may be delayed another year or two. It is far preferable (when one considers the effort that went into collecting the specimens in the first place) to sow in flats or containers of some sort and place in the cold frame over winter. Bury the container to the rim in sand and when the soil is frozen, cover with a light mulch. Cover the frame, leaving open a crack for ventilation. I shade the frame with a section of snowfencing (it is heavy enough so that it won't blow off, a consideration in this windy country!). Most seed from our area require that period of freeze and thaw to break the dormancy. It is possible to "trick" the seed by stratifying and refrigerating it for 1 or 2 months before sowing in the spring (see Chapter I).

Although these are wild flowers, it is not safe to assume they are rock hardy and will survive treatment you would not mete out toward the cultivated kinds. I prefer to carry the seedlings on in the frame or shaded nursery bed the first year; this encourages the plant to grow a large enough root system to sustain it through the adverse conditions it will face later on. Transplanting seedlings to the garden in fall is rather hazardous because this time of year is usually very dry and they very possibly would freeze down before becoming established.

Field Collection of Plants

Moisten the soil around the specimen if the ground is too dry; the soil particles should cling together when squeezed. One may dig the plant, using great care not to disturb the root system, or dig and shake off the soil.

(1) If you are not far from home and the plant will be resettled the same day, dig the speciment along with a good soil ball. Roll it up in wet paper and then enclose in a plastic wrap to retain necessary moisture and hold back evaporation.

(2) However, if you are a long way from home and it may be up to 2 weeks before the plant is put back in the ground, use the following method: shake off most of the soil from the roots (don't wash) and slip the whole plant into a plastic bag (each plant in its own bag). Do not add water. Seal the bag with a rubber band or wire twistem. Keep the plants cool and out of sunlight—some light is necessary for photosynthesis to continue. Be sure to remove the flower heads and some of the top growth if it is too luxuriant.

As in seed collection, be sure to label, jotting down as much information concerning the plant's environment as possible. I prefer to label with numbers which I have keyed in a small notebook (saves writing the same information twice).

If soil peculiar to the plant is needed, take an extra supply to use when relocating the plant in your garden. At the most, it wouldn't be more than a quart.

When I arrive home with my collection, I allow them to recover from their ordeal either in the greenhouse or the cold frame (the latter is preferable for the high-altitude species). Set the plant at the same depth that you found it, water well, and shade. In other words, treat as you would a cutting; much the same principle is involved. Finally, set the plant out in the garden. Ideally copying as nearly as possible the same conditions as it was accustomed to where you found it. Mulch to prevent it from being heaved out of the soil the first winter. The alpines love a stone mulch all of the time.

Wood land Garden

Woodland gardens require more water because of the competing tree roots, and they also need more fertilizer. Add humus at least once a year. Mulch every spring with well-rotted manure (really very beneficial!) leaf mold, and pine needles or forest duff.

The shallow-rooted trees such as elms, Norway maple, linden, and cottonwoods are not the wisest choice for a woodland garden, and yet those are the very ones we have to use because they endure our climate. The only solution is to build up a forest floor for the woodland plants to counteract those greedy tree roots.

Ferns

A woodland garden would be poor indeed without ferns; therefore, it is well to know their rather different cultural needs. Most grow well in neutral soil with plenty of humus added and adequate moisture.

They may be planted at any time (if in summer, cut back to the ground). Set with the crowns just at ground level, not entirely covered with soil but well mulched. This rule applies mainly to the large types such as Ostrich fern or the Osmundas.

The types with creeping rootstalks are moved just as one would move a clump of sod (examples: Marshfern, Hay scented fern). The smaller sorts with creeping rootstalks (examples: Oakfern, Beachfern) should be set about 2 inches deep.

III

Culture

Plant Hardiness

Basically the hardiness of plant tissue is inherited, and this is really more important to trees and shrubs than it is for herbaceous perennials which die to the ground in winter anyway; cold hardiness for perennials pertains to the root system and is the only factor we are concerned with here. I have observed through the years that good drainage is far and above the most important consideration — water must not stand around the roots or the crown all winter. Given wind protection and good drainage, plants may be grown far north of their native habitat.

I have also found it advisable not to be overly tidy in fall. Allow the dead stems to stand and catch all the snow possible; allow the leaves to fall and lie where they naturally will. Humus and snow cover are the best aids we have to wintering through the perennial garden. One may obtain a plant hardiness zone map from the United States Department of Agriculture. Again, this pertains more to trees than to flowers. It is not a huge chore to dig up and store those tender sorts from warmer climes; a tree is a different matter altogether.

Soil

To understand what it takes to grow plants to a healthy maturity, it is vital to know something of the environment .nat supports and aids their growth—namely, the soil. Soil provides (1) physical support for the plant, and (2) moisture. The soil should have the ability to hold moisture in sufficient amounts for the plant's use between irrigations (you can't count on rainfall in the highlands). When the plant wilts, this is an indication that it is losing more water through transpiration than is being supplied via the roots. Water is also the means by which the minerals (in solution) are absorbed and transported throughout the plant. Soil also provides (3) aeration. A desirable soil provides movement of air. If the spaces between the soil particles are too small, they fill with water, and aeration is reduced until the water is gradually dissipated by evaporation or transpiration. (4) The soil must contain mineral nutrients; 12 chemical elements are necessary for a plant's growth. Nitrogen, phosphorus, and potassium are the most important; others are calcium, magnesium, sulphur, iron, zinc, manganese, copper, boron, and molybdenum.

Soil Testing

An essential chore for every highland gardener, and one which will save him money in the long run, is to have his soil and water tested. Your local county agent will be happy to assist in advising how to prepare and where to send your samples. There is also available on the market home soil testing kits which are not a bit difficult to figure out. Wait until the soil is warmed in spring and plants are starting to grow, then take samples from many areas in the garden—the soil will probably vary considerably from place to place. Take your sample from 4 to 5 inches deep, using a clean utensil.

Don't let that pH hocus-pocus throw you. It is merely a method invented by chemists for labeling the range of acidity or alkalinity present. For instance a pH of 5 would indicate an acid condition, 7 neutral, and 9 would be very alkaline. The majority of plants do well at pH 6 to 7. Testing once every other year or so should be adequate. Watching plants for physical signs of stress is another way. Yellowing of leaves in our area usually indicates a lack of iron for which I apply iron chelates (in solution). Iron is present in the soil but is in a form that the plant cannot utilize.

Lowering the pH

To lower the pH when soil alkalinity is above 7.5, water in a solution of iron sulphate such as Copperas or Ferrous Sulphate (1 ounce to 2 gallons water). Be careful to wash off any of the solution that may get on the foliage.

Another helpful aid for acid-loving plants which you are contrarily attempting to grow in limy soils is to add Sequestrene 138 (an iron chelate powder) to water (1 teaspoon to 1 gallon water), mix, and apply to the soil below the leaf spread of the plant in spring or at any time the plant shows a need. If the weather is dry, water in thoroughly. Outward signs of the plant's need for this treatment are poor, straggly growth, pale leaf color, and a scorched appearance of the leaf edges.

Aluminum sulphate is also beneficial in treating acid loving plants (1 pound to 5 gallons water). It may be necessary to make as many as 5 or 6 applications during the season. For large plants (trees and shrubs) that require acid conditions, changing the soil from alkaline to acidic is ridiculous, if not impossible. For small plants, it is fortunately fairly simple. In addition to the above aids, there is also sulphur. One-half cup of sulphur per 9 square feet will lower the pH 1 point. Humus also helps: peat moss, pine needles, leaf mold, and sawdust (To change to a more alkaline condition is a problem we don't have to give a thought.)

Alkaline Problems

There are few remedies for gardeners who live in areas where extreme salinity is a problem. Water excessively (called leaching) over and beyond the plants needs. The poorer the quality of the water, the more frequently this should be done. Do not grow dry—that is, maintain an even condition of soil moisture; do not allow the soil to become bone dry, because the salts concentrate on the surface through evaporation.

Good drainage must be stressed—it is absolutely necessary. Leaching is of no help if there is a hard, impervious layer of hardpan underneath the surface. In that event, I would concentrate my efforts to raised beds and container growing.

Be very careful with the addition of fertilizers, especially chemicals. Use the smallest amount possible and always water liberally! Overfertilization is one factor that contributes to excess soluble salts.

Humus

Without humus there is no life in the soil. It absorbs and holds moisture, provides greater aeration for the roots, prevents the soil from becoming like cement, and maintains a continuing release of nutrient compounds through the action of microorganisms which are then available to the plant as food. Although you are somewhat restricted by the over-all texture of your soil (clay is the finest, increasing gradually to the larger sand particles), it may be greatly improved by adding humus, which refers (by and large) to any material that will help in increasing the capacity of the soil for water and air.

Whether inorganic (perlite or vermiculite) or organic (peat, sawdust, shredded bark, leaf mold, or manure) in order to be effective, it should measure 25 to 50 % of the total volume cultivated (actually worked up). The process of tilling also adds air to the soil.

It is well to remember that organic materials are decomposed by soil organisms that need nitrogen and if you do not add an extra amount of nitrogen at the time the humus is added, they will use what is available in the soil—robbing the plants. This is especially true of material that breaks down slowly such as sawdust, straw, or bark. Therefore, for each 1,000 square feet of humus, 3 inches deep, add and mix in 35 pounds ammonium nitrate.

Peat is an excellent form of humus, and I use large quantities of it. It is not a fertilizer; use it to improve the soil's aeration and water-holding capacity and as an aid to the soil organisms in their task of making nitrogen available to the plants.

When a house is built, the subsoil is often haphazardly filled in about the house by the builders—in which case, there is not much you can do about the soil other than having it all removed—and I have yet to see that happen. But all is not lost. There is a way of improving that poor soil so that it will support plant life again. Spread the following mixture over each 1,000 square feet of the area:

> 2½ cubic yards well-rotted manure
> 1 cubic yard coarse sand
> 100 pounds commercial fertilizer, high in nitrogen.

Harrow or roto-till in well and allow to settle for at least 2 weeks before planting. This tonic is also beneficial to any area of the garden that is intensively cultivated; use your own judgment as to the addition of sand.

Composting

I hate to see all that lovely humus go up in smoke; far better, indeed, that it is deposited in an out-of-way corner of the garden and built up into compost. If you do not have a shredder, another means of cutting up leaves and plant residue is to pile it up and use your rotary mower. Some of us perfer to bury plant scraps in shallow trenches in the garden and then till in (do not forget to do this with your discarded pea vines for they are high in nitrogen and decompose rapidly).

Organic materials may also be composted along with sawdust or wood chips, using a half-to-half ratio. This type of compost does not have to be turned over periodically as is necessary with the others. All composting should be kept moist to aid the process of decay.

Summer Mulching

Important? I'll say. Mulch saves on weeding (ghastly chore) but must be deep enough to block out the light, making it impossible for photosynthesis to take place in the sprouting weeds. It maintains moist and cool soil conditions, adds to the top soil, improves the texture, and increases soil bacteria. There are many materials which are useful as mulches, both organic and inorganic in substance.

Inorganic materials may be paper or plastic (black), stone chips, gravel, or sand. a 2 to 3-inch layer of sand is an inexpensive mulch for every part of the garden. The soil remains moist underneath, and weeds are surprisingly easy to yank out.

In addition, the organic mulches add to the soil as well as controlling weeds. They may consist of tree leaves, grass clippings, wood chips (this robs the soil of nitrogen; therefore, once a year add 2 pounds nitrogen fertilizer per 100 square feet), pine needles (which are my favorite as they take years to disintegrate), peat moss, well-rotted manure, straw, or sawdust. The latter two materials also rob the soil of nitrogen, and so additional nitrogen must be added to make up the loss (1 pound nitrogen fertilizer to 100 pounds of sawdust).

The following sources make up 1 pound of nitrogen:
> 2.2 pounds urea
> 3.3 pounds ammonium nitrate
> 6.25 pounds sodium nitrate
> 5 pounds of 20-10-5 fertilizer
> 10 pounds of 10-6-4 fertilizer
> 20 pounds of 5-10-10 fertilizer

Fertilizers

The ingredients of the packaged inorganic fertilizers are given as proportions and read as follows: nitrogen, phosphate, potash—always in that order. Perennials, for the most part, are not heavy feeders: a light top dressing in spring (1 pound per 100 square feet is usually adequate. In general, one can easily remember that nitrogen promotes leaf growth, phosphate is for roots, and potash is for the branches.

Organic fertilizers include dried blood, bone meal, cottonseed meal, animal manures, and fish emulsions. Bone meal is an excellent soil builder, but it takes all of 6 weeks to be effective. For those who may wish to use chicken or sheep manure, remember that these materials will burn your plants unless mixed with soil before application (about 4 parts soil to 1 part manure). This rule does not apply to well-rotted cow manure which is quite safe to use as is. Fresh manure should never be applied near or on vegetation.

Liquid manure is a wonderful tonic for all plants. Using whatever covered container you may have, add 1 cup manure to 2 gallons water and allow to steep at least overnight. A small garbage can with lid is not unsightly or smelly and, kept filled with this manure tea, is always handy.

It is preferable to add phosphate to the soil when setting out plants. Mix it into the soil down where the roots are, for it is least effective when merely broadcast on the surface.

Soil bacteria do not work when temperatures are below 40 degrees, and so organic fertilizers are of no direct aid until the soil warms up. Another word to the wise: avoid feeding plants on cloudy days as the food is only utilized to its fullest extent on sunny days.

IV
Uses

Perennial Border

The perennial bed should be at least 5 feet wide; it is most effective if 8 to 10 feet or so and either backed by a hedge or fence or located so that it may be approached from all sides. The following are a few basic rules to consider:

(1) Low plants should be toward the front, graduating in size to the tallest in the back.

(2) Three or more of one species to a grouping; usually plants are more attractive when planted in groups.

(3) Pay attention to the color; there are some shades that definitely do not blend well together. Always use white and yellow for contrast and to help other colors live together. Interesting color, shape, and texture of the foliage should be considered. The form or habit of growth of the plant also dictates its placing.

(4) Know the season of bloom of the various species so that there will be a constant succession of flowers all summer. Including annuals, such as petunias and marigolds, in the border helps to overcome any shortcomings and delay of bloom.

(5) Label specimens for identification and location to prevent digging them up during their dormant periods.

Rock Gardens and Walls

For a rockery, one needs a slope which should be naturally rocky. If it is not, transplant the rocks; observe nature for your inspiration and plans. If the site is flat, don't despair; dig a valley and so create a slight hill. It doesn't have to be much of a grade for rock plants to be happy. My neighbor has a small rockery only two feet high near her back door. It is utterly charming.

Rocks should be all of one kind or, at any rate, the same that are found strewn about in your locality. If you will notice, they are usually arranged (in nature) in layers. Half bury the rocks so that their surfaces slant back into the slope, thereby making it possible for the moisture to run back into the soil and not cascade off like a waterfall. Avoid monotony by using various sizes.

If you have to build a slope or wish to alter the one you do have, it will be necessary to add some soil or change what you do have in order that the rock plants will be happy with their environment. This soil mix may also be used for all rocks crevices:

> 1 part soil
> 1 part coarse sand or gravel
> 1 part peat moss

Remember: rock plants do not require fertilizer!

In creating a rock scree (on the mountain side, you would call it a rock slide and stay off of it), which you may want to include as a part of the rockery, place rocks of 3 to 4 inches in diameter at the bottom of the slope and cover with a 2-inch layer of peat or leaf mold, then top with this mix:

> 10 parts stone chips (not over 1 inch in size)
> 1 part soil
> 1 part peat or leaf mold
> 1 part sand

Saxifraga and draba, for example, prefer this type of location.

Planting a Rock Wall

Use only small plants. Wrap the bare roots in wet sphagnum moss and slip into a crevice. Fill every little crack and crevice with the mix recommended for rock plants. Firm in and water by laying the hose on top of the wall and letting the water slowly trickle over the rocks, absolutely saturating all (a canvas soaker hose is perfect for this).

The Water Garden

If you contemplate establishing a water garden, it is well to follow nature's laws and locate it in a natural low part of the garden. Don't place it under trees unless you don't mind the constant chore of removing leaves. It is important to remember that hardy water lilies need at least 4 hours of sun per day, and tropicals require 5 to 6 hours of sunlight.

What type of pool you build depends on whether you lean toward the formal or informal manner of life style. The instructions I include here refer to the informal plan which is also appropriate for the wild garden. It is a simple construction that anyone, who is at all handy with his hands, can build. Taking into account the cost of labor these days, that is an important consideration.

The simplest pool is one which nature (with an assist on your part) has formed. If by chance you have (as I do) a natural water course on your property which tends to dry up, or almost, during the dry season, build a series of small dams—in effect creating small pools. They need not be great feats of engineering, just stones built up and chinked and wedged with mud and vegetation will do.

Unfortunately the rigid or flexible plastic pools will not withstand our terrific summer hailstorms (neither does the garden, but the plants are capable of repairing themselves); cement is the only material I would recommend, other than galvanized or wooden tubs sunk in the ground, which have their place but are limited in size.

There are many books and pamphlets devoted entirely to the building of pools, and so I shall not go into the ABCs of construction; however, here are a few tips I'd like to pass on. Use a rope or hose laid out on the ground to plan where to put the pool, its shape and size, and how much shade will overcast the area, if any (it's much easier, by far, to move a hose than a hole in the ground). Stake and dig. The earth will be your form.

The cement will have to be reinforced for our winters. Reinforcing wire may be purchased, or if you live in the country, as I do, you know there is plenty of old wire lying around. Hold it in place with short lengths of wire bent like hairpins and stuck into the ground; this will pin it in place. Do not make the walls with a steeper grade than 45 degrees. The wet concrete will tend to slide off.

The end of the pool having the outlet should, of course, be about 2 inches lower with the floor sloping to it. The pool may be emptied with a drain plug, installed when it is built, or siphon with a hose (a section of old hose will do) by filling the hose with water, double over the ends to keep the water in as you place it into position, then release.

The cement should set up overnight. Put a plank across it the next day for ease of access, spread wet burlap sacks over the surface, and keep them wet for 7 to 10 days. The new cement will create quite alkaline conditions and it is wise to cure the pool before using.

If the pool is built in fall, it is possible to let nature do the curing for you; however, most of us are spurred to gardening endeavors in spring and im-

patient to see results immediately. Use a litmus paper test before using the pool; if the pink litmus turns blue, it is still too alkaline for plant and fish life. The following is the method recommended by commercial fisheries for curing pools. Fill the pool and allow the water to stand for 5 days. Drain. Mix a solution (1 quart vinegar to 10 quarts water) and scrub vigorously with an old broom, sloshing generously over every inch of the surface. Mix more of the solution if needed. If it bubbles, don't be alarmed; that is just a chemical reaction. Rinse well, and the pool should be ready for use. If any new cement work is ever added (repairs or additions), this process must be repeated. I would also recommend the vinegar treatment for pools made of galvanized metal just to be on the safe side. It isn't necessary to paint the inside of the pool, but there are many of us who consider the dark background more attractive.

Planting the Pool

It is advisable to plant in a container rather than directly on the floor of the pool (also not as messy). Prop the container off the floor with bricks. In this manner you can raise or lower the height of the container according to the plant's needs. If planting in a farm pond or reservoir that livestock have access to, planting in containers will, to a large degree, prevent the animals stepping on them. (If you can, however, it is

preferable to fence animals out.) Boxes may be whatever you have available—that is, tubs, buckets, old dishpans, etc. Soil mix for this:

> 3 parts good garden loam
> 1 part well-rotted manure
> Fertilizer 10-10-10
> (about 1 pound or 2 handfuls per tub)

The commercial type manure is stronger, so use less. Never use fresh manure, as it will foul the water. The soil mix must be moist when planting.

Lay the rhizomatous-type water lily (odorata and tuberosa) horizontally, 1 inch beneath the surface of the soil with the growing tip just showing. Place a stone over the root so that it won't come bobbing up when you lower the box into the water, and cover the soil surface with gravel as well (do not cover the growing tip). This will aid in keeping the water clear. Without the weight of rocks and gravel, the whole contents of the box will come floating to the surface—I speak from experience! Adjust the height of the box as the plant grows, gradually lowering as the plant elongates and the water warms. Start out with just a few inches of water over the tip.

Plant the pineapple-like Marliac roots upright with the crown just showing above the surface of the soil. Hardy lily types may be left in the pool over winter; tropicals naturally must be set out anew every season.

For bog plants, build a leaky wall across one end of the pool and fill with a mixture

of peaty soil, topping with a deep layer of live sphagnum moss.

Container Growing Outdoors

Hardy perennials, trees, and shrubs are very attractive when grown in containers. This method also makes possible collecting and enjoying those half-hardy species which we would never encounter otherwise. Growing in containers adds color where you want it, making it possible to move your planting scheme to suit your purpose and site, and lastly (but most important), it makes possible a longer growing season. With protection, the plant material in containers may be started earlier and will maintain their flowering period longer, especially if placed on a large expanse of concrete like a patio which retains and radiates solar heat.

Outdoor containers are only limited by your imagination; they may be built-in planters, tubs, urns, pots, or whatever receptacle will hold soil and allow drainage. If the container is of wood (other than redwood which does not rot), it is wise to treat with Cuprinol, a wood preservative which is not harmful to plants. Metal or masonry containers may be coated with a moisture-proof paint or asphalt. Remember, the larger the containers, the less attention to watering will be required.

If you would like to try your hand at making a simple planter of a light weight cement mix, here is a formula:

1 part cement
1½ parts sphagnum peat (coarse)
1½ parts perlite

The forms may be cardboard cartons of varying sizes, or plastic, wood, or damp sand, but all need reinforcement with 1-inch mesh chicken wire; be sure to add drainage holes while the cement is still soft (wooden dowels inserted). Remove the dowels when the concrete is set up.

Other lightweight mixes are:

4 parts vermiculite to 1 part cement
or
2 to 3 parts vermiculite
2 parts sand
1 part cement

Mixes using vermiculite require a longer setting-up time because they hold water longer. When mixing, be sure that each particle of sand and vermiculite is coated with cement. Add the water slowly until the mixture is plastic; too little water is preferable to too much.

Plant containers should always have drainage holes. Place pieces of wire or plastic screening over the holes, then gravel, then coarse soil. Finally, holding your plant at the proper level (usually 1 inch below the rim), fill in with one of the soil mixes recommended in Chapter I, taking care to work and firm the soil around and between the roots, using fingers or a stick. For a potted plant, merely set into a hole in the mix, firm in, and water.

It is preferable to choose plants with a naturally shallow, fibrous root system. Proportion also plays an important part in choice of plant material. For small planters, use low plants, not over 12 inches high, some of which should have a trailing habit. For large planters and tubs, plants should be 15 inches or more in height (this includes shrubs and trees). A trellis may be added to espalier a woody plant; this is most effective when backed up to a wall or fence.

Before setting out plants in large (usually built-in) planters, wait several days after filling with soil for the mix to settle. If you don't, you will wish you had, for the only remedy for that hindsight will be to dig up the plants and add some more soil. Cover the soil, after the plants are set out, with ½ inch of sand. It prevents the soil from washing and holds down evaporation to some degree.

Routine care of container plants includes watering daily and placing, if possible, where there is high shade during the hottest part of the day and where it is airy but not windswept.

Overwintering of the hardy sorts requires storing in an unheated building, a deep cold frame, cold cellar, or cold greenhouse. Half-hardy species will have to winter at a minimum of 40 degrees. Do not cut back before storing. Water once a month (about a pint), just enough to keep the plant alive. Be very careful, though, not to overwater; I killed an agapanthus that way—the roots rotted.

In spring, cut back the tops of the perennials and move them into heat and light. Do not be too hasty about putting them directly outdoors.

Hanging Baskets or Containers

Where should these be used? Just about anywhere—outdoors, at the entrances, from the eaves, under the carport, or from the trees (my neighbor used her clothes poles)—indoors, at a sunny window, under fluorescent lights, or in the greenhouse. Give the outdoor containers some protection from our drying winds and place where there is shade part of the day.

Any of the potting soil mixes given in Chapter I may be used, but here is one specifically recommended for the hanging basket:

1 part soil
1 part peat
1 part sand
1 part leaf mold

Add 1 cup dried cow manure per peck of the mix. Fill in with soil mix, adding plants as you go. Trailing plants seem most appropriate since you are usually observing the container from below.

The only aspect of a hanging plant which annoys me is the drip; however, there is a new type of hanging pot on the market which has a saucer arrangement underneath. This would be especially useful in the home where the problem

is more acute. The dripping really doesn't matter outdoors.

Wire Baskets

The wire-basket type of hanging plant container dries out extremely fast in our dry air, and so I line the basket with plastic film (cut to fit and punctured with holes for drainage) before lining with sheet moss. I don't suppose the sheet moss is needed with the plastic liner, but it does hold a lot of moisture and looks attractive. You may omit the plastic lining, but be warned that evaporation will be a problem. As a matter of fact, I have finally come to using the wire basket only in the greenhouse where there is enough humidity. Other types such as redwood, metal, plastic, or ceramic are a wiser choice for outdoors.

Soak the sheet moss in a bucket of water prior to lining the basket (the moss may be purchased at a florist shop or nursery) and then fill with your potting soil mix, leaving room for the plants, of course. Allow the moss to lop over and cover the rim, adding the soil so that it is rather dished toward the center. Sometimes (not always) I sink a 2½-inch clay pot (hole plugged with a cork or wad of clay) in the center, and by keeping this filled with water, it helps to maintain a moist soil as a certain amount seeps through the porous clay. Depending on the mature size of the plant, about 3 plants is, as a rule, the limit for a 10-inch basket.

When watering any of the hanging containers, really soak it (if in the house, place in the sink and let drain there before hanging up again). Feed once a month with a soluble fertilizer.

Some of the plant material that I have found useful in hanging containers are petunias, dianthus barbatus (limited season of bloom), nasturtium, campanula (both garganica and fragilis; these are very beautiful but prefer cool conditions which are hard to maintain in July and August), arabis alpina, and alyssum saxatile (rather short season of flowering). Annuals or tropical perennials are practical selections for hanging containers, as they are not so restricted in length of bloom.

Forcing Hardy Bulbs

Plant tulips, daffodils, and crocus when obtained in fall, usually about October; hyacinths from September to December. Set tulip and daffodil bulbs ½ inch apart with the tips just showing above the surface; hyacinths should have ¼ of the bulb above the surface. Cover the crocus altogether. Pot one bulb to a 4 - or 5-inch pot or five bulbs per 8-inch bulb pan. An excellent potting mix for bulbs is:

> 1 part soil
> 1 part peat
> 1 part sand, with ½ cup bone meal added per each 2 potfuls.

Water thoroughly. Rooting requires darkness and a cool temperature (40 to 45 degrees). These requirements may be met by storing in a cool cellar, unheated garage, or cold frame, or by burying about 6 inches deep in a trench dug in the garden. Be sure to keep the pots moist.

The pot should be full of roots in 8 weeks or so. As a general rule, hyacinths may be brought in soon after Christmas, daffodils the middle of January, and tulips in February. The bulbs will begin to show sprouts. Bring indoors to 50 degrees, but the pots should remain in the dark until the sprouts are 3 to 4 inches high. Then place in full sun and water as needed. They may also be forced into bloom under incandescent or fluorescent lights, raising the lights as the plants grow. The crocus must be kept cool (60 degrees) all the time.

After flowering, allow the foliage to ripen. Store in a rather cool (less than 60 degrees) place and plant outdoors when conditions allow in spring. Do not attempt to force the same bulbs two years in succession; they would not do well.

The hyacinth forced in water is most attractive. Use the beautiful glass vases especially created for this process. The bulb and water should just meet—not over! Place in a cool dark place for 8 to 10 weeks and then handle just as though grown in a pot.

V

Catalogue

of

Ferennials

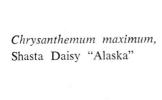

Chrysanthemum maximum,
Shasta Daisy "Alaska"

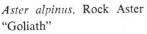

Aster alpinus, Rock Aster
"Goliath"

Stachys lanata, Lamb's Ears

Dianthus "Old Laced Pinks"

Dianthus barbatus auriculae-florus, Old Fashioned Sweet
william

Campanula persicifolia,
   Peachleaf Bellflower and
Campanula medium, Can-
      terbury Bells

Dianthus allwoodii, Garden
   Carnation

Campanula medium, Canterbury Bells

27

Sempervivum tectorum, Hen and Chickens

Lychnis coronaria atrosanguinea, Mullein Pink

Salvia sclarea vatican, Vatican Sage

Verbena bipinnafida, Fern Verbena

Digitalis purpurea, Foxglove "Excelsior hybrids"

Heuchera sanguinea, Coral Bells "Bressingham hybrids"

Veronica incana, Wooly Speedwell

Linum narbonense, Flax "Heavenly Blue"

Glaucium flavum, Horned Poppy

Helenium autumnale, Helen's Flower "Riverton Gem"

Aquilegia canadensis, American Columbine

Corydalis lutea, Golden Bleeding Heart

Kniphofia uvaria, Red Hot Poker

Trollius ledebouri, Siberian Globeflower "Golden Queen"

Linum flavum, Yellow Flax

Gilia rubra, Skyrocket and Shasta Daisies

29

Aubrietia rosea splendens, Purple Rock Cress

Euphorbia polychroma, Yellow Spurge

Chelidonium majus, Great Celandine

Aquilegia caerulea candissima, Columbine "Snow Queen"

Santolina chamaecyparissus, Lavender Cotton

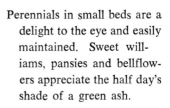

Perennials in small beds are a delight to the eye and easily maintained. Sweet williams, pansies and bellflowers appreciate the half day's shade of a green ash.

With giant cottonwoods for background, fireweed points skyward. Bellflowers and western yarrow compliment its vertical outline.

Hybrid moschata rose "Kathleen" clambers over a fallen willow, sharing the mixed company of delphinium, anchusa and columbines.

Catalogue

of

Perennials

Achillea

Family: *Compositae* (Daisy).

Common name: Milfoil. Yarrow.

Propagation: Seed sown at 65 to 70 degrees. Germination in 6 to 14 days. Scattered bloom the first year if sown in early spring. Named varieties may not come true from seed.

Division in spring.

Culture: Sun. Light, well-drained soil. Drought resistant. Space the tallest species 18 to 20 inches apart, the 12- to 15-inches species 12 inches apart, and the dwarfs 6 inches apart.

Use: Border. Cut flower. Rock garden. Dried bouquets. Wild flower garden.

Species and Varieties:

A. ageratifolia aizoon (syn. *Anthemis aizoon*): 6 to 8 inches high. Silvery foliage. Solitary, daisy-like white flowers. June/July. Rockery.

A. ageratum (Golden Sweet Yarrow. Sweet Maudlin): 2½ feet. Compact habit. Small yellow flowers in corymbs. July/ August.

A. clavennae (Silver Yarrow): 12 inches. Prostrate stems. Deeply divided gray leaves. White flowers. June/ July. Rock garden.

A. filipendulina (syn. *A. eupatorium*) Fernleaf Yarrow: 3 to 5 feet high. Robust habit. Light green fern-like foliage. Flowers in large corymbs, 4 inches or more

Achillea filipendula, Fernleaf Yarrow "Cloth of Gold"

across, yellow. July /September. Asiatic origin. Varieties: "*roseum,*" 1½ feet, rose-red; "Cloth of Gold"; "Gold Plate"; "Coronation Gold".

A. lanulosa (Western or Wooly Yarrow): 1 to 3 feet. Lance-shaped, very divided, fern-like leaves. White flower heads in flat-topped clusters, 2 to 4 inches across. White rays with yellow discs make up the individually tiny flowers. May/September. Found in the Rockies from the valleys to above timberline. A spreading habit makes this a desirable native plant for erosion control on banks. It is also attractive in the garden and not invasive.

A. millefolium (Common Yarrow. Red Milfoil): 2 feet. Finely cut foliage. Yellow or white flowers from July on. Originally from Europe.

Varieties: "*roseum,*" *rose pink;* "Cerise Queen," rose-cerise; "Crimson Beauty," dark red; "Fire King."

A. moschata (Musk Yarrow): 6 inches. Tufted habit. White flowers. May/June. Rock garden.

A. ptarmica (Sneezewort): The only ones worth growing are the varieties of this. "The Pearl," 2½ feet, dense heads of double white flowers. July on; "Perry's White"; "Boule de Neige (Snowball)"; "Angels' Breath".

A. taygetea: 1½ feet. Grey leaves. Flowers soft primrose in clusters. June/August. Greece.

A. tomentosa aurea (Wooly Yarrow): 9 inches. Spreading

Achillea millefolium, Common Yarrow "Cerise Queen"

Achillea lanulosa, Western Yarrow

mats of ferny wooly grey foliage. Umbels of bright golden yellow flowers. July/September. An alpine that prefers sandy soil. Useful as a sunny ground cover, edging, or rock garden.

Aconitum

Family: *Ranunculaceae* (Buttercup).

Common name: Monkshood. Aconite. Wolfsbane.

Propagation: Seed must be fresh, but even then germination is slow and erratic. Sow in fall. Spring sowing requires cold treatment to start. Prechill in freezer and then refrigerator for several weeks. Remove to 45 degrees. Germination may take up to 2 months.

The tuberous root of a mature plant is difficult to transplant or divide.

Culture: Light shade. Enriched humus-type soil. Add superphosphate. Moist. Cool. Take great care in handling any part of this plant, as it is extremely poisonous.

Space 8 inches apart in groups of three or more.
Use: Border. Cut flower. Woodland garden.

Species and Varieties:
A. anthora (Pyrenees Monkshood): 1 to 2 feet. Pale yellow flowers. July/August.

A. columbianum: 2 to 5 feet. Purple-blue flowers to 1 inch long in loose racemes. The sepal forms a hood covering the other flower parts. June/August. Naturally wet sites

6,000 to 9,000 feet. Rocky Mountains from Montana to New Mexico.

A. fischeri (syn. *A. carmichaelii*): 3½ feet. Brilliant blue to dark blue flowers. Also a white form. August/ September. China.

A. henryi (*A. autumnale*): 4 feet. Dark blue, lilac, or white flowers in open branching clusters. July/September.

A. japonicum: 4 feet. Deep blue or purple flowers with a red sheen. August/September.

A. lycoctonum (syn. *A. vulparia*) Yellow Monkshood: 3 to 4½ feet. Leaves very divided. Rather small flowers in variable shades of yellow. July on. Rare. European.

A. napellus (Common Monkshood. English Monkshood): 3 to 4 feet. Bright blue spike-like racemes. July/ August. European.

Varieties: *"alba magnifica,"* 3 feet, yellowish-white flowers; "bicolor," 3 feet, helmet-shaped flowers, white and edged with blue, August on; "Bressingham Spire," 3 feet, pyramid habit, glossy green leaves much like a delphinum, close-set violet-blue flowers in spikelike racemes. July to frost.

A. uncinatum: Semi-climber for the wild garden. Pale, striped flowers. Native to the Appalachians.

A. volubile: Climber with rich blue flowers.

A. wilsonii: The only good one is "Barkers Variety" 6 feet. Amethyst to violet-blue flowers. August/September.

Actaea

Family: *Ranunculaceae* (Buttercup).

Common name: Baneberry. Cohosh.

Propagation: Sow in fall or spring. Collect seeds in fall (September on), separate from the pulp and sow immediately. Germination is slow with spring-sown seeds because they have dried (hard-shelled little devils). Stratification of several months or overwinter is advised; even then it may take 2 years for sprouting to take place.

Root division in spring or late fall.

Culture: Shade. An easily grown woodland plant. Neutral soil (add leaf mold and peat when planting). Moist, at least in spring, to boggy sites.

Use: Shaded border or rockery. Margin or stream or pond. Woodland garden.

Species:

A. alba (syn. *A. pachypoda*) Doll's Eyes. White Baneberry. White Cohosh: 1½ to 3 feet. Short, dense terminal clusters of small white flowers from May to July followed by white berries having a distinctive purplish-black eye. Native from Quebec to Minnesota and southward.

A. arguta (Western Baneberry): 1 to 3 feet. Compound leaves made up of toothed, lobed, ovate-shaped leaflets. Dense terminal racemes of small white flowers. May/July. Conspicuous, shiny, white or red berries are poisonous. This is the western species found in moist, shady sites from valley to 9,000 feet in the Rockies.

A. arguta rubra (Red Baneberry): Native to most of North America. Prefers a more acidic soil than the Rocky Mountain cousin. The leaves are not so deeply lobed or toothed, and the red berries are not so distinctively eyed.

A. spicata (Herb Cristopher. Black Baneberry): 1½ feet. Yellowish-white flowers followed by shiny, purplish-black fruit. European.

Adenophora

Family: *Campanulaceae* (Bellflower).

Common name: Ladybell.

Propagation: Seed sown in spring at 45 to 50 degrees. Seed must be fresh. Collect seed and sow at regular intervals each or every other year, because the plants are short-lived.

Cuttings in early summer.

Culture: Sun or light shade. Light, well-drained soil, humus added. A fleshy rooted plant that resents being disturbed. Group plants 9 to 12 inches apart.

Use: Rock garden (especially *A. tashiroi* and *A. nikoensis*). Border. Woodland garden.

Species:

A. lamarcki (Mt. Gland Bellflower): 18 to 20 inches. Blue flowers. A rock-garden type from Transylvania.

A. lilifolia (syn. *A. communis*) Common Ladybell: 2½ to 3 feet. Erect, open racemes of fragrant, nodding pale blue bells to 1¼ inches long. July/September.

A. nikoensis: 12 inches. Leaves form rosette. Spikes of dark blue bells. July/August. Japanese.

A. potaninii (Bush Ladybell): 1½ feet. Spikes of large blue bells to 1 inch across. July/August.

A. tashiroi: 12 inches. Another Japanese species having spikes of roundish, violet-blue bells, often shading to pale blue or white. July/August.

Adenophora potaninii, Bush Ladybell

Adonis

Family: *Ranunculaceae* (Buttercup).

Common name: Pheasant's Eye.

Propagation: Seed sown in fall or early spring. 45 degrees. Seed flat exposed to light. Seed must be fresh.

Root division in spring.

Culture: Sun or light shade. Average to rich, loamy soil. Space 6 to 8 inches apart. Plant in masses for effect.

Use: Border. Rock garden. Cut flower.

Species:

A. amurensis (Amur Floss Flower): 1 to 1½ feet. Leaves not so finely cut as *A. vernalis*. Orange to golden-yellow flowers, 2 inches across, appear before the leaves are fully mature. May. There is a double form.

A. vernalis (Spring Adonis. Spring Ox-eye): 1 to 1½ feet. Delicate, finely divided foliage. Solitary, large bright yellow flowers, 2 to 3 inches across. May/June. Often white and doubled variations. Native to Europe and western Asia.

Aethionema

Family: *Cruciferae* (Mustard).

Common name: Stonecress. Persian Stonecress or Candytuft.

Propagation: Sow seed at 65 degrees. Germination in 8 days. Named varieties rarely reproduce true from seed.

Division in early spring, using the outer shoots.

Stem cuttings in July.

Culture: Sun. Sandy, gritty, alkaline soil. Dry. Transplant when young, for the roots are long, long! Space 6 inches apart.

Use: Front of border. Rock garden. Cut flower. Dry walls. Naturalize.

Species and varieties:

A. arnenum: 3 to 8 inches. Blue-grey leaves. Round heads of pink flowers, veined. May/June.

A. cordifolium (Lebanon Stonecress): 4 to 10 inches. Small rose-lilac or pink, lilac veined, flowers in short racemes. May/June.

Variety: "Warley Rose," 12 inches, blue-green leaves with pinkish edges, rose-red flowers in May.

A. grandiflorum (Persian Stonecress): 12 inches. Habit of growth much like iberis. Long prostrate stems to 1 foot in length. Blue-green, silver-edged leaves persist through the winter. Rose flowers in long terminal racemes. May/June. Persia.

A. iberideum: 6 inches. Mound of grey foliage. White flowers. May. Rare.

A. pulchellum: 6 to 9 inches. Trailing habit. Blue-green leaves. Clusters of fragrant, large, rose-lilac to pale pink flowers freely produced. June/July. Asia Minor.

A. schistosum: 9 inches. Bluish foliage and pink flowers. June.

Agapanthus

Family: *Liliaceae* (Lily).

Common name: Lily of the Nile. African Lily.

Propagation: Seed needs warmth, use heating cable, 70 degrees. Germination in 20 days. Will take from 3 to 5 years to flower from seed.

Division in spring (fleshy root).

Culture: Sun or light shade. Light sandy soil enriched with well-decayed manure. Moist during the growing season. Allow to dry and go dormant in fall. Remove roots from the pot or tub and store in vermiculite in frost-free place over winter. (I have had some which rotted when left in the soil) Container planting—should have at least a 12- to 18-inch tub or pot; plant with the tip of the tuber just below the soil level. If setting in outdoor bed, the tuber should be 2 inches below surface, and protect the crown in winter (still risky).

Use: Tubbed for patio. Garden border. Cool greenhouse.

Species and varieties:

A. africanus (syn. *A. umbellatus*): 3 feet. Basal linear leaves. Huge umbels of lily-like, sky-blue flowers.

Varieties: "*albus*" a white form; "*mooreanus*," 1½ feet, smaller clusters of darker blue flowers, multiplies rapidly. A good cut flower.

A. "Headbourne Hybrids": 3 feet. A hybrid offered by the English seedsmen, Thompson & Morgan, who assert this to be a hardier sort. Handle from seed as you do lilies. Plant in flat for first year and winter over in frame or greenhouse. Seedlings will not survive being set directly into the garden.

A. orientalis: 4 feet. More robust habit than *A. africanus*. "*alba*" is a white form.

Agastache

Family: *Labiatae* (Mint).

Common name: Giant Hyssop.

Propagation: Seed collected and sown in fall or sow in spring at 45 degrees.

Division in spring.

Culture: Sun or open shade. Average soil. Moist during the growing season. Space 30 inches apart.

Use: Border. Wild flower garden.

Species:

A. foeniculum (Blue Giant Hyssop): 1½ to 5 feet. Scented leaves, undersides white and hairy. Dense spikes of blue to deep purple-blue flowers. June/September. Native to the eastern slope of the Rockies.

A. urticifolia (Giant Hyssop): 2 to 5 feet. Mint scented, toothed, ovate leaves, 2 inches long and opposite each other on square-sided stems. Dense, terminal spikes of purple or white flowers. June/ August. Native to the Rockies, foothills to 8,500 feet, Montana to California.

A. mexicana: 2 to 3 feet. Spikes of rose flowers. Blooms the first year from seed.

Ajuga

Family: *Labiatae* (Mint).....

Common name: Bugleweed. Alpine or Geneva Bugle.

Propagation: Sow in fall or in spring. 45 degrees. Cool soil needed for germination.

Division after flowering, or really anytime for the runnering types.

Cuttings in summer of *A. genevensis*, *A. metallica*, and *A. pyramidalis* which do not form runners.

Culture: Shade, but tolerates some sun. Tolerant of poor soil. Space 8 inches apart, plant in masses.

Use: Ground cover in shade. Rock garden. Edge paths. Front of border.

Species and varieties:

A. genevensis (Geneva Bugle): 3 to 4 inches. Mat-forming habit but does not form runners. Shiny, dark green leaves are the real attraction, as the flowering season is very short. Deep

blue flowers on 6 - to 8-inch spikes. June. Rarely pink or white forms. European.

Varieties: "Pink Spire"; "Bronze Beauty" has bronze colored leaves.

A. metallica crispa: Metallic blue flowers.

A. pyramidalis: Very slowly spreads; does not runner. 6 - to 9-inch spikes of gentian blue flowers. May/June.

A. reptans (Carpet Bugle): Prostrate habit. Long stems root easily at the nodes. Shiny green leaves. 8-inch spikes of white, blue, or purple. May.

Varieties: "*alba*," light green foliage and white flowers; "*atropurpurea*" bronze leaves and blue flowers; "multicolor," varicolored leaves, red, brown and yellow; "*purpurea*," dark purple foliage; "*rubra*," dark purple; "*variegata*," leaves mottled cream-yellow.

Alchemilla

Family: *Rosaceae* (Rose).

Common name: Lady's Mantle.

Propagation: Seed sown at 65 degrees. Germination in 8 days. Division in early spring.

Culture: Light shade preferred, but tolerates sun. Humus-type soil. Space 8 inches apart.

Use: Rock garden. Border. Cut flower. Dried bouquet. Naturalize.

Species and varieties:

A. alpina (Alpine Lady's Mantle): 6 to 9 inches. Mat forming. Silvery palmate leaves. Greenish flowers. July.

A. major (syn. *A. mollis*): 1½ feet tall. Fan-like leaves. Sprays of delicate cream-colored flowers. July. Europe.

A. vulgaris: 1½ feet. Round, fan-like, grey-green leaves. Spikes of greenish-yellow flowers. July.

Allium

Family: *Liliaceae* (Lily).

Common name: Ornamental Onion.

Propagation: Seeds sown in spring at 65 degrees. Germination in 10 days. Some of the species are quite slow.

Offsets, removed and planted spring or fall.

Aerial bulblets in flower heads.

Division of clumps just as the green growth starts in spring.

Bulbs purchased for fall planting.

Culture: Sun. Well-drained, sandy, or gravelly soil. Moist during the growing season. Set bulbs fairly shallow, 3 to 5 inches deep, depending on size of the bulb. Plant dwarfs 6 inches apart, taller species 12 to 18 inches apart.

Use: Border. Rock garden. Wild flower garden. Long-

lasting cut flower. Dried bouquet.

Species and varieties:

A. acuminatum (Hooker's Onion): A rock garden type from the Rocky Mountain area. Stems 3 to 6 inches high, topped by rose, purple, pink, or white umbels, 2 to 3 inches across.

A. aflatunense: 3 to 8 feet tall. Pale violet umbels in May.

A. albopilosum (syn. *A. christophi*) Star of Persia. Giant Allium: 1 to 2 feet high. Leaves have downy white undersides and are to 1½ feet long. Flower heads 8 to 12 inches across, made up of star-like flowers of lavender to deep purple with a metallic sheen. June.

A. beesianium: 15 inches. Nodding flower heads of bright blue to purple-blue. July/August.

A. caeruleum (syn. *A. azureum*) Blue Allium: Flowering stems 1 to 4 feet tall topped by dense round umbels of deep blue flowers, 2 inches across. June.

A. cernuum (Nodding Onion): 6 to 18 inches. Grass-like basal leaves. Long-stamened, rose-purple, pale pink, or white flowers in nodding umbels. June/ August. For the wild garden, this is native to the Rocky Mountains to 9,000 feet elevation. It is also found in many of the northern states and Canada.

*A. cyaneum*s 9 inches. Small clusters of nodding blue

flowers. July. A rock garden type.

A. cyrillii: 1½ feet. White or violet flowers in dense umbels.

A. douglasi: 12-inch-high stems topped with umbels of deep pink.

A. farreri: 12 to 15 inches. A chinese species with reddish-purple bells in loose umbels.

A. flavum: 12 inches. Bells of shiny yellow. Self-sows readily.

A. geyeri: 6-inch dwarf with pale pink flowers.

A. giganteum (Giant Allium): Blue-green leaves to 1½ feet long and 2 inches wide. Woody stems 4 to 8 feet high topped by large globular umbels 4 to 9 inches across, made up of myriads of tiny star-like violet flowers (often blue or rose-lavender shades). June/ July.

A. grillii: 1½ feet. Globular heads of rose flowers.

A. karataviense (Turkestan Allium. Rainbow Leek): Interesting tulip-like leaves, 2 to 5 inches across, blue-green with violet veins. Flowering stems to 10 inches tall crowned by globular umbels of pink, beige, lavender-pink, or white flowers to 3 inches across. May/June. Prefers a limy soil.

A. moly (syn. *A. luteum*) Lily Leek. Golden Garlic: 12 to 18 inches. Leaves 1 foot long by 2 inches wide. Globular umbels of shiny, bright yellow flowers, 3 inches across. June/July. Multiplies freely. Tolerant of shade.

A. narcissiflorum: 12 inches. Nodding umbels of bright rose bells in July. A difficult type to propagate; slow to germinate.

A. nevii: 5-inch dwarf. Deep wine flowers.

A. ostrowskianum: Rock garden sort, 4 to 12 inches high with glaucous blue-green leaves. Rose flowers in large, loose umbels. May/June.

Variety: "Zwanenburg," 6 inches, deep red flowers.

A. pulchellum: 1½ feet. Flowers reddish-purple to red.

A. rosenbachianum: 2½ to 4 feet. Large flowers of rose-purple, purple to lilac hues. May/June. There is a white variety "*album.*"

A. roseum: 1 to 1½ feet. Rose flowers in loose umbels. June.

A. schoenoprasum (Chives): Usually thought of as an herb used for seasoning, it is also an attractive border flower. Planted among the roses, they will thwart the aphid population. Globe-like heads of lilac flowers. June/July.

Variety: "*sibiricum*" is taller, has larger flowers.

A. senescens: 3 foot high stems topped with dense umbels of rose to lilac flowers. July.

Variety: "*glaucum*" 12 inches high with glaucous leaves and lavender flowers. August/September.

A. siculum: 3-foot flowering stems with nodding dark red flowers.

A. sikkimense: 12 inches. Purple-blue bells.

A. spherocephalum: 1½ to 2 feet. Globular umbels of purple to reddish-purple flowers in July.

A. stellatum: 1½ to 2 feet. Thickish leaves with length-wise grooves. Lavender to lilac-pink flowers. July/September. Admirable type for the wild garden. Found on the dry prairies from Saskatchewan to Texas.

A. tanguticum: Dense umbels of bluish-lilac.

A. tibeticum: A 6-inch dwarf from Tibet with deep blue flowers.

A. triquetrum: 12 inches. White bell-shaped flowers in July.

A. unifolium: 1 - to 2-foot-high flowering stems. Lavender-pink flowers in June. California.

Alstroemaria

Family: *Amaryllidaceae* (Amaryllis).

Common name: Golden Peruvian Lily. Chilean Lily.

Propagation: Seed must be fresh. Sow as soon as ripe in fall. Purchased seed sown in spring in warmth, 60 to 65 degrees. Germination slow and erratic, will occur in 1 to 2 months.

Culture: Sun. Light, rich soil with humus added. Moist. Cool. Dig and store for the winter. Not hardy. Plant tubers 6 to 8 inches deep in tubs or sheltered spot.

Use: Border. Cut flower. Cool greenhouse. Pot plant.

Species and varieties:

A. aurantiaca: 2 to 3 feet. Clusters of yellow-orange lily-like flowers. July/August. Chile.

Varieties: "*lutea,*" yellow; "Moerheim Orange," deep orange; "major," larger than type, orange.

A. brasiliensis: 3 feet. Reddish-yellow flowers.

A. chilensis (Chilean Lily): 2½ feet. Variable colors, ranging from pastels to red and pink shades.

A. haemantha: Copper-colored flowers. Var. "*rosea*" rose or pink.

A. Ligtu Hybrids: 2 feet. Flowers pale pink to deeper crimson.

A. pelegrina: Lilac flowers, spotted dark purple.

A. pulchella (syn. *A. psittacina*): 3 feet. Red flowers, tipped green, 1½ inches long. June/September.

Althea

Family: *Malvaceae* (Mallow).

Common name: Hollyhock.

Propagation: Sow in spring or summer at 65 degrees. Germination about 5 days. Collected seed will not remain true to color or form. Any desirable plant you wish to increase, make root divisions in fall.

Self sows.

Cuttings in spring. Use bottom heat.

Transplant to permanent site when a seedling for this has a long tap root.

Culture: Sun. Average soil. Stake in windy sites. Space 18 inches apart. Red spider mites are always a problem with this genus; spray at intervals with a miticide (Kelthane). The all-purpose insecticides are not very effective. For rust, dust with sulphur.

Use: Background of border. I prefer an open area as against a wall, because the grasshoppers are attracted, I suppose, by the reflected warmth, and they shred the leaves no matter what you do until the plant looks very unsightly.

Species and varieties:

A. ficifolia (Antwerp or Figleaf Hollyhock): Biennial. 5 to 6 feet. Toothed, deeply lobed leaves. Lemon-yellow to orange flowers.

A. officinalis (Marsh Mallow): 4 feet. Coarsely toothed, hairy leaves. Clusters of flowers in leaf axils, pale pink to rose shades, 1 to 2 inches across. August/September. Found from Europe to western Asia and North Africa. Naturalized in eastern America.

A. rosea: Biennial or perennial. 3 to 5 feet. Large, round, coarse leaves to 12 inches

across. Single or double flowers to 3 inches across in leaf axils, may be white, pink, rose. lavender, purple, or yellow. June/August. The double strain, "Powder Puff," is quite an improvement over the older types. Original home was China.

Alyssum

Family: *Cruciferae* (Mustard).

Common name: Basket of Gold. Madwort. Dwarf Goldentuft. Gold-dust.

Propagation: Sow in spring at 45 to 65 degrees. Germination in 9 days.

Self sows.

Division in spring.

Cuttings in midsummer.

Culture: Sun. Sandy to gravelly well-drained soil. Dry. Rocky site if possible. Divide about every third year. Shear after blooming to promote new growth and neater appearance. Space 6 to 8 inches apart; 4 inches for alpines.

Use: Rock garden. Border edging.

Species and varieties:

A. alpestre (Alpine Madwort): 3 to 6 inches. Tufted habit. Mound of small, grey downy leaves. Small yellow flowers in dense racemes. May/July.

A. argenteum (Yellow Tuft): 12 to 15 inches. Shrubby habit

(shear severely after blooming). Silvery foliage. Deep yellow flowers. June/August.

A. creticum: 12 inches. Silvery foliage. Short racemes of yellow flowers.

A. flexicaule: 3-inch dwarf. Tufted habit. Fragrant, yellow flowers.

A. moellendorfianum: 4 inches. Silvery leaves. Yellow to white flowers in umbels. June

A. montanum: 3 to 6 inches. Neat tufted habit. Grey-green leaves. Small clusters of fragrant yellow flowers. May/June.

A. saxatile (Basket of Gold): 12 inches. Spreading mat of greyish foliage. Tiny yellow flowers in corymb-like clusters. April/May.

Varieties: "*citrinum*" (syn. '*luteum*'). 6 inches, pale yellow flowers in May (color not true from seed); "*compactum*," 6 to 9 inches, bright yellow flower clusters and silvery foliage, May/June, Mediterranean; "*flore pleno*," double flowers in June.

A. serpyllifolium: 2 inches. Exquisite tiny foliage. Racemes of yellow flowers.

A. spinosum: to 12 inches. Shrubby mound of silvery foliage, spiny. White flowers in May/ July. Var. "*roseum*" in shades of pink to rose. Germination is slow and poor. Transplanting only possible when young.

Family: *Apocynaceae* (Dogbane).

Common name: Blue Shadow. Willow Amsonia.

Propagation: Collect seeds in fall and sow, or pre-chill for several weeks in the refrigerator and sow in spring at 45 degrees. Germination in 3 weeks.

Division in very early spring.

Cuttings in summer.

Culture: Sun or part shade. Average soil. Moist. Cool. Space 12 to 18 inches apart. Slow-growing clumps. Use: Border. Cut flower. Naturalize. Rock garden.

Species:

A. montana: 12 to 15 inches. Pale blue flowers. Rock garden.

A. tabernaemontana (Blue Star of Texas): 2 to 3 feet. Willow-like foliage. Pale steel-blue, funnel-shaped flowers, ¾ inch long, in terminal panicles. May/June. Natively found from New Jersey to Oklahoma. You may want to pinch the tips of the shoots in spring to induce a bushier habit of growth.

Anacyclus

Family: *Compositae* (Daisy).

Common name: Atlas Daisy.

Propagation: Seed sown in spring at 50 to 65 degrees.

Anacyclus depressus, Atlas Daisy

Seed must be fresh.

Division in spring.

Cuttings in summer.

Culture: Sun. Sandy, gravelly, porous soil. Dry. Tolerant of limy soils.

Use: Rock garden.

Species:

A. depressus: 6 inches. Spreading, mat forming. Finely divided leaves. Single, daisy-like flowers to 2 inches across, at the tips of procumbent stems. White rays, red underneath, yellow disc; flowers may also be yellow or purple. July/August.

Family: *Compositae* (Daisy).

Common name: Pearly Everlasting.

Propagation: Seed sown in fall, or in spring at 45 degrees. The plant is easily collected from the wild at any time.

Creeping underground rootstocks.

Division in spring.

Culture: Sun. Average to sandy, well-drained soil. Dry or moist; very tolerant.

Use: Rock garden. Border. Wild flower garden. Dried flower bouquet (cut just before the flower matures).

Species:

A. margaritacea: 8 to 24 inches. Lance-shaped leaves, 2 to 6 inches long, silver-white, wooly hairs on the foliage give a silvery effect to the plant. Flower heads are either male or female, in terminal flatish clusters to 6 inches across. Small pale yellow disc florets are surrounded by papery, petal-like, white bracts. June/September. Flower heads when dried turn silvery and may be dyed. Native to the Rockies as well as most of North America.

A. triplenervis: to 12 inches high. Hairy foliage. White flower heads. An everlasting.

Family: *Boraginaceae* (Borage).

Common name: Bugloss. Alkanet. Summer-forget-me-not.

Propagation: Sow seed in spring at 50 to 65 degrees. Germination in 14 days. (*A. mysotidiflora* requires actual freezing conditions for one week prior to sowing. Germinate at 45 degrees).

Division in spring.

Root cuttings.

Culture: Sun. Light, well-drained soil with humus added. Spring application of well-rotted manure. Moist. (Exception is *A. caespitosa* which prefers a dry site). Space tall species 15 inches apart, singly or in groups; dwarf, 8 inches apart in groups of 3 or more.

Use: Border. Rock garden. Naturalize in woodland garden.

Species and varieties:

A. azurea (syn. *A. italica*) Italian Bugloss: 3 to 5 feet. Sturdy branching habit. Very coarse, hairy foliage. Bright blue flowers in loose racemes. June/August. Mediterranean.

Varieties: "Dropmore," 4 feet, deep blue, June/July; "Loddon Royalist," 3 feet, bright blue flowers; "Morning Glory," 4 feet, large gentian blue flowers; "Opal," light blue.

A. barrelieri: 2 feet. Small blue flowers with white or yellow centers. May/June.

A. caespitosa: 1½ feet. Cushion habit. Blue flowers. May/July. Mediterranean specie that prefers dry conditions.

A. myosotidiflora (syn. *Brunnera macrophylla*) Siberian Forget-me-not. Siberian Bugloss. Dwarf Anchusa: 12 inches. Broad, heart-shaped, hairy, basal leaves to 8 inches across. Open clusters of small blue forget-me-not flowers. May/June. A woodland garden type from Siberia.

A. officinalis: 2 feet. Blue or purple flowers in July/August.

Family: *Primulaceae* (Primrose).

Common name: Rock Jasmine.

Propagation: Cold treatment required. Sow in fall or stratify and sow in spring at 45 degrees. Germination may take a year. If any first-year seedlings develop buds, pick off and do not allow to flower, or the plant will not survive the winter.

Division in spring.

Cuttings of soft wood.

Culture: Sun. Sandy, gritty soil. Dry. If possible give this a rocky, gravelly site.

Use: Rock garden. Rock wall.

Species:

A. helvetica: 3 inches. Dense tufts. Solitary flowers that are rose in bud but open white. Native to the Alps. Easiest to grow.

A. lanuginosa (Silver Rock Jasmine): 4 inches. Trailing, prostrate habit of growth, mat forming. Leaves to ¾ inch long and covered with silky white hairs. Lavender-pink flowers in dense umbels. August/September. Himalayas.

A. obtusifolia: 6 inches. Umbels of white or pink flowers, ¼ inch across. Alps.

A. sarmentosa (Himalayan Rock Jasmine): 3 to 5 inches. Silvery rosettes formed by basal leaves that are wooly and to 1½ inches long. Clusters of rose, verbena-like flowers, ¼ inch across. May/ June. Easily propagated by the rooting stems which form tiny new rosettes. A very tolerant alpine; sites may be sunny and dry or more moist and shady.

Anemone

Family: *Ranunculaceae* (Buttercup).

Common name: Anemone. Windflower.

Propagation: Seed of most species needs cold to start.

Prechill by refrigeration for several weeks and germinate at 45 degrees. (Exception is *A. coronaria*, a bulbous type requires warmth, sow 65 to 70 degrees). In all cases, the seed must be fresh. Collect and sow when ripe in fall for best results if you are fortunate enough to have established plants.

Division in spring or fall. *A. canadensis* tolerates moving at any time.

Root cuttings (2 inches long) of *A. hupehensis* and *A. nemorosa* taken in late fall or early spring before top growth begins.

Culture: Sun or part shade. Neutral, humusy but well-drained soil. Moist. Cool. Shelter from wind. Fertilize with well rotted manure in spring. Set tubers 2 inches deep, claws downward, in spring. (Not all are tuberous rooted.) *A. coronaria* is not hardy here, and so the bulb is dug and stored cool.

Use: Border. Cut flower. Rock garden. Pot plant. Naturalize as ground cover *A. apennina* and *A. blanda*.

Species and varieties:

A. alpina (Mountain Windflower. Pasque Flower): 8 to 12 inches. Cup-shaped flowers, white, tinged with rose, 3 inches across. June. Rock garden type. Plant 4 to 6 inches apart. Tuberous roots resent transplanting; therefore, set in permanent place when a seedling. Give this a peaty soil mix, moisture, and shade.

Variety: "*sulphurea*," 12 inches, sulphur-yellow

flowers, 2½ inches across. Rare. Germination the second spring following sowing.

A. appennina: 3 inches. Tuberous rooted. Daisy-like blue and white flowers. May. Prefers shade. Mediterranean.

A. blanda (Sapphire Anemone. Blue or Grecian Windflower): 6 inches. Neat, silky-haired mounds. Blue and white in combination or azure-blue, white, or pink flowers. May.

Variety: "*atrocoerula*" has fern-like foliage and violet-blue flowers; it prefers shade. Tuberous-rooted species, plant 2 inches apart and 3 inches deep. Mediterranean.

A. canadensis (American Meadow Anemone. Canada Anemone): 1½ feet. Starry-white flowers to 2 inches across. May/August. Has a creeping rootstock and will form colonies. Prefers partial shade. Space plants 6 to 10 inches apart. A wild-garden specie found natively in Canada and the northern states in meadow and open woodland.

A. coronaria (Poppy Anemone): 1½ feet. Finely cut leaves. Solitary flowers, white, purple, red, or blue, 2½ inches across. May/June. Tuberous rooted, set 2 to 3 inches deep and 6 inches apart in a sunny site. Spring planting only (not hardy enough to leave outdoors over winter); they must be purchased in the fall, and you will have to store until spring.

Varieties: "His Excellency," 12 inches, scarlet flowers; "Lieutenant" (Blue Poppy), large, single blue; "St. Brigid"

and its "Creagh Castle strain," 1 to 1¼ feet, double and semi-double flowers in brilliant colors; "sylphide," 12 inches, light purple flowers.

A. de Caen or Giant French: 12 inches. Single, saucer-shaped flowers in various colors.

A. fulgens (Flame or Scarlet Anemone): 12 inches. Scarlet flowers, 2 inches across. Tuberous rooted. Dry, porous soil and sunny spot.

Variety: "*annulata grandiflora*," vivid scarlet which multiplies and forms clumps.

A. hupehensis (syn. *A. japonica*) Dwarf Japanese Anemone: 2 to 3 feet. Single or double flowers, 3 inches across, in clusters, pink, rose, purple, mauve, or white. August/September. Asiatic origin. Fibrous root resents disturbance, but root cuttings and division are sometimes successful methods of increase. Mulch with leaves or pine needles over winter.

Varieties: "*alba*," white; "*rosea superba*," rose; "*rubra*," red; "*Margarette*," double pink; "Profusion," deep rose; "September Charm," silvery pink.

A. leveillei: 1¼ feet high with branching habit. White flowers.

A. magellanica: 12 inches. Cream to sulphur-yellow flowers. From Straits of Magellan.

A. multifida (syn. *A. hudsoniana*) Globe Anemone: 12 inches. Flowers vary in color from red, green, blue, purple, white, or yellow, 1 inch across, have no petals (the sepals are petal-like), 1 to 3 at the end of the stem. Odd globe-shaped seed head at maturity resembles a ball of cotton. Tuberous root. Western states from 4,000 to 12,000 feet elevation.

A. narcissiflora: 1¼ feet. White or cream-colored flowers, rarely purple, to 1 inch across. Europe and Asia. Moist, sunny site.

A. nemorosa (European Wood Anemone): 6 to 8 inches. Solitary, cup-like flowers, quite variable in size and color, may be white, often tinted rose, purple, or reddish-violet, to 1 inch across. May/June. Dormant after flowering. Moist conditions at least in spring. Colonize 4 to 6 inches apart in shady woodland.
Varieties: "*alba-plena*," double white; "*robinsoniana*," flowers are larger than type, often blue; "Royal Blue."

A. palmata: 6 inches. Golden-yellow flowers.

A. patens nuttalliana (Prairie Anemone. American Pasque Flower): 6 to 15 inches. Silky-haired basal foliage. Bluish-purple, cup-shaped flowers made up of sepals (there are no petals), solitary, to 1½ inches across. Plumed, feathery seeds. Blooms from April/June. Native to the western states from 4,000 to 9,000 feet. A rock-garden type preferring sun and dry, limy soil.

A. pulsatilla (see PULSATILLA).

A. quinquefolia (American Wood Anemone): 8 inches. Mat forming. Solitary, nod-

Anemone multifida, Globe Anemone

ding, white flowers. May. Smaller than *A. nemorosa* and prefers a moist, more acid soil.

A. rivularis: 12 inches high. Flowers white, violet outside.

A. sylvestris (Snowdrop Anemone): 12 inches. Nodding, fragrant, creamy-white flowers, 2 inches across, 1 or 2 to a stem. June/July. Native to Europe and Asia. A woodland type, plant in colonies 6 inches apart. Easily divided in spring.

A. vernalis: A 6 inch rock-garden type with white flowers.

A. virginiana (Tall Anemone. Thimbleweed): 2 feet. White or greenish flowers to 2½ inches across. May/August. For the wild-flower garden.

A. vitifolia (Grape Leaf Anemone): 2 to 3 feet. Profuse, many flowered clusters of large pale pink flowers, 2 inches across. August/October. From Nepal. Prefers shade.

Anomatheca

(see LAPEYROUSIA) ....

Antennaria

Family: *Compositae* (Daisy).

Common name: Pussy Toes. Catspaws. Ladies or Indian Tobacco.

Propagation: Seed collected and sown in fall or spring. Seed must be fresh. Germinating temperature about 45

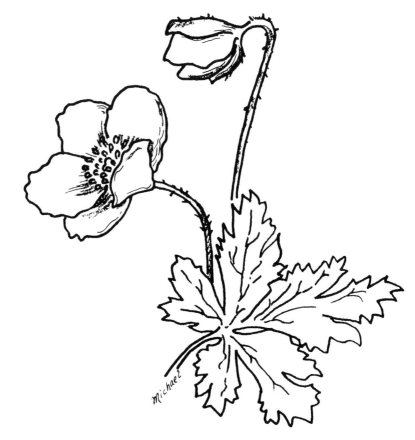

Anemone sylvestris, Snowdrop Anemone

degrees. Seed houses sometimes offer *A. rosea.*

Division in spring.

Cuttings in August.

Culture: Sun. Sandy to rocky, limy soils. Dry. Plants may be collected from the wild at any time; they are easily transplanted.

Use: Rock garden. Ground cover for dry places. Wild garden. Dried bouquet.

Species:

A. luzuloides: 6 to 24 inches. Not mat forming. Flower stems rise in clusters from woody crown. Native to the western states.

A. plantaginifolia: 2 to 3 inches high. Mat-forming

habit. Small silvery, wooly leaves. Plants dioecious ie one plant male, another may be female. Flowers, whitish, tubular, in small heads (dry papery bracts surround each head). April/June. Found from Maine to Minnesota and southward.

A. rosea (syn. *A. dioica rosea*) Rose Pussytoes: 3 inches. Mat forming. Prostrate, creeping habit. Narrow, silvery-white, wooly foliage in basal rosettes. Dioecious. Clusters of flower heads, ⅛ to ¼ inch across, enclosed by dry papery bracts of white to rose. May/August. Native to the Rocky Mountain states from prairie to 9,000 feet; it is also found from Europe to Siberia.

Anthemis

Family: *Compositae* (Daisy).

Common name: Chamomile. Golden Marguerite.

Propagation: Seed sown at 65 degrees. Reproduces true from seed. Germination in 21 days.

Self sows.

Division in spring.

Cuttings in August.

Culture: Sun. Sandy to gravelly soil. Dry. Divide *A. tinctoria* every other year or the clump is inclined to die in the center. Space 9 to 12 inches apart for most, 2 feet apart for the taller sorts.

Use: Border. Cut flower. Rock garden, walls and crevices. Ground cover. Wild garden.

Species and varieties:

A. aizoon (see *ACHILLEA ageratifolia*).

A. biebersteiniana: 12 inches Mounds of silvery foliage. Yellow, daisy-like flowers in June.

A. cinera: to 12 inches. Wooly, greyish foliage. White flowers.

A. cupaniana: 12 inches. Silvery foliage. White flowers all summer. Appenine Mountains of north Italy.

A. nobilis (*Chamomile*): 12 inches. Spreading, prostrate habit. Feathery, green leaves. White flowers. Set plants 6 inches apart if using as a ground cover or to take the place of grass; wait until the second year to mow. Camomile Tea is made from the dried flower heads.

Varieties: "*simplex*" has larger flowers; "*florepleno*" is a double form; "Treneague" spreads by stolons and does not flower.

A. montana: 10 inches. Hairy foliage. White flowers.

A. tinctoria (Golden Marguerite. Yellow Camomile): 2 to 2½ feet. Fragrant, finely cut foliage. Single flowers with golden-yellow rays and discs. June/August. This is the parent of most of the garden cultivars including: "Kelwayi," 2 feet, dark green leaves, lemon-yellow flowers, July to frost; "Moonlight," very floriferous, pale yellow

Anthemis tinctoria, Yellow

flowers to 2½ inches across; "Sancti Johannis" (often catalogued as a separate species) 2 to 3 feet, grey-green leaves, golden-yellow flowers, 2 inches across, Bulgarian origin.

Anthericum

Family: *Liliaceae* (Lily).

Common name: St. Bernard's Lily.

Propagation: Sow seed in early spring at 45 to 50 degrees. Germination is slow and may take 2 years. Shade.

Division in spring of fibrous rooted clumps.

Creeping stolons.

Culture: Sun or partial shade. Enriched, well-drained soil. Top dress with manure in early spring. Moist. *A. liliago* is hardy in my garden, enjoying a sheltered spot huddled against a hedge of caragana. Most effective when planted in masses, space 6 inches apart.

Use: Rock garden. Border. Naturalize.

Species:

A. algeriense: 1¼ feet. White flowers. From Spain.

A. liliago (St. Bernard's Lily): 1 to 1½ feet. Clumps of narrow, linear leaves, 12 to 16 inches long. Racemes of dainty, white, lily-like flowers on unbranching stems July/August. Southern Europe.

Antholyza

ANTHOLYZA (syn. *CURTONUS*).

Family: *Iridaceae* (Iris).

Propagation: Seed sown in warmth, 65 to 70 degrees.

Separation of corms.

Culture: Sun or light shade. Average well-drained soil. Set corms 3 to 5 inches deep, 6 to 8 inches apart, when danger of frost is over. Not hardy, so dig and store in cool place over winter. To extend the season, start early in pots in house or greenhouse.

Use: Border (must be massed for effect).

Species:

A. aethiopica: to 4 feet. Reddish-yellow flowers, 2½ inches long.

A. caffra and *A. cunonia*: are both about 12 inches tall with spikes of bright red flowers.

A. paniculata: 2½ feet. Narrow leaves. Panicles of orange-red flowers, somewhat resembling montbretia or small gladiolus.

Anthyllis

Family: *Leguminosae* (Pea).

Common name: Lady Fingers.

Propagation: Seed sown at 45 degrees. Germination within 10 days.

Division of runners.

Culture: Sun. Sandy, well-drained soil. Rocky site.

Use: Rock garden.

Species:

A. montana rubra: 2 inches high. Mat forming, shrubby. Greyish foliage. Fragrant,

clover-like, deep rose flowers
in showy spikes in June.

A. vulneriaria (Lady
Fingers): 12 inches. Matting
habit. Clusters of pea-like
flowers, may be white, yellow,
pink or reddish-purple.
June/July.

Anthyllis montana rubra,
Lady Fingers

44

Aquilegia

Aquilegia caerulea, Columbine "Crimson Star"

Family: *Ranunculaceae*
(Buttercup).

Common name: Columbine.

Propagation: Seed sown in
early spring at 50 to 65
degrees. The alpines require
a period of cold to germinate;
sow in fall or stratify prior
to spring sowing. Germination will vary from 10 to 30
days according to species.

Clumps may be divided in
spring just as new growth
starts if you wish to preserve
and increase any favored
selection. Treat as cuttings in
a shaded frame until the
plant recovers.

Culture: Sun or light shade.
Well-drained, humusy soil.
Tall species need staking in
windy sites. Space 6 inches
apart for the dwarfs, 12
inches apart for the taller
kinds. Plant in masses for
effect. All of the columbines
do extremely well in our
highlands.

Use: Border. Rock garden.
Cut flower. Wild garden.

Species and varieties:

A. alpina (Alpine Columbine): 9 inches. A rare
species having long-spurred,
blue flowers in July.

Variety: "Hensol Harebell,"
1½ feet, flowers a vivid,
deep violet-blue.

A. bertolonii: 6 inches. Large
light violet-blue flowers.

A. caerulea (Colorado Blue
Columbine): 8 to 24 inches.
Compound, deeply divided

Aquilegia alpina, Alpine Columbine

Aquilegia alpina, Alpine Columbine "Hensol Harebell"

45

leaves. Flowers white to deep blue to 3 inches across (petals often white and sepals in shades of blue), spurs to 2 inches long. June/August. Look for it in the mountains from Montana to New Mexico at 6,000 to 11,000 feet.

Varieties: "Blue King," 2½ feet, very large, medium blue, long-spurred flowers, June/July; "*candidissima* or Snow Queen," (see illustration. p. 30), 1 to 2 feet, white with long spurs in June/July (a hybrid but reproduces true from seed); "Crimson Star." 2½ feet, white petals and crimson sepals and spurs,

June/July (true from seed); "*cuprea* or Copper Queen," 1 to 1½ feet, long-spurred, copper flowers; "Dragonfly Hybrids," 1 to 1½ feet, long-spurred, bicolored flowers in shades of rose, blue, yellow, crimson, pink, and white (I found these to be very outstanding); "Mrs. Nicholls," 2½ feet, long-spurred, blue flowers. Very like the native *A. caerulea* but taller; "Mrs. Scott Elliot" 2 to 3 feet, pastel shades of blue, purple, pink, yellow, and red; "*rosea* or Rose Queen," 2½ feet, long-spurred, bright rose flowers.

Aquilegia caerulea, Columbine "Dragonfly hybird"

Aquilegia canadensis,
American Columbine

A. canadensis (American ....
Columbine): 2 to 2½ feet.
Flowers are red and yellow
with short, straight red spurs.
Blooms all summer if not
allowed to go to seed.
Natively found in a variety of
soils and conditions from
open woodland to hot sunny
ridges. (See illustration,
p. 29.)

A. chrysantha (Golden or
Yellow Columbine): 2½ to
3 feet. Fragrant, golden-
yellow flowers with long
spurs. June to frost. Native
to the Rockies.

A. clemitiflora hybrida
(Clematis Flowered Colum-
bine): 1½ feet. Large spurless flowers to 3 inches across
in variable colors. Distinct
petal form resembles the
clematis. June/July. (This is
a sport of the Elliot hybrids.)

A. ecalcarata (see
SEMIAQUILEGIA)

A. flabellate: 9 inches. Nodding flowers, white with tints
of blue or lavender-pink.
Japanese.

A. formosa truncata: 1½ to
2 feet. Flowers are yellow or
brick red and yellow
with short, thick spurs (quite
similar to A. canadensis).
June/July. Indigenous to the
Rockies.

A. fragrans: 1½ feet. White
or purple flowers. Needs a
warm sheltered position.

A. glandulosa vera (Altaian
Columbine): 9 to 18 inches.
Large, nodding, bright Ox-
ford-blue flowers. A rare
type from Siberia.

Aquilegia chrysantha,
Golden Columbine

Aquilegia formosa truncata,
Columbine

Aquilegia fragrans, Columbine

Aquilegia hybrid, **Columbine "Helenae"**

Aquilegia vulgaris erecta **Edelweiss, European Columbine**

A. "Helenae": 1½ feet. Flowers are blue and white. June/July. A hybrid (*A. caerulea* x *A. flabellata*) but comes true from seed.

A. longissima (Long Spurred Columbine): 3 feet. Flowers are pale yellow with long spurs, 4 to 6 inches. June/August. Found from Texas to New Mexico but perfectly hardy here in Wyoming.

A. pyrenaica: 6 to 9 inches. Short-spurred, deep blue flowers. May/June. A really lovely sort but likely to be short lived.

A. skinneri (Mexican Columbine): 1 to 2 feet. Flowers are crimson red with greenish mouth. June/July.

A. viridiflora: 12 to 15 inches. Fragrant flowers of blackish hue. An oddity for the rock garden. June.

A. vulgaris (European Columbine): 2 feet. Short, hooked spurred flowers may be blue, purple, or white. June/July. Crossed with *A. caerulea*, it is the parent of many hybrids.

Variety: *"erecta* Edelweiss," 12 inches, white flowers. Rock garden dwarf.

Arabis

Family: *Cruciferae* (Mustard).

Common name: Rock Cress.

Propagation: Seed sown in early spring at 45 to 65 degrees. Germination in 10 days.

Division in early spring or immediately after flowering.

Cuttings as you would mums.

Culture: Sun. Light, sandy soil. Dry. Prune back about one-third after flowering is over. Space 6 inches apart.

Use: Edge of border. Rock garden.

Species and varieties:

A. albida (syn. *A. caucasica*) Wall Rock Cress: 12 inches. Sprawling, matting habit. Light, grey-green, wooly leaves. White flowers in short, open racemes. May.

Varieties: *"flore-pleno,"* long-lasting, white, double flowers; *"variegata"* white margins on leaves.

A. alpina grandiflora (Mountain or Alpine Rock Cress): 6 inches. Tufted habit. Hairy, silvery-grey leaves. Short racemes of white flowers. April/May.

Varieties: *"rosea"* soft rose or pink flowers (fairly true from seed); *"flore-pleno"* double flowers.

A. aubretioides: 9 inches. Small, wooly, grey to greenish-white leaves in tufts. Spikes of pink or purple flowers. May. An alpine.

A. blepharophylla: 6 to 12 inches. Neat mounds. Fragrant, large, deep rose to vivid red flowers. From California; this needs to be mulched over winter as insurance against our open, dry winters.

A. ferdinandi-coburgii: 10 inches. Matting habit. Deep

green leaves. White flowers in June.

A. hirsuta: 10 inches. Tufted habit. Hairy leaves. Flowers white or rose. Biennial.

A. petraea: 3 inches. For the rockery. White flowers in June.

A. procurrens (syn. *A. mollis, A. sturii*): 8 inches. Tufted, creeping habit (underground stolons). Dark green, shiny leaves. Open racemes of white flowers in May.

A. purpurascens: 6 inches. Hairy, grey-green leaves. Umbels of rose flowers. From Oregon.

Arenaria

Family: *Caryophyllaceae* (Pink).

Common name: Sandwort.

Propagation: Seed collected in early fall and sown, or sow in spring following a pre-chilling treatment in the refrigerator. Germination at 45 degrees, may take up to 3 months.

Division by easily rooted plugs.

Cuttings in summer.

Culture: Sun or shade. Light, well-drained soil. Tolerates aridity. Space 4 to 6 inches apart.

Use: Rock garden. Crevices and cracks in stone walk or terrace. Rock wall.

Species:

A. balearica (Corsican Sandwort: 3 inches. Trailing or creeping habit. Tiny white flowers above glossy, green, minute, oval leaves in June. Neat, turf-like, it stands being walked on. Alpine.

A. congesta (Ballhead Sandwort): 4 to 12 inches. Prickly, grass-like leaves, ½ to 3 inches long. Woody underground stem. White flowers in small terminal clusters, one or several to a stem. July/August. Rocky Mountain native found from 5,000 to 12,000 feet.

A. montana (Alpine Sandwort): 4 inches. Trailing habit, carpet forming. Rather large white flowers. May/June. Much like *A. balearica* but having linear leaves about 1 inch long. Division is difficult; propagate by seed for best results.

A. obtusiloba: Matting habit. Linear leaves less than ¼ inch long. Solitary, small, white to greenish flowers. An alpine, native to the Rockies.

Arisaema

Family: *Araceae* (Arum).

Common name: Jack-in-the-pulpit. Indian Turnip.

Propagation: Collect seed, remove pulp, and sow when ripe in September, or stratify in moist sand in the refrigerator for 1 month and sow in spring at 45 degrees.

Division of tubers in fall.

Culture: Shade. Neutral, humusy soil. Moist. Tuberous roots transplant best in fall, but young plants may be moved anytime. Set tuber 4 to 6 inches deep and 15 inches apart.

Use: Woodland garden. Shady side of walls or buildings.

Species:
A. triphyllum (syn. *A. atrorubens*): 1 to 3 feet. Two, large, three-parted leaves on long stems. The pulpit or spathe which forms at the fork of the leaf stems may be striped green, purple, or brown. Flowers are on the spadix inside the pulpit. May/June. Clusters of red berries ripen in September. Native from Manitoba to Kansas and eastward.

Armeria

(syn. *STATICE*) ....

Family: *Plumbaginaceae* (Leadwort).

Common name: Thrift.

Propagation: Seed must be fresh as it is short-lived. Seed sown in fall, or soak in water several hours and sow in spring at 65 degrees. Germination in 4 days. Will bloom the first year from seed.

Division of tufts in early fall.

Culture: Sun. Light, sandy soil. Dry. Divide about every third year. Space 6 to 8 inches apart, and plant in groups of at least three.

Use: Border. Cut flower. Rock garden. Rock crevice.

Species and varieties:

A. alpina: 4-inch tuft with bright rose flowers.

A. caespitosa (syn. *A. juniperifolia*): 2 inches. Prickly rosettes of foliage. Almost stemless flowers in small heads of pale lilac or pink. From Spain. Rosettes branching from parent plant may be severed and rooted in sand.

A. formosa (syn. *A. cephalotes, A. litifolia, A. pseudo-armeria*) Sea Thrift: 1½ to 2 feet. Tufted habit. Lance-shaped, blue-green leaves to 10 inches long. Globular flower heads of white to rose, 2 inches across, atop naked wiry stems. June/August. Parent of most named varieties.

Varieties: "Bees Ruby," 1½ feet, red; "Vindictive," crimson; "Glory of Holland," pink.

A. maritima (Sea Pink. Common Thrift): 6 to 12 inches. Tuft of narrow, blue-green leaves. Globular flower heads to 1 inch across, white to rose-purple. May/June. Found throughout the northern parts of America and Europe from sea level to the mountain heights.

Varieties: "*alba*," white; "*laucheana*," 4- to 6-inch dwarf with bright rose flowers; "*rosea*" dark pink.

Armeria formosa hybrida,
Sea Thrift

Arnica

Family: *Compositae* (Daisy).

Common name: Arnica. Mountain Tobacco or Snuff.

Propagation: Sow in fall or stratify prior to spring sowing. A period of cold is required. Germinate at 45 degrees.

Division of underground rhizome (young plants only)

Root cuttings.

Culture: Sun or preferably open shade. Loamy soil on the acid side, leaf mold added. Moist. Transplant only when young. Set out in colonies, 2 to 18 inches apart.

Use: Border. Rock garden. Woodland garden.

Species:

A. cordifolia (Heartleaf Arnica. Woodland Daisy): 6 to 24 inches. Creeping rootstock. Dark green, heart-shaped leaves, 1 to 4 inches long—foliage is slightly hairy. Single stemmed plant with 1 to 3 flower heads made up of yellow rays and discs, 2 inches across. May/July. A lovely plant of the aspen woods, found throughout the western states from the foothills to 11,000 feet.

A. latifolia (Broadleaf Arnica): Another Rocky Mountain species differing from *A. cordifolia* in that the leaves are bright green and smooth and the flowers rise from the upper leaf axils, 1 to 5 flowers to a stem.

A. montana (Mountain Tobacco or Snuff): 1 to 2 feet tall. Creeping underground rhizome. Basal leaves, soft-textured, and lanceolate. Flower heads, 2 inches across, composed of yellow ray and disc florets; flowers 3 to 4 in a cluster. July. A showy alpine from Europe. Requires sun, plenty of peat moss when planting, and a gravel mulch.

Arum

Family: *Araceae* (Arum).

Propagation: Seed collected and sown when ripe, or sow in spring at 50 to 65 degrees.

Self sows.

Offsets from tubers.

Culture: Shade. Loamy soil enriched with leaf mold. Moist. Set tubers rather deep for their size. Mulch in fall.

A. maculatum is the hardiest of the lot.

Use: Shaded border. Woodland garden. Pot plant.

Species:

A. italicum (Italian Arum): 15 inches. Arrow-shaped leaves, about 8 inches long and short-stemmed, appear in fall. Spaxdix may be white to yellowish, rarely green to purplish. May/June. Clusters of red fruit.

A. maculatum (Lords-and-Ladies. Cuckoo Pint): 12 to 15 inches. Resembles the Jack-in-the-pulpit. Long-stalked, arrow-shaped leaves often blotched with dark markings. Pale green spathe with purple spots and margins in May. Red berries. European woods plant.

A. pictum: 6 inches. Long-stalked, heart-shaped, light green leaves to 10 inches long. Flowers are white inside with purple margins.

Aruncus

Family: *Rosaceae* (Rose).

Common name: Goat's Beard.

Propagation: Seeds sown at 45 degrees. Germination in 2 weeks.

Division in spring.

Culture: Sun or shade. Loamy soil. Moist. Space 1½ to 2 feet apart.

Use: Border background. Woodland garden.

Species:

A. silvester (syn. *A. dioicus*): 4 to 6 feet. Compound leaves. Terminal racemes of tiny creamy-white flowers resemble large plumes. June/July. Plant is dioecious (separate plants are male or female). The staminate or male is a bit more showy than the pistillate (female). Found natively from New York to Missouri.

Aruncus silvester, Goat's Beard

Asarum

Family: *Aristolochiaceae* (Birthwort).

Common name: Wild Ginger.

Propagation: Period of freezing required. Stratify 1 to 2 months and sow in early spring or sow when ripe in fall, germination will follow in spring.

Division of creeping root in spring and early summer.

Summer cuttings rooted in sand.

Culture: Shade. Neutral to slightly acid soil, humus enriched. A leaf mulch is excellent to help preserve moisture. Moist.

Use: Excellent shady ground cover. Woodland garden.

Species:

A. canadense (Canadian Snake Root): 6 inches. Deciduous, heart-shaped, hairy leaves in pairs, 3 to 6 inches across. Inconspicuous, long-lasting flowers are close to the ground, bell-shaped, brownish-purple. April/May. Found in the woodlands of the northeastern states and as far west as Manitoba.

A. caudatum: 10 inches. Aromatic, evergreen, heart-shaped leaves to 7 inches across. Odd reddish-brown, bell-shaped, tailed flowers hide under the leaves in May. Native to the Pacific range, this is of borderline hardiness in the Rocky Mountain area.

A. europeaum (European Wild Ginger): Small, evergreen leaves, dark green, shiny and leathery, round or kidney shaped, create a dense carpet.

A. virginicum (Heartleaf): Evergreen, heart-shaped leaves, often mottled grey, turn bronze in fall. Native to the southern states but hardy in the North.

51

Asclepias

Family: *Asclepiadaceae* (Milkweed).

Common name: Butterfly Weed. Orange Milkweed.

Propagation: Seed sown in spring or fall. Germination is aided by prechilling treatment given to spring-sown seeds; sprouting will follow in about 20 days.

Root cuttings taken in early spring before growth starts, set upright, barely covered with sand.

Stem cuttings in early summer.

Culture: Sun. Average to light, sandy, well-drained soil. Dry. Long taproot makes transplanting difficult for a mature plant. Space 6 inches apart in groups.

Use: Border. Wild garden. Cut flower (sear cut end of stem with flame).

Species:

A. tuberosa: 2 feet. Coarse, hairy leaves. Red-orange flowers in large umbels. July to frost. The flower is attractive to butterflies as the name implies. Interesting seed pod. Indigenous to most of the states from New England to Colorado.

Asperula

Family: *Rubiaceae* (Madder).

Common name: Woodruff.

Propagation: Seeds require a freezing period. Sow in fall or stratify 1 month and sow in early spring.

Division in spring of trailing, rooting rootstock.

Culture: Part shade. Average soil. Moist.

Use: Woodland garden. Shaded edge of border, rock garden or ground cover.

Species:

A. odorata (Sweet Woodruff): 6 to 9 inches. Aromatic foliage attractive all year. Narrow leaves arranged in whorls on square stems. Flowering spikes held above the foliage. Small, scented, lily-like, white flowers in loose cymes. May/July.

A. tinctoria: 12 inches. Trailing, procumbent habit. White flowers, petals red outside.

Asphodeline

Family: *Liliaceae* (Lily).

Common name: Asphodel. Jacob's Rod. King's Spear.

Propagation: Seed needs cold to start. Prechill in refrigerator several weeks. Germination at 45 degrees, in 4 weeks.

Divide in spring.

Culture: Sun. Loamy soil. Space 9 to 12 inches apart.

Use: Border.

Species:

A. lutea: 2½ feet. Long narrow leaves form clumps.

Long fleshy roots like a day lily. Spikes of fragrant, yellow flowers to 1 inch across. June/July. Mediterranean.

Aster

Family: *Compositae* (Daisy).

Common name: Hardy Aster. Michaelmas Daisy.

Propagation: Seed sown in spring at 45 degrees. Sow rather thick; percentage of viable seeds seems rather poor. Germination in 12 days.

Division in spring.

Cuttings when spring growth is about 4 inches high. Some will bloom the first year.

Culture: Sun. Good drainage. Light soil, preferably alkaline. Moist. Divide clumps every third or fourth year, and discard the old center. Pinch tips of tall kinds in early summer when about 1 foot high. Space the large kinds 1½ to 2 feet apart, dwarfs 8 to 9 inches apart.

Use: Border. Rock garden. Cut flower. Wild garden.

Species and varieties:

A. alpigenus (Alpine Aster): A dwarf of the Rocky Mountains. Foliage slightly pubescent (hairy). Solitary flowers having lavender rays and yellow disc. August/September.

A. alpinus (Mountain Daisy. Rock Aster): 6 to 12 inches. Large, solitary violet-blue flowers. May/June. Found in the alpines of Europe and North America. (See illustration p. 27).

Varieties: *"albus,"* white form; *"roseus,"* pink; "Goliath," soft blue; "Dark Beauty," deep purple.

A. amellus hybridus (Italian Aster. Italian Starwort): 1½ to 2 feet. Branching habit. Greyish-green leaves and rather hairy stems. Flowers to 2 inches across in clustered heads, purple rays, yellow disc. July/August.

A. cordifolius elegans (Heart-leaf Aster. Blue Wood Aster): 4 feet. Branching habit. Numerous small (½ inch), soft blue or pale lavender flowers in loose panicles. August/September. Tolerates part shade. For the wild garden. Found from Quebec to Wisconsin.

A. diplostephioides: 12 inches. Flowers made up of long, feathery, violet rays and orange discs.

A. divaricatus (syn. *A. corymbosus*) White Wood Aster: 1 to 1½ feet. Rosette of basal foliage. Creeping rhizome. Flowers in flat corymbs, to 1 inch across, white rays and pale yellow or purplish discs. August/September. Makes an attractive ground cover in a dry open woodland garden. Native from New England to Ohio.

A. ericoides (Wreath or Heath Aster): 3 feet. Bushy habit. Heath-like foliage. Creeping roots. Small flowers in one sided racemes, rays white, pink or lavender with dark discs. July/August. Dry, sunny, wild garden. From Maine to British Columbia and southward.

A. farreri (Big Bear): 12 inches. Flowers in solitary

heads, narrow violet rays, red-orange discs, to 3 inches across. June on. Native to China. Variety "Berggarten" resembles "Napsbury" but is earlier.

A. frikartii "Wonder of Stafa": 2 feet. Rather sprawling habit. Greyish foliage. Lavender-blue flowers. Blooms all summer.

A. laevis (Smooth Aster): to 4 feet. Stout smooth stem often glaucous. Blue flowers to 1 inch across in loose panicles. August/September. Parent of many garden varieties. Prefers dry, sandy soil. Native to the Rockies from British columbia to New Mexico.

A. novae-angliae (New England Aster): to 4 feet. Branching habit. Downy, grey-green leaves. Flower rays, deep purple, blue or white, and narrow; the discs, yellow to orange. September/October. Moist, sunny site. Indigenous from New England west to Wyoming.

Variants come true from seed and often flower the first season. "*Roseus*," rose flowers; "September Ruby," deep ruby shade. August to frost.

A. novi-belgii (New York Aster): 3 feet. Bushy habit. Glossy foliage. Creeping roots. Flowers in dense paniceles, color is variable, blue, pink or white, but usually a violet-blue. Parent of many cultivated forms. Native from New England south to Georgia.

A. sericeus (Silvery Aster): 2 feet. Branching. Silvery foliage. Violet-blue flowers to

1½ inch across. August/September.

A. subcaeruleus: 9 inches. Matting. Nonbranching habit. Large flowers in solitary heads, pale blue to lilac-blue. August.

A. yunnanensis "Napsbury": 1 to 2 feet. Solitary flowers with ray florets a soft heliotrope shade and orange discs, fragrant. June/August. China.

Astilbe

Family: *Saxifragaceae* (Saxifrage).

Common name: Astilbe. False Spirea. Meadow Sweet.

Propagation: Difficult and slow from seed. Sow in fall or in spring following a period of prechilling in the refrigerator, germination at 45 degrees, very slow and erratic. Does not come true from seed.

Simplest method is division in spring or fall. Divide every 4 to 5 years to rejuvenate old clumps (at least one eye to a section). Very tolerant of transplanting, may even be moved when in flower.

Culture: Shade (tolerates sun if there is a constant source of moisture). Well-drained but rich soil; add peat and leaf mold. Moist. Set plants 1½ to 2 feet apart in groups of at least three.

Use: Border. Beside pond or stream. Very beautiful when tubbed for patio. May be forced for winter bloom (plant in pot in fall, sink the pot in the ground until Janu-

Aster yunnanensis, Hardy Aster "Napsbury"

ary, bring indoors to light and moderate temperature, keep very moist). Cut flowers (cut when the buds are half open, split the stems up about an inch and place in cool spot overnight).

Species and varieties:

A. x arendensii: This cross includes most of the named horticultural varieties. The main flowering period is from June/July. "Deutschland," 2 feet, white; "Avalanche," 1½ feet; "Bremen," 2 feet, robust growth, salmon-carmine; pink varieties include "Europa," 1½ to 2 feet. "Irene Rotseiper," to 30 inches, "Hyacinth," 2½ to 3 feet, "Peach Blossom," 1½ to 2 feet, red flowers and bronze foliage, "Red Sentinel" also has reddish-green leaves.

A. astilboides: 2 to 3 feet. Sharp-toothed, hairy, divided leaves. White flowers in dense spikes. Japanese.

A. chinensis: 1½ feet. Finely divided leaves. Slender, branching panicles of white to soft pink flowers. July/August. Self-sows if happily sited.

Rock garden variety "Pumila," 8 inches, flowers in stiff spikes, rose with a bluish cast. July/August.

A. x crispa (cross of *A. simplicifolia* x *A. x arendsii*): 4 to 6 inches. Crinkled, deep-bronze leaves; "Parkes" and "Crispa" are also dwarfs with pink flowers in June.

A. davidi (often catalogued as a variety instead of species): to 6 feet. Hairy leaves. Dense panicles of rose-pink flowers with dark

blue anthers; also found in colors white, salmon, and reds. Often forced by florists. There are many named varieties. Of Chinese origin.

A. grandis: 6 feet. Another Chinese species with hairy foliage and creamy-white flowers. There is also a rose variety.

A. japonica: 1 to 3 feet. Finely cut foliage. Plumy panicles of white, pink, or red flowers. June to July. Many named varieties. Prized by florists for forcing. Purchased plants may be set out in the garden when weather permits. They will not flower again that year but are perfectly hardy and will be an asset later on.

A. rivularis: 5 feet. Creeping rootstock. Yellowish-white flowers.

A. simplicifolia: 12 inches. Leaves, 3 to 5 lobed. Rather open panicles of starry white flowers (often pale pink) on arching stems. June/July. Japanese. There is a rose variant.

A. thunbergi: 2 feet. Hairy, toothed leaves. White flowers fade to pink.

Astrantia

Family: *Umbelliferae* (Parsley).

Common name: Masterwort.

Propagation: Seed sown in early spring at 45 degrees. Germination rather slow.

Division in spring or fall.

Culture: Shade. Rich, humusy soil. Moist. Does not like to be moved; once it is established, leave it alone.

Use: Woodland garden. Shady place beside water, in the rock garden, or in the border.

Species:

A. biebersteinii: 6 to 12 inches. Silvery leaves. White flowers surrounded by pinkish bracts. Caucasus.

A. major (or sometimes listed as *A. carniolica major*): 1 to 3 feet. Toothed and lobed, long-stemmed, palmate leaves. Flowers, 1 to 2 inches across, white, pink, or rose with notched petals, in umbels surrounded by greenish-pink or purple bracts. June/September. European mountain plant found to 6,500 feet elevation; have become naturalized in the British Isles.

A maxima (syn. *A. heleborifolia*): 1½ feet. Robust habit of growth. Pink flowers in June.

Aubrieta

Family: *Cruciferae* (Mustard).

Common name: False or Purple Rock Cress. Rock Mustard.

Propagation: Seed sown in spring at 50 to 65 degrees. Germination in 6 to 14 days.

Division in spring.

Layer (root) trailing shoots.

Cuttings in July or August.

Culture: Sun or open shade. Light, porous soil. (Limestone ledges if you are fortunate to own any). Shear after blooming for neatness. Space plants 4 inches apart.

Use: Rock garden or wall. Low border adjoining paved area.

Species and varieties:

A. deltoidea: 6 inches. Mat forming. Small, hairy leaves. Flower color varies from red to purple. April/June. From Greece.

A. rosea splendens: 3 to 6 inches. Mat-forming plant of trailing habit. Bright rose flowers in May/June. (See illustration. p. 30).

Varieties: "Crimson King"; "Dr. Mules," deep purple; "Gloriosa," large rose-pink flowers; "Mrs. Lloyd Edwards," violet-purple; "leichtlini," reddish-pink; "graeca," light blue; "Borsch's White"; "bougainvillei," dark blue.

Balsamorhiza

Family: *Compositae* (Daisy).

Common name: Balsam Root.

Propagation: Seed collected and sown in August; sow thickly as viability is low. Sow in spring at 65 degrees.

Culture: Sun or partial shade. Well-drained, sandy soil. Dry. A long tap root makes this almost impossible to transplant except for young plants.

Use: Very brilliant sheets of color for the wild garden.

Species:

B. hookeri (Hooker Balsamroot): Leaves arranged in a basal rosette; deeply divided, arrow-shaped, silvery-white, and wooly. Solitary flowers atop a leafless stem 4 to 12 inches tall, composed of golden-yellow ray and disc florets. Flower heads 1½ to 2½ inches across. June/July. Native to the western states from prairie to 5,500 feet.

B. saggittata (Arrowleaf Balsamroot): 8 to 24 inches. Silvery-grey, long-stalked, arrow-shaped leaves, 12 inches long and 6 inches wide. Solitary flower head, 2 to 4 inches across, with bright yellow rays, on mostly naked stems. April to July, depending on the altitude. The plant becomes dormant in late summer. Also from the western states, valley to 8,000 feet.

Baptisia

Family: *Leguminosae* (Pea).

Common name: False or Wild Indigo.

Propagation: Collect seeds in fall and sow anytime, or sow in spring at 50 to 65 degrees. Germination in 10 to 30 days.

Division in spring.

Culture: Sun or part shade. Average to sandy soil. Slow growing. Space 1 to 2 feet apart. Best placed in permanent position while young for

it is deep-rooted and not easy to transplant.

Use: Single specimen. Border background. Cut flower. Wild garden. Winter bouquet of seed pods.

Species:

B. australis (Blue False Lupine): 3 to 5 feet. Branching habit. Compound leaves. Arching branches with indigo-blue, lupine-like flowers in long terminal racemes. June/July. Moist, enriched soil. Fat, 2-inch-long, black seed pods an asset for winter bouquets. Found from New England to Texas.

B. bractea: 1½ to 2 feet. Cream to pale yellow flowers in axillary racemes. May/June.

B. leucantha (Prairie False Indigo): 4 feet. White flowers in racemes. June/July. Midwestern states. Prefers part shade and moisture.

B. leucophaea (Plains False Indigo): 2½ feet. Hairy foliage. White or cream-colored flowers to 1 inch long in arching racemes. May/June. Downy seed pods. From Michigan to Arkansas. Requires sandy soil.

B. tinctoria (Yellow Wild Indigo. Yellow False Lupine): 4 feet. Bushy plant having small, blue-green leaves to 1 inch long. Small, bright yellow flowers in terminal clusters. June/July. Native to the eastern states from Massachusetts to Minnesota. Good for the dry wild garden.

Belamcanda

(syn. *PARDANTHUS*) ....

Family: *Iridaceae* (Iris):

Common name: Blackberry or Leopard Lily.

Propagation: Seed sown in early spring at 45 degrees. Germination in 15 days.

Division of rhizomatous tuber in spring, much as you would an iris clump.

Culture: Sun. Light, sandy soil. Space 10 inches apart in colonies; not very showy unless planted in large groups.

Use: Border. Naturalize. Fall bouquets of dried seed heads.

Species:

B. chinensis: 2 to 3 feet. Iris-like leaves and habit. Branching flower stems with star-like, orange to yellow flowers, 2 inches across, in loosely arranged clusters. Flowers are often spotted blackish-red. July/August. Shiny, black seeds in pods. Var. "avalon hybrids." China and Japan.

Bellis

Family: *Compositae* (Daisy).

Common name: English or Meadow Daisy.

Propagation: Seed sown in spring at 50 to 60 degrees. Germination in 7 to 14 days.

Does not always reproduce true to type from seed. Will bloom the first year if sown in April.

Self-sows.

Division in fall.

Culture: Sun or part shade. Rich, humusy soil. Moist, cool conditions. Plant wilts rapidly without sufficient moisture. Space 6 inches apart. These often behave as biennials. Not rock hardy; give winter protection.

Use: Edge of border. Rockery. Pot plant.

Species and varieties:

B. perennis: 6 inches. Rosette or tufted habit. Downy, spatulate leaves, 2 inches long. Solitary, single flowers, 2 inches across, with white rays and yellow discs. May/July. European.

Varieties: "Longfellow," a double, deep rose; "Etna," double scarlet with quilled petals; "*nana* Red Buttons," double red; "Stromboli," bright red; "*monstrosa tubulosa*," quilled form of dark red, rose shades, or white.

Bergenia

(syn. *MEGASEA*) ....

Family: *Saxifragaceae* (Saxifrage).

Common name: Siberian or Heartleaf Bergenia.

Propagation: Sow seed in spring at 45 degrees. Germination within 20 days.

Division in spring.

Culture: Sun or filtered shade. Enriched, humusy soil. Moist. Space 10 to 12 inches apart. These will form colonies in lightly shaded, moist sites.

Use: Woodland garden. Rock garden. Border. Stream or pondside.

Species:

B. cordifolia: 1 to 1½ feet. Foliage is large, fleshy, and decorative. The shiny, evergreen leaves turn purple in winter. Reddish flowers in nodding panicles in May. Siberian.

Variants: "*alba*," white flowers; "*purpurea*," deep rose.

Bocconia

(syn. *MACLEAYA*) ....

Family: *Papaveraceae* (Poppy).

Common name: Plume Poppy. Tree Celandine.

Propagation: Sow in spring at 65 degrees. Germination very erratic; it may occur in 10 days or a year.

Division in spring.

Suckers.

Culture: Sun. Average to poor soil (likely to get out of bounds in rich soil). Clumps enlarge; should be kept to the back of the border and given room. May need dividing every fourth year.

Use: Border background.

Species:

B. cordata: 5 to 8 feet. Grey-green, heart-shaped leaves with pale undersides. Erect feathery panicles of small, petal-less, beige to pinkish flowers. July/August. Attractive drooping seed heads. Native to China and Japan.

Borage

Family: *Boraginaceae* (Borage).

Propagation: Sow in early spring or fall at 45 to 50 degrees.

Division.

Cuttings.

Culture: Sun. Average garden loam.

Use: Rock garden. Wall crevice.

Species:

B. laxiflora: Low trailing habit. Hairy foliage. Long-stemmed, saucer-shaped, pale blue flowers. April/August. Like the annual species *B. officinalis*, this plant attracts bees. Mediterranean.

Boykinia

Family: *Saxifragaceae* (Saxifrage).

Propagation: Purchased or collected seed sown in late summer or in spring (spring sowing requires a period of prechilling). Germinate at 45 degrees, sprouting occurs within 15 days.

Division of creeping rootstock in spring.

Culture: Partial shade. Very well drained, stony, gritty soil with leaf mold and peat added for *B. jamesii*, others require a humusy, woodland loam. Moist, at least in spring. Space 5 to 8 inches apart.

Use: Shaded rock garden. Woodland garden.

Species:

B. aconitifolia: 1½ feet. A woodland type with whitish flowers.

B. jamesii (James Boykinia): 3 to 12 inches high. Mostly basal leaves, to 2 inches across, toothed and kidney-

Boykinia aconitifolia

shaped. Flowering stems are clustered along thick branching rootstocks. Flowers to ½ inch long, in dense panicles of bright, deep pink to reddish-purple. June/July. A native of the Rockies; look for it in rocky sites, 7,000 feet and above.

Brodiaea

Family: *Liliaceae* (Lily).

Common name: Triplet Lily.

Propagation: Sow seed in early spring at 45 degrees. Germination within 28 days. Sow in a deep flat that may be carried through the first season until the bulbs are large enough to set out.

Small bulb produces offsets.

Culture: Sun or open woodland. Soil must be well drained, preferably sandy, gritty consistency with humus added for moisture retention. Moist in spring and dry in summer (conditions which are normal for Wyoming). All are indigenous to the West Coast, except for *B. douglasii* and *B. hyacintha*, which are found in the Rockies. Space plants 6 inches apart, setting bulbs 2 to 3 inches deep. Arrange in colonies and situate where they will not be irrigated during the summer.

Use: Rock garden. Naturalize at edge of or in the open woodland.

Species:

B. capitata (Blue Dicks): 1½ to 2 feet. Umbels of deep violet-blue, funnel-shaped flowers to ¾ inch long.

B. coccinea: 2 to 2½ feet. Rich crimson flowers.

B. coronaria: 1½ feet. Violet-purple to deep blue flowers to 2 inches long. June.

B. crocea: 9 to 12 inches. Bright yellow flowers, ¾ inch long.

B. douglasii (Wild Hyacinth): 1 to 3 feet. Basal grass-like leaves. Edible bulb. Blue, tubular flowers to 1 inch long, 5 to 15 inch umbels at top of leafless stems. April/July. Found to 9,000 feet in the Rocky Mountains from Montana to Utah.

B. grandiflora: 8 to 12 inches. Large purple-blue, trumpet-like flowers.

B. hendersonii: 9 inches. Large yellow flowers with a center band of purple.

B. hycintha: Another Rocky Mountain species very like *B. douglasii*, but this has white flowers.

B. ixioides (Pretty Face): 1½ feet. Salmon-yellow flowers, veined dark purple, about ¾ inch long.

B. lactea: 1 to 1½ feet. White or lilac flowers, ½ inch long.

B. laxa (Ithuriel's Spear): 1 to 1½ feet. Deep purple-blue bells, 2 inches long, in umbels (30 to a cluster) atop slender stems. May/July.

B. uniflora (Spring Star Flower): 8 inches. Solitary flowers, white, tinged blue, 1 inch long.

B. volubilis (Snake Lily): 3 feet. Variable in habit may be upright or grow to 8 feet as a twining vine. Rose-pink flowers, ¾ inch long.

Brunnera marcrophylla

(see ANCHUSA .... *mysotidiflora*

Bulbinella

Family: *Liliaceae* (Lily).

Propagation: Seed sown in spring, germinates at 65 degrees.

Division of tuberous roots.

Culture: Sun or part shade. Enriched, light soil, well drained. These are not completely hardy here; plant the fleshy tubers in spring after the ground has warmed. In fall treat as you would dahlia tubers; dig and store over winter.

Use: Border. Cut flower.

Species:

B. hookeri: 2 to 3 feet. Grass-like leaves. Bright yellow or white flowers in dense racemes 10 inches long atop naked stems.

B. robusta (*B. setosa*): Narrow, grassy leaves. Numerous, yellow, bell-shaped flowers in dense 4-inch spikes atop flowering stems. From South Africa.

Callirhoe

Family: *Malvaceae* (Mallow).

Common name: Poppy Mallow. Buffalo Rose.

Propagation: Seed sown at 50 to 65 degrees. Germination in 9 days. If sown in spring, it will flower the same season. Transplant when seedlings because they have long roots.

Culture: Sun. Sandy well-drained soil. Dry. Space 8 inches apart. Prostrate stems are inclined to die back in winter.

Use: Border. Rock garden. Naturalize on rocky hillside.

Species:

C. involucrata: 12 inches. Trailing habit. Mallow-like, wine-crimson flowers to 2 inches across. July to frost. Native to the dry plains from Wyoming to Texas.

Calochortus

Family: *Liliaceae* (Lily).

Common name: Sego or Mariposa Lily. Globe or Star Tulip.

Propagation: Seed collected and sown immediately, usually late July/August, or sow in spring at 50 to 65 degrees. Germination may not occure until the second season—do not discard the flat in despair. It requires 3 to 4 years to attain blooming size from seed.

Bulb (corm) separated when plant is dormant in late summer. It is quite easy to transfer to your own wild garden at this time if you have staked the plant's location. I have moved them with success when in full bloom; they must be taken up with a large clump of sod so that the roots are not disturbed.

Culture: Sun or open shade. Perfect drainage is an absolute must; porous, gravely soil is the best. As with brodiaea, set your plants where there is little or no irrigation during the summer. The foliage ripens within weeks after flowering at which time it is possible for the bulbs to be dug and stored for next spring planting (if you do not have the dry summer conditions advised). Space 6 inches apart in colonies.

Use: Wild garden or rocky slope. Many are indigenous to the western highlands. Look for them from April to June.

Species and varieties:

C. albus (Fairy or Diogenes Lanterns): 2 feet. A globe type, this prefers shade and more humus in the soil. Nodding, roundish, white flowers, fringed with hairs and having a deep blotch at the base of the petals.

C. amabilis (Golden Globe Tulip): 1½ feet. Nodding, golden-yellow flowers.

C. amoens (Purple Globe Tulip): 1½ feet. Hanging, globe-shaped, purplish-rose flowers.

C. clavatus: 3 feet. Yellow flowers, 2 to 3 inches across,

often having brownish-red blotches. April/June. California.

C. coeruleus (Cat's Ears): 3 to 6 inches. Blue flowers, 1 inch across. April/May. From the Sierra Nevada Mountains.

C. kennedyi (Scarlet Mariposa Tulip): Yellow, orange, or red flowers. April/June. Native to Nevada and Arizona.

C. macrocarpus (Green-banded Mariposa Lily): 2 feet. Purple flowers, 2 to 4 inches across, petals have a green stripe down the center of each. July/August.

C. monophyllus (Yellow Star Tulip): 10 inches. Bright yellow, cup-shaped flowers, often with black or brown markings at the base of the petals.

C. nitidus (Purple-eyed Mariposa): to 1½ feet. Resembles *C. nuttallii* in habit but does not have the basal markings. Flowers are lavender to deeper purple. Found from Montana to Nevada.

C. nutallii (Sego Lily or Lavender Sego Iily): 8 to 20 inches. Few, fleshy, onionlike leaves (hardly noticeable). 2 to 5 large, cup-shaped, white flowers in loose clusters, petals have crescent-shaped, purple markings in the center and the bases are yellow. June/July. Found on the dry plains of the western states from the Dakotas to California.

C. uniflorus (syn. *C. lilacinus*) Star Tulip: 10 inches high. Fragrant lilac flowers. May/June. Native to the Pacific coastal ranges.

C. venusta (White Mariposa Lily. Butterfly Mariposa): 10 to 12 inches. Flowers may be yellow or purple to red; they often have basal markings. May/July. California.

Varieties: "*citrinus*," yellow with a dark eye; "*oculatus*," white with purple shadings and dark basal blotches.

Caltha

Family: *Ranunculaceae* (Buttercup).

Common name: Marsh Marigold.

Propagation: Seed is slow to germinate; best results are obtained if sown while seeds are fresh. Sow the seed in a pot, plunge in water, keeping the soil surface constantly moist. Will bloom the third year from seed.

Division in early spring after flowering or when dormant in late summer.

Culture: Sun in spring, shade in summer. Neutral, heavy, rich, humusy soil. Easily adapted to a moist place in the garden even though it is a marsh plant. Protect the crown from the sun and dry winds in winter. As long as the site is very wet in spring, it may be dry later on in the year without injury to the plant. May be transplanted at any time. Space 8 to 12 inches apart.

Use: Edge of stream or pond. Moist wild garden. Long-lasting cut flower.

Species:

C. leptosepala (Marsh Marigold): 4 inches high. Basal, ovate leaves are large, shiny and dark green. Large, buttercup-like flowers, 1 to 2 inches across, white. Numerous yellow stamens give it the appearance of having a yellow center. May/August, depending on elevation. Found in subalpine (7,000 to 10,000 feet) wet meadows or at the margins of stream or pond in the Rockies from Alberta to New Mexico.

C. palustris: 1 to 2 feet. Leaves mostly basal, fleshy, roundish or kidney-shaped. Large, deep yellow, waxy flowers, 2 inches across, in clusters on hollow stems. May/June. There is a double variety "*flore-pleno*."

Spreads by runners but is easily controlled. If planting beside water, the root crown should be barely covered by the water. Found in eastern states to as far west as Saskatchewan; also native to Europe and Asia.

Calypso

Family: *Orchidaceae* (Orchid).

Common name: Fairy Slipper.

Propagation: This is very difficult and should be attempted only if conditions can be met. Other than field collection, there is one commercial source of plant material that I know of, the Jamison Valley Gardens of Spokane, Washington.

Corms (size of marble).

Culture: Shade. Coniferous woods soil, composed of decayed wood and pine needles (see Cypripedium). Moist, especially in the spring. Transplanting is possible anytime but will not be successful unless the site is very like the original. It must be moved as a clump, without disturbing the roots or the necessary mycorrhiza adaptation. It is preferable to move when dormant in late June or July.

Use: Woodland garden.

Species:

C. bulbosa: 3 to 6 inches. One, clasping, broad, basal leaf. Solitary, fragrant, nodding pink to rose, orchid-like flower to 1½ inch long. Unlike the cypripedium which has an inflated pouch, this has a flattish lip. May/June. Found in coniferous woods from 5,000 to 8,000 feet elevation in the Rockies as well as other cold northern areas of North America, Europe, and Asia.

Camassia

Family: *Liliaceae* (Lily).

Common name: Quamash. Camash. Camas Lily. Swamp Sego.

Propagation: Sow in fall; the seeds need a period of freezing. Stratify seeds prior to spring sowing, remove to 45 to 50 degrees. Germination is slow. As with other members of the lily family that form a bulb, it is preferable to leave the seedlings in the

seed flat the first season, overwintering in the cold frame. Do not transplant to the garden until a large enough bulb has formed; they will not survive.

Bulbs purchased for fall planting. These rarely produce offsets.

Culture: Sun or part shade. Neutral, humus-enriched soil. Naturally moist site in spring, as moisture is needed during the growing period. The plant is dormant by late summer. Set out bulbs in fall, 4 inches deep, spaced about 4 inches apart in colonies.

Use: Border. Rock garden. Pond or streamside. Wild garden.

Species:

C. cusicki (Cusick's Camass): 3 - to 4-foot flowering stem decorated with dense clusters of pale blue to lavender flowers. More and wider leaves to each basal clump than other species. Mountains of Oregon and California.

C. leichtinii (Leichtlin's Camass): 1½ to 2½ feet. A western coast species of very robust habit. Glaucous foliage. The large cluster of flowers are variable in color, ranging from creamy-white and pale blue to deep violet-blue.

C. quamash (Common Camass): 2 to 3 feet. Long narrow, basal leaves. Flowers in loose clusters, deep violet-blue (rarely white). The 3 sepals and 3 petals are the same color. May/July. Seed pods stand erect. Found in the western states from Alberta to California.

C. scilloidea (syn. *esculenta* is often confusingly applied to both eastern and western species) Wild Hyacinth. Eastern Camass: 1 to 2 feet. Basal grass-like leaves. Starry flowers on unbranching stems, with spike-like racemes of pale blue, lavender, or white. May. Found in open woodland and wet meadows from Pennsylvania to Wisconsin southward to Texas.

Family: *Campanulaceae* (Bellflower).

Propagation: Seed sown at 65 degrees. Germinating time will vary with the species.

Division in spring.

Root cuttings.

Stem cuttings, include part of the root at base of the shoot.

Culture: Sun or light shade. Well-drained, humusy soil. *C. medium* is easily transplanted even when in bloom. The season of bloom may be lengthened considerably by careful removal of faded flowers.

Use: Border. Rock garden. Wild garden. Cut flower (sear cut end with flame).

Species and varieties:

C. barbata: 12 inches. Leaves in a basal clump, 2 to 5 inches long, narrow, and hairy. Nodding, bearded bells of pale lilac or porcelain blue, 1 inch long. July. This has a long root—transplant when young. Prefers sun. Space

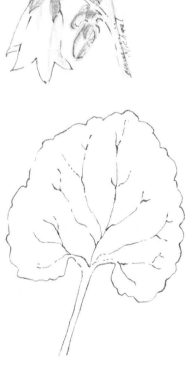

Campanula alliariifolia,
Bellflower

plants 6 inches apart. Germination within 11 days from
seeding. Allow to self-sow,
for they are not long-lived.

C. caespitosa: 12 inches.
Clear blue bells. Plant in the
sun, 6 inches apart. Sow
thickly, as viability is low.
Germination takes up to
3 weeks.

C. carpatica (Carpathian
Harebell or Bellflower. Tus-
sock Bellflower) : 6 to 12
inches high. Tufted habit or
growth. Smooth, wavy,
toothed leaves, 1 to 1½
inches long; the lower leaves
are ovate, 1½ inches long,
and long stemmed. Erect,
up-facing, cup-shaped,
solitary flowers, 1 to 2 inches
across, in shades of light to
deeper violet are held well
above the foliage. July on.
Plant in the sun, 6 inches
apart. Moist. Germination
in 7 to 18 days.

Varieties come true from
seed: *"turbinata,"* 4 to 6
inches, hairy foliage, flowers
small and more bell-like than
type and a deeper violet-
blue; *"turbinata pallida,"* pale
blue flowers; "White Star,"
12 inches, the white flowers
are flat rather than cup-
shaped; "Convexity," 6
inches, large, wide-open,
purple-blue flowers; "Blue
Chips and White Chips," 9
inches. July/September.

C. cochlearifolia (syn. *C.
pusilla*) : 2 to 6 inches.
Leaves form tiny rosettes.
Solitary blue harebells on
wiry stems. Prefer a gritty
soil. Var. *"alba,"* white
form.

C. collina: 9 inches. Clumps
of narrow, rough leaves. Deep
blue flowers in June. From
the Caucasus.

Campanula carpatica,
Carpathian Harebell
"White Star"

Campanula formanekiana,
Bellflower

Campanula carpatica, Carpathian Harebell "Convexity"

60

C. fragilis: 4 inches high of trailing habit. Long-lasting light blue flowers in clusters. Variety "Jewel." Two plants in a 10-inch basket make a wonderful display under cool conditions; in the heat of midsummer, I move them to the garden (easily transplanted). Of borderline hardiness, they should really be taken up and kept indoors during the winter.

C. garganica (syn. *C. elatines*) Adria Bellflower. Italian Harebell: to 6 inches. Spreading tufted growth. Small, greyish leaves, 1 inch wide, sharp-toothed, heart-shaped, with long petioles. Pale violet-blue starry flowers, often with small white eyes, solitary or a few atop the stem. June/July. Set plants 4 inches apart in rock garden, window box, or baskets. Variety *"hirsuta"* has hairy foliage and pale blue flowers; it is also a trailer.

C. glomerata (Clustered Bellflower. Twelve Apostles. Danes Blood): 1½ to 2 feet. Erect habit. Light-colored flowers in shades of purple-blue, blue, or white, of rather small, narrow bell-shape and found in dense clusters in the leaf axils and ends of stem and branches. June/July. Space 12 inches apart. Tolerates dry, poor soil. Native to southern Europe.

Varieties: *"acaulis,"* 3 to 6 inches, dwarf tufted habit, rough-textured, narrow, pointed leaves, stemless umbels of violet-blue flowers in July; "Crown of Snow," 12 inches, stiff growth, thick, sturdy stems, white flowers in leaf axils and terminal clusters; *"dahurica,"* 12 inches, deep violet-purple.

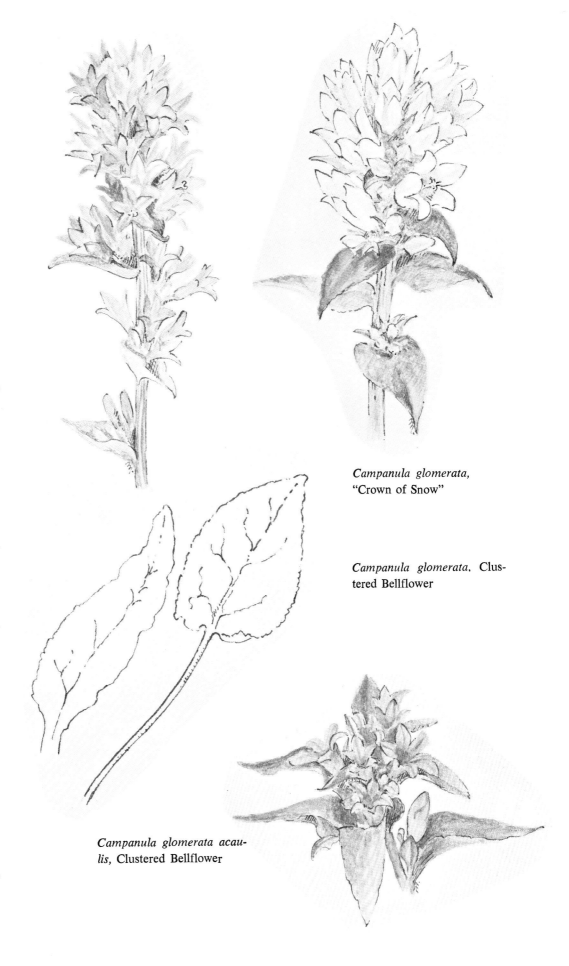

Campanula glomerata, "Crown of Snow"

Campanula glomerata, Clustered Bellflower

Campanula glomerata acaulis, Clustered Bellflower

61

C. lactiflora (Milk White Bellflower): 2 to 4 feet. Branching habit. Slightly hairy foliage. Upfacing flowers of white to pale blue, 1 inch long by 1 inch wide, in terminal clusters. July/August. Add peat to soil as well as annual applications of iron chelates, for this shows a need for a more acid soil. Plant 12 inches apart. Germination takes 9 days. Native to the Caucasus.

Variety "Loddon Anna," 4 feet, flesh-pink flowers, will not reproduce true to type from seed.

C. latifolia (Great Bellflower): 2 to 4 feet. Lower leaves are long-stemmed, toothed, rugose, hairy, and 5 to 6 inches long: upper leaves have shorter stems and are more narrow and pointed. Very large violet-blue flowers in leafy, terminal clusters. June/July. Give it a sunny spot; plant 12 to 18 inches apart.

Varieties: "*alba*," a white form; "*macrantha*," 3 feet, large, flaring bells to 2 inches across, of deep violet shade. July.

C. latiloba: 2 feet. Pale violet bells to 2 inches across. Resembles C. persicifolia. Germination within 3 weeks. Plant 8 to 10 inches apart in sunny spot. From Asia Minor. Variety: "Highcliffe varieties."

C. medium (Canterbury Bells): Biennial. 3 feet. Erect, stout-stalked bushes. Foliage is coarse and hairy. Single, upfacing flowers, one or more in upper leaf axils and terminal clusters may be

white, pink, lavender, or purple-blue. June/July. Originally from southern Europe. (I discovered that careful removal of each faded flower with a small sharp-nosed scissors will extend the blooming season to frost. Although a biennial, the canterbury bells are so delightful they are well worth the trouble.) (See illustration p. 27.)

Varieties: "*calycanthema*" (Cup and Saucer Bellflower), 2½ feet, the calyx forms a saucer under the corolla or bell—white, lilac and rose forms; "*flore-pleno*" (Hose-ing-Hose), 2½ feet, double (the calyx resembles the corolla in that it is also bell-shaped), may be white, violet-blue or rose; "*nana* Musical Bells," 1½ feet, very compact, profuse blooms in shades of blue, purple, pink, and white. (See illustration p. 27.)

C. muralis (syn. *C. portenschlagiana*): 6 inches. Tufts of tiny, ivy-like, shiny leaves. Panicles of purplish-blue, upfacing bells. Light shade. Outer rosettes of the clump may be separated and rooted anytime.

C. persicifolia (Peachleaf Bellflower. Beach Bells): 2 to 3 feet. Open racemes of blue flowers on erect stems. July/August. Space 12 inches apart. Division of the basal tuft every other year will improve flowering capacity and allow increase of a selection. European. (See illustration p. 27.)

Varieties: "*alba*" white; "Wedgewood Blue"; "Telham Beauty," 2½ feet; double chromosomes are responsible

Campanula persicifolia, Peachleaf Bellflower

for the larger flowers; china blue bells in loose, open racemes. July/August.

C. planiflora: 12 inches. Rosettes of round, wavy-edged, deep green leaves. Flattish, pale blue bells in leaf axils on stiff stems. Variety *"alba"* is a white form. Germination in 11 days. (Not true from seed, some are dwarfs and some resemble tall *C. persicifolia*.) Space 6 inches apart in the sun.

C. poscharskyana: 4 inches. Spreading habit. Sprays of pale lavender-blue stars. Similar to *C. garganica* but larger leaves and more abundant bloom. Requires shade and a gritty, stony soil.

C. punctata: 1½ feet. Nodding 2-inch-long, creamy-pink flowers, dotted red within; the spots show faintly to the outside. Hairy foliage.

C. pyramidalis (Chimney Bellflower): 3 to 5 feet. Long-stemmed, heart-shaped leaves, 2 inches long. Racemes of white or pale blue bells, 1 inch long; blooms from June to frost. Var. *"alba"* a white form. Germination in 19 days. Space plants 12 to 18 inches apart.

C. raddeana: 9 inches. Toothed, heart-shaped leaves with prominent veins. Violet-blue, funnel-shaped flowers on branching stems that are often not sturdy enough to hold up the blossoms. July/August.

C. raineri: 3 inches. Spreading and mat forming. Hairy, grey-green foliage. Upfacing, short-stemmed, lavender-blue bells.

Campanula pyramidalis,
Chimney Bellflower

C. rapunculoides (Rover Bellflower. European Bellflower): 3 feet. Nodding, violet-blue, funnel-shaped flowers in open racemes on one side of the stem only. July/August. Germination in 9 days. Space plants 10 inches apart. Creeping rootstock but not invasive. A good choice for the wild garden.

C. rhomboidalis: 1½ to 2 feet. Drooping, blue bells. Germination in 22 days. Sunny position, 6 to 8 inches apart. Not completely hardy in Wyoming (1 in 5 survival).

C. rotundifolia (Harebell. Bluebell of Scotland): Altitude affects height of this plant, 4 to 12 inches. Many variations of form but usually found with loose clusters of pale blue flowers on slender wiry stems. June on. Var. "Olympica" has large deep lavender flowers. The species is found from Alaska to Texas, prairie to 10,000 feet; oddly enough, it is also native to Scotland.

C. sarmatica: 12 inches. Stout stems and large grey leaves. Pale grey-blue flowers on one-sided raceme. August/September. Germination in 23 days. Space plants 5 or 6 inches apart in the sun.

Carlina

Family: *Compositae* (Daisy).

Common name: Silver Thistle. Westherglass Thistle.

Propagation: Sow in late summer, or prechill in the refrigerator and sow in early spring. Germinate at 50 to 60 degrees.

Division.

Culture: Sun. Stony, rocky site. Dry.

Use: Rock garden.

Species:

C. acaulis: 9 inches. Rosette of spiny, thistle-like, deep-cut leaves. Stemless white flower, to 6 inches across rises from the center of the rosette. June/August. European.

Castilleja

Family: *Scrophulariaceae* (Figwort).

Common name: Paintbrush. Painted Cup.

Propagation: Seed and plants of some of the species may be purchased commercially; otherwise, it must be gathered locally. Sow seed in unsterilized soil taken from a site where this plant is growing. Germinating temperature, 65 degrees.

The plant is difficult to collect from the wild. A large clump of earth must be taken, including the plants surrounding the chosen specimen, for Castilleja is partially parasitic (depending for food on the roots of other plants) or has a mycorrhizal association with a soil-like fungus (the fungi act like root hairs and feed the plant).

Culture: Sun or open shade. Well-drained sandy soil. Dry or moist. Do not cultivate around these species.

Use: Wild flower garden; it will not survive cultivation.

Species:

C. chromosa (Early Paintbrush): 6 to 12 inches. Deeply divided leaves having linear to lanceolate lobes. Bright red bracted flowers. May/June. One of the more easily grown western mountain species.

C. flava: to 12 inches high. Resembles C. sulphurea, but the hairy grey leaves are divided into narrow linear sections. Flowers have yellow bracts.

C. integra: Very like C. chromosa, but the color is variable.

C. linariaefolia (Wyoming Paintbrush): 1 to 3 feet. Semi-parasitic type. Foliage may be smooth or hairy, leaves narrow or linearly divided. Terminal spikes of brilliant red (what appear to be the petals are really the bracts and calyx of the flower which is inconspicuous). June/August, depending on elevation which ranges from the dry plains to 9,000 feet. Found throughout the Rocky Mountain region.

C. miniata (Scarlet Painted Cup): 1½ feet. Leaves lanceolate and entire (not divided). Red flowers, 1½ inches or more long. June/August. A western mountain species found in open woodland.

C. rhexifolia (Splitleaf Painted Cup): Another western mountain type with bright red flowers to 1 inch long. Narrow to ovate, entire leaves.

C. sulphurea (Yellow Paintbrush): 4 to 16 inches. Smooth, entire, lanceolate leaves emerge from woody crowns. Rising from the center of the crowns there are a cluster of flowering stems having dense spikes of yellow flowers. May/July. Found from plains to timberline from Montana to Colorado.

Catananche

Family: *Compositae* (Daisy).

Common name: Cupid's Dart. Blue Succory.

Propagation: Seed sown in early spring will bloom the first year. Germination at 45 degrees in 10 days.

Division. Selections may be divided; however, it does not require dividing and prefers not to be disturbed.

Culture: Sun. Well-drained garden loam. Dry. Space 8 inches apart in groups; should be massed for effective display.

Use: Border. Cut flower. Dried winter bouquet.

Species and varieties:

A. caerulea: 2½ feet. A dozen or more naked flower stems to each crown of narrow, pubescent leaves. Solitary flowers of blue, white, or bicolored, to 2 inches across. June/August. Mediterranean.

Variants: "*major*," 2 feet, greyish foliage, large blue flowers on strong wiry stems; "*alba*," white; "*bicolor*," 2½

feet, blue rays edged white; "Perry's White."

Catananche caerulea, Cupid's Dart

Caulophyllum

Family: *Berberidaceae* (Barberry).

Common name: Blue Cohosh.

Propagation: Seed sown in fall or stratified overwinter and sown in early spring. Germination is sporadic over two years.

Self-sows.

Root cuttings.

Division in spring.

Culture: Shade. Neutral, humusy woods soil. Moist

Use: Woodland garden.

Species:

C. thalictroides: 1 to 3 feet. Erect habit. Large compound leaves. Panicles of yellowish-green flowers in spring, followed by large, rich, blue seeds in fall. Native from Ontario to Manitoba and southward.

Centaurea

Family: *Compositae* (Daisy).

Common name: Perennial Cornflower.

Propagation: Seed sown in early spring is preferable. Germination at 65 degrees.

Self-sows freely(too freely, if seed heads are not removed).

Division in spring.

Softwood stem cuttings in summer of *C. rutifolia* and *C. gymnocarpa.*

Culture: Sun. Light, well-drained soil. Space 12-inch species 9 inches apart; taller kinds 12 to 18 inches apart with the exception of *C. macrocephala* as noted below.

Use: Border. Rock garden. Cut flower. Wild garden.

Species and varieties:

C. dealbata (Persian Centaurea): 2 to 3 feet. Delicate, pinnate foliage; toothed, wooly leaves, white undersides. Large rose-purple flowers.

C. gymnocarpa (Velvet Centaurea. Dusty Miller): 1 to 2 feet. Grown for its ornamental foliage. Wooly, silver-white, fine-cut, pinnate leaves. Panicles of rose to purple flowers. Not always dependably hardy in the western highlands.

C. fritschii: 6 feet high. Rose flowers, ½ inch across.

C. jacea: 3½ feet. Narrow leaves. Rose-purple flowers to 1½ inch across.

C. montana (Perennial Cornflower. Mountain Bluet): 2 feet. Beautiful deep blue flowers to 3 inches across (the deepest blue in the garden). May/June. Cut the plant back after blooming as the foliage becomes ragged and rather unsightly.

C. macrocephala (Showy Knapweed): 2 to 4 feet. Very large leaves make this a very distinctive plant, better used as a single specimen than in groups. Thistle-like, large,

double, yellow flowers, 3 to 4 inches across. July/August. Armenian.

C. nigra (syn. *C. endressii*) Knapweed: 2 feet. Wooly foliage. Rose-purple flowers, 1 inch across.

C. orientalis (syn. *C. rigidifolia*): to 3 feet. Yellow flowers, 2½ inches across.

C. pulcherrima (syn. *C. aethiopappus*): 2½ feet. Brilliant rose flowers.

C. ruthenica: 3 feet. Pinnate foliage, leaves deeply lobed. Pale yellow flowers, 2 inches across. Russian.

C. rutifolia (syn. *C. candidissima, C. cineraria*) Dusty Miller: 1 to 3 feet. Finely cut, silvery-white, wooly foliage; leaves mostly basal. Solitary, large, yellow or purple flowers, 1 inch across. July/September.

Centaurea montana, **Perennial Cornflower**

Cephalaria

Family: *Dipsaceae* (Teasel).

Common name: Giant Scabiosa. Cephalaria.

Propagation: Seed sown in early fall or spring. Germinating temperature 60 degrees.

Cuttings in summer.

Division in spring.

Culture: Light shade. Average garden loam. Adequate moisture. Space plants 1½ to 2 feet apart and place in the background (it has a rather coarse appearance).

Use: Border. Cut flower. Wild garden.

Species:

C. tatarica: 5 feet. Divided leaves with hairy undersides. Flowers resemble scabiosa, cream to sulphur-yellow flower heads to 2 inches across atop slender, naked stems. July/August. Native to Russia and western Asia.

Cephalaria tatarica, Giant Scabiosa

Cerastium

Family: *Carophyllaceae* (Pink).

Common name: Mouse-ear or Meadow Chickweed.

Propagation: Sow seed in spring at 50 to 60 degrees. Germination in 15 to 28 days.

Division in spring.

Rooted layers.

Cuttings in August.

Culture: Sun. Poor to average soil. Dry. Prune after flowering for neatness. Space 10 to 12 inches apart; the creeping stems will gradually fill in.

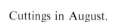

Use: Rock garden. Ground cover. Edging for paved area.

Species and varieties:

C. alpinum: 6 inches. Dense, silky-wooled tufts. Large white flowers on short stems. April/May. From the Arctic regions. Variety "*lanatum*" 2 inches high, very desirable rock-garden type.

C. arvense (Starry Grasswort): 10 inches. Green tufts. Clusters of white flowers. April/May. Variety "*compactum*" 3 inches, form a dense rounded mound covered with white flowers in June.

C. biebersteinii: Resembles *C. tomentosum* except it does not spread, and the leaves and flowers are larger. Asia Minor.

C. grandiflorum (syn. *C. argenteum*): 8 inches. Creeping habit. Greyish-white leaves. Very large white flowers.

C. tomentosum (Snow in Summer): 6 to 8 inches high. Prostrate, spreading habit. Silvery foliage. Small white flowers on wiry stems. June/July. Native to Europe, Asia, and North America. Variant "*columnae* Silver Carpet." Best used for carpeting; its spreading habit may make it a nuisance in the rock garden or border.

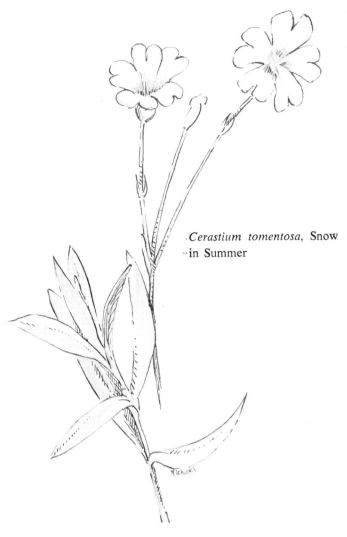

Cerastium tomentosa, Snow in Summer

Chaenactis

Family: *Compositae* (Daisy).

Common name: Morning Brides. Dusty Maiden.

Propagation: Seed of *C. douglasii* is offered by a few seed houses. *C. alpina* would probably have to be collected in the field. Sow when ripe or in spring at 45 degrees.

Division.

Culture: Sun. Average soil. Dry. Tap root makes transplanting difficult, except for

C. alpina which is small enough to be moved without injury.

Use: Rock garden. Wild garden.

Species:

C. alpina: 2 to 4 inches. Dusty-appearing basal leaves are the attractive feature of the plant. Pink flowers.

C. douglasii: Biennial. 1 to 2 feet. Divided leaves; the larger leaves form a basal rosette. One to several flowering stems to a clump, terminal flower heads, ½ inch across, composed of small tubular

flowers, white to flesh colored (only disc florets are present). June/August. From valley to timberline in the Rocky Mountains, Montana to New Mexico.

Chamaenerion *augustifolium*

(see EPILOBIUM) ....

Family: *Cruciferae* (Mustard).

Common name: Wallflower.

Propagation: If sown in February, *C. allonii* and *C. cheiri* will bloom the first year. Germination at 50 to 60 degrees within 6 days.

Cuttings in midsummer.

Culture: Sun. Native to limestone areas. On poor soil, *C. cheiri* may be perennial and become quite woody; however, seedlings must be wintered in the frame. They are not hardy enough to survive our winters without protection. Space 10 inches apart in the garden.
Use: Border. Cut flower. Rock garden. Container.

Species and varieties:

C. allioni (syn. *ERYSIMUM asperum*) Siberian Wallflower: Biennial or short-lived perennial. 9 to 12 inches. Clusters of orange flowers from June on. Self-sows. Varieties "Golden Bedder"; "Orange Queen." Native to North America.

C. cheiri (English Wallflower): Biennial. 1½ feet. Bushy habit. Flower racemes in shades of yellow to pink, red, copper, orange, or reddish-brown. June. From southern Europe. There are numerous named varieties, single and double. The largest listings are to be found in English catalogues.

C. kewensis: 12 inches. Fragrant flowers, pale primrose changing to orange-yellow and violet. Winter flowering, so are to be used in the cool greenhouse.

C. linifolius: Perennial. 12 inches. Lilac-mauve flowers. Good for the dry rockery.

C. semperflorens (syn. *C. mutabilis*) 2½ feet. Cream-colored flowers that turn purple with age.

Chelidonium

Family: *Papaveraceae* (Poppy).

Common name: Great Celandine.

Propagation: Sow seed in spring at 45 degrees. Germination in 8 days.

Self sows to some extent.

Culture: Sun. Average garden loam. Remove faded flowers to extend the flowering season. Space 10 inches apart.

Use: Border. Wild garden.

Species:

C. majus: 1 to 1½ feet. Branching habit. Small

Chelidonium majus, Great Celandine

September. Moderately acid soil. Northern states from Ontario to Minnesota.

C. lyoni (Purple Turtlehead): 3 feet. Rose-purple flowers to 1 inch long; lip has yellow beard and purple lines. July/ September. Native to the southern states but hardy in the North.

C. obliqua (Pink Turtlehead): 1½ to 2 feet. Terminal clusters of deep rose flowers, 1 inch long. July to frost. Another southern species.

Chiastophyllum oppositifolia

(see COTYLEDON .... *simplicifolia*) ....

Chionodoxa

Family: *Liliaceae* (Lily).

Common name: Glory of the Snow.

Propagation: Seed collected and sown when ripe, or in the spring at 50 to 60 degrees.

Bulb offsets.

Bulbs purchased and planted in early fall.

Culture: Sun (tolerates some shade). Fertile, loamy soil. Plant in colonies, 2 to 3 inches deep and 1 to 2 inches apart (about 18 bulbs to the square foot). They will self-sow and perpetuate themselves for years. Always allow the foliage to ripen when the flowering season is over.

Use: Naturalize in the grass. Rock garden. Good cut flower. Underplanting of trees and shrubs. Edging for woodland path.

Species:

C. gigantea: Somtimes classified as a variant of *C. luciliae,* this has larger leaves and flowers. Pale blue flowers.

C. luciliae: 5 to 7 inches. Basal leaves, narrow and strap-like appear at the same time as the flowers. Short racemes of starry, upfacing flowers, 6 to 8 to a stem, usually blue with white centers. April/May. Hybrids of this also include pink and white shades. Native to the mountains of Asia Minor.

Chrys- anthemum

Family: *Compositae* (Daisy).

Common name: Mum. Hardy Chrysanthemum.

Propagation: Seed sown in spring at 50 to 60 degrees. Germination between 4 and 14 days.

Division in spring.

Cuttings in spring very easily rooted; when 3 to 4 inches of new growth appears in spring, sever just below a leaf node. Insert in rooting medium with bottom heat and air temperature of 65 degrees. When roots form around the cut ends, transplant to peat pots and place in cold frame for a week or so. Moist and shaded.

Culture: Sun. Well-drained,

double, yellow flowers. June/ July. Attractive pale, apple-green leaves, deeply divided. European. (See illustration, p. 30.)

Chelone

Family: *Scrophulariaceae* (Figwort).

Common name: Turtlehead. Shellflower.

Propagation: Sow in spring at 45 degrees.

Division in spring.

Cuttings in summer.

Culture: Filtered shade. Light well-drained soil with peat added. Moist (found in the wild in open woodlands). Easily transplanted. Plant in groups, 8 to 10 inches apart.

Use: Border. Cut flower. Naturalized in damp, shady site.

Species:

C. barbata (see PEN-STEMON *barbatus*).

C. glabra (White Turtlehead. Snakehead): 2 to 3 feet. Slender, erect habit. Leafy stems topped by dense, terminal spikes of white or pinkish, snapdragon-like flowers, to 1 inch across; the lip has a white beard. July/

fertile, loamy soil. Fertilize with manure and superphosphate. Tolerant of aridity. Most species need division every third year as the clump spreads and the center dies. Very tall sorts may need to be staked. Space them 15 to 18 inches apart, the dwarfs 6 inches apart.

Use: Border. Rock garden. Wild garden. Cut flower (cut when a single bud shows color; the others on the stem will open in the water).

Species and varieties:

C. achilleaefolium (Yarrow Chrysanthemum): 2 feet. Downy leaves. Yellow flowers.

C. alpinum (Pyrethrum): 2 to 6 inches. Silvery, finely divided, basal leaves. Short-stemmed, solitary flowers, ¾ to 1 inch across, white rays are yellow at the base, yellow disc. June. Rock-garden type. Sow seed when ripe; it must be fresh for good germination.

C. arcticum (syn. C. leucanthemum arcticum) Arctic Daisy: 15 inches. Single flower. Ray florets vary from shades of red to yellow or white. Yellow disc. Flowers are 2 to 3 inches across. Very hardy but blooms in October which is often too late for mountain country. Parent of the Northland Daisy hybrids and the de Petris hybrids.

C. balsamita (Costmary. Lavender or Mint Geranium): 2 feet. Fragrant, downy foliage. White flowers to 1 inch across. August/September. Var. "tanacetoides" has no ray florets.

C. broussoneti: 2 to 3 feet. Flowers to 3 inches across, lilac rays shading to yellow at the base.

C. cinerariaefolium (Dalmatian Chrysanthemum. Insect Powder Plant): 1 to 2 feet. Silvery foliage. White flowers to 1 inch across.

C. coccineum (see PYRETHRUM).

C. indicum: 3 feet. Early flowering, single bloom. Variety "Charm," 1½ feet, fragrant, star-shaped flowers in shades of red, pink, yellow, orange, or white. Will flower 5 months from sowing.

C. koreanum (syn. C. sibericum, C. coreanum) Korean Chrysanthemum: 1½ to 2 feet. Sturdy, bushy habit; does not require staking in spite of fall winds. Flowers may be single or double in colors of yellow, gold, pink, crimson, and bronze. August on. Not as spectacular as the cultivars of C. morifolium but very hardy. Var. "Korean Sunset" has larger flowers and the colors are brighter. Native to Siberia.

C. leucanthemum (White-weed. Ox-eye Daisy): 3 feet. Free-flowering common daisy of eastern states; better suited to the wild garden. Variants "compactum Little Silver Princess," 1½ feet, dwarf form; "Diener's Double Giant," to 3 feet; "May Queen."

C. macrophyllum (Tansy Chrysanthemum): 2 to 3 feet. Flat cluster of small white or yellow flowers.

C. maximum (Shasta or Max Daisy): 2 to 3 feet. Bushy.

Single or double white flowers to 3 inches across. June/August. Originated in the Pyrenees. Many named variants: "Alaska," single; "Marconi," frilled, double (my favorite); "Mount Everest," largest flowers; "Polaris," 4 feet, flowers to 7 inches across; "Thomas Killin" double row of rays and crested gold centers; "Mount Shasta," a double sort with high-crested disc florets. (See illustrations, p. 29.)

C. morifolium (syn. C. hortorum): Most of the types offered for the garden and greenhouse are derived from this species. I am especially fond of the cultivars developed at the Cheyenne Horticultural Experiment Station: "Aztec," copper red; "Inca," amber-orange; "Powder River," white; "Shoshone," yellow. They are very hardy cushion mums of mound habit. 1½ feet high and as wide, blooming from August on.

C. nipponicum (Nippon Daisy): 2 to 3 feet. Hardy sub-shrub. Single flowers, white rays and yellow disc, 3½ inches across. September/October. Parent of the hybrids, "Milky Way" and "Burma."

C. parthenium (syn. MATRICARIA parthenium) Feverfew. Matricaria: 2 feet. Bushy, branching habit. Strong scented flowers and foliage. Open clusters of small white double or single flowers to ¾ inch across, yellow centers. July/August. European. Not completely hardy in the highlands.

Varieties: "aureum Gold

Feather," 12 inches, green-yellow foliage, single white flowers; "Silver Ball," globular double white flowers;

"Golden Ball," yellow disc (no ray florets); "Lemon Ball," soft pale yellow (no rays).

C. rubellum: 2 to 3 feet. Spreading clumps. Pinnate foliage. Solitary or a few flower heads to a stem. Single flowers pink or red, yellow disc, 3 inches across. August/September.

Varieties: "Clara Curtis," salmon-pink, very hardy; "Royal Command," red; "Anna Hay," salmon; "Jessie Cooper," bronze.

C. tchihatchewi (Turfing Daisy): 6 inches. Spreading habit. Finely cut foliage. This can be used as a substitute for lawn; it can be mowed.

C. uliginosum (High or Giant Daisy): 4 to 6 feet. Very sturdy, does not need staking. Large white flowers in August. European.

Cimicifuga

Family: Ranunculaceae (Buttercup).

Common name: Bugbane. Fairy Candle.

Propagation: Seeds collected and sown in fall. Prechill in the refrigerator several weeks before sowing in spring. Germinating temperature, 45 to 50 degrees. Germination is very slow and erratic.

Division in early spring is the best means of increase.

Culture: Partial shade (this is natively a woods plant). Soil rich in humus. Moist Space 12 to 18 inches apart in colonies of four or more.

Use: Shaded border specimen. Cut flower. Woodland garden.

Species and varieties:

C. americana (syn. C. cordifolia) American Bugbane: 3 to 6 feet. Large compound leaves are smaller than C. racemosa. Racemes of creamy-white flowers. August/September. Range from Pennsylvania to Georgia.

C. dahurica: 5 feet. Black stemmed. Spikes of creamy-white flowers from August to frost. Asian origin.

C. racemosa (Cohosh Bugbane. Black Snakeroot. Black Cohosh): 4 to 8 feet. Large palmate leaves. Fragrant, small white flowers with numerous stamens in long racemes. July/September. Native from Ontario to Missouri and eastward.

C. simplex (Kamchatka Bugbane): 3 feet. Upright racemes of creamy-white flowers. August/September. Same native range as C. racemosa. Variety "White Pearl" 3 to 4 feet. September/October. Growth habit more compact than type.

Clintonia

Family: Liliaceae (Lily).

Common name: Bead Lily.

Propagation: Seed sown in spring at 60 degrees. Seed gathered when ripe in fall; remove pulp and sow immediately. Slow to germinate. It takes 3 years to bloom from seed.

Division in spring or fall. Spreads by rhizomes or underground stems but is not weedy. New plants form at the nodes. Transplant in large clods.

Culture: Shade. Humusy woodland soil. Moist. Adapts quite well to the same cultural practices used for lily-of-the-valley. Feed at yearly intervals with well-rotted manure and bone meal. Set plants 6 inches apart in order to form colonies. Plant with the eye or bud just below the surface.

Use: Shady rock garden. Woodland garden. Edge of pond or stream. Ground cover.

Species:

C. andrewsiana: to 1½ feet high. Nodding, pink to rose-purple, lily-like flowers. From northern California, it is not absolutely hardy in the mountains but worth a try in a protected spot.

C. borealis (Bluebead Lily): 12 to 18 inches. Leaves very like those of the lily-of-the-valley, 2 to 4 shiny, dark green, hairy-edged leaves, 6 to 8 inches long and 3 inches wide. Three to six nodding, bell-like, greenish-yellow flowers to 1 inch long in loose, small terminal umbels atop naked stems 8 to 18 inches high. May/June. Brilliant, large, blue berries in late summer. This species prefers a rather acid peaty

soil. It is found in cool moist woods and bogs from Manitoba to Minnesota and southward.

C. umbellulata (White Clintonia. Speckled Bead Lily): Resembles C. borealis but is much more amenable to cultivation. Requires neutral soil conditions which are easier met in the western highlands. The clusters of white flowers, spotted brown and purple, are held erect. May/June. Blackish berries. Mountain woodlands of New York south to Tennessee.

C. uniflora (Queencup): 2 to 5 bright green, lance-shaped, basal leaves. Flowering stems, 3 to 8 inches high, carry one large, fragrant, starry white flower, 1 inch across. May/July. Blue berries. Look for this in the moist, peaty woodlands or streamsides of the Rocky Mountains from Alaska to California.

Clivia

Family: Amaryllidaceae (Amaryllis).

Common name: Clivia. Kafir Lily.

Propagation: Sow seeds at 70 degrees. Often blooms 18 months from seed.

Division of fleshy root.

Culture: Outdoors: Plant so the top of the tuber is just above the surface of the soil. Shade. Rich, humusy, loamy soil with sand added. (For container growing, add a bit of charcoal to the mix). This is a half-hardy plant so must

be potted or stored over winter in frost-free place. Moist during the flowering period, allow to dry off afterwards (which would normally be during the summer).

Indoors: Pot up from June to October. Average temperature of 65 degrees. In January, increase moisture and fertilize with liquid manure or fish emulsion as the plant blooms. Reduce the water after the flowering period is over. A potted plant can remain undisturbed for years in its container.

Use: Protected garden planter or bed. Container.

Species:

C. miniata: 2 feet. Clump of glossy, dark green, drooping, strap-like leaves, 1½ feet long. Lily-like flowers, 2 to 3 inches long, deep orange-red, in umbels on stiff stems. Spring bloom. Ornamental red berries. African.

Codonopsis

Family: Campanulaceae (Bellflower).

Propagation: Seed sown in spring at 50 degrees. Germination is erratic.

Cuttings in midsummer.

Division in spring.

Culture: Partial shade. Fertile loamy soil. Transplant when young, as this has a long tap root. Climbing types are best displayed by allowing them to naturally clamber over rock walls or stumps and brush. All are mountain plants from central Asia. Fall mulching is advised, for they are not reliably hardy without snow cover.

Use: Border. Rock garden. Wild garden.

Species:

C. clematidea: 1 to 3 feet. Blue or white bell-shaped flowers with white or yellow centers.

C. ovata: 1 to 2 feet. Half-twining habit. Rock garden type. Pale lavender to greyish-blue flowers, yellow and white spotted insides.

Colchicum

Family: *Liliaceae* (Lily).

Common name: Meadow Saffron. Autumn Crocus.

Propagation: Sow seed in fall or stratify prior to spring sowing. Germinate at 50 degrees.

Offsets.

Corms purchased and planted by August (almost immediately begin to bloom).

Culture: Sun or light shade. Light sandy soil. Plant in fall, 4 to 5 inches deep. Leaves appear in spring, allow to mature without disturbance.

It is possible to dig this corm in July and set upright in bowl containing 1 to 2 inches of pebbles, fill with water to the base of the corm; they will flower normally. Afterward plant outdoors again.

Use: Rock garden (give it enough room). Border. Create colonies in woodland gardens or under trees and shrubs.

Species and varieties:

C. autumnale: 12 inches. Several tulip-like, pointed leaves, 6 to 12 inches long, appear in spring, mature, and then die down. They are followed in fall by clusters of fragrant flowers, to 4 inches across, on naked stems, pale purple, rose, or white in color. August/October. The ovary is below ground; the mature seed capsule does not appear until the following spring. Native to Britain and Europe.

Varieties: "Waterlily," double, orchid-pink flowers in clusters of 6 or more; "*album*," white; "*roseum plenum*," double pink.

C. luteum: 12 inches. Himalayan species that (unlike the others) blooms in spring. Long, tubular, yellow flowers, often tinged purple on outside.

C. speciosum: 12 inches. Autumn flowering. Colors vary from rose to lilac. Varieties "Autumn Queen" deep rose; "The Giant" lavender.

Convallaria

Family: *Liliaceae* (Lily).

Common name: Lily-of-the-valley.

Propagation: Seed sown in fall. Prechill in refrigerator

prior to spring sowing. Germination at 50 degrees.

Division a more successful method of increase; usually in spring but actually is possible at any time.

Culture: Shade. Enriched humusy soil. Moist. Top dress with manure spring or fall. The fleshy crown known as a pip acts like a bulb; given warmth and water, a flowering stem will arise, making it possible to force bloom in winter. Space 6 to 9 inches apart, in colonies. It has a creeping rootstock and will normally spread.

Use: Shady ground cover. Cut flower.

Species and varieties:

C. majalis Fortunei (Giant Lily-of-the-valley. Fortin's Variety): 6 to 12 inches. The flowering stem rises between a pair of lance-shaped leaves. This variety has larger leaves and flowers than type. Small, white, nodding bells on short racemes, fragrant. May/June. From Europe and Asia.

Other variants: "*flore-pleno*," double form; "*rosea*," 9 inches, pale pink; "Parson's Giant."

Coptis

Family: *Ranunculaceae* (Buttercup).

Common name: Goldthread.

Propagation: Seed sown in fall when ripe, germinates by next spring. Spring sown seed must be stratified and refri-

gerated for several months prior to sowing. This seed must germinate in the dark; be sure to cover with brown paper.

Division in spring.

Root cuttings in spring; start in peat, shade.

Culture: Shade. Slightly acid, peaty soil. Moist. Mulch for coolness. Transplant in sodded clumps if necessary.

Use: Rock garden. Ground cover under evergreens. Terrarium.

C. groenlandica (syn. *C. trifolia*): 4 inches. Small, creeping plant (yellow thread-like roots just under the surface of the ground). Evergreen. Shiny, dark green, three-lobed, long-stemmed leaves. Solitary, white (rarely, yellow) flowers, ½ inch across. May/June. Requires moist rather boggy situation. Natively found across Canada from Labrador to the Pacific and as far south as Iowa.

Coreopsis

Family: *Compositae* (Daisy).

Common name: Tickseed.

Propagation: Sow in spring at 50 to 60 degrees. Germination time, 9 to 20 days.

Self-sows.

Division in spring.

Culture: Sun. Light sandy soil. Space plants 12 inches apart.

Use: Border. Cut flowers. Wild garden.

Species and varieties:

C. grandiflora: Biennial. 3 feet. Rather hairy foliage. Large, deep yellow flowers, rays are three-lobed at tips.

Var. "Badengold," 3 feet, very large deep yellow, variable from seed; "Baby Sun," 1½ feet, bushy dwarf, golden yellow.

C. lanceolata (Lance Coreopsis): 2 feet. Mostly basal, narrow, shiny leaves. Bright yellow, three-lobed rays, yellow disc. May/July. Found from Maine to Michigan. Easily naturalized.

Varieties: "*flore-pleno*," double; "Mayfield Giant," 3½ feet, taller and more vigorous than type; "Sunburst," 2½ feet, large, semi-double, golden yellow flowers from July to frost.

C. pubescens superba (syn. *C. auriculata*): 3 feet. Bushy. Hairy foliage. Large yellow-orange flowers with a dark blotch in the center, rays toothed at tips. July/August. Blooms all summer if faded flowers are removed. I have found this to be short lived but self-sown seedlings often appear. Natively found from Illinois to Virgina.

Var. "*nana*" 3 to 8 inches, orange-flowered rock garden type. June/August.

C. verticillata (Fern or Thread-leaved Coreopsis): 1 to 2 feet. Dainty, fern-like, grey-green leaves. Creeping roots, but not invasive. Clusters of fragrant, small, pale yellow flowers, 2 inches

Coreopsis lanceolata, Lance Coreopsis "Sunburst"

across. July/September. A southern species but hardy North. Var. "Golden Shower."

Cortusa

Family: *Primulaceae* (Primrose).

Propagation: Fresh seed important, sow when ripe or stratify and sow in spring at 50 to 60 degrees.

Division of clumps.

Root cuttings in early fall.

Culture: Shade. Woodland soil. Requires a winter mulch.

Use: Shady rock garden. Woodland garden.

Species:

C. matthioli: 6 to 9 inches. Hairy, geranium-like leaves in a basal crown. Terminal clusters of small, nodding, purple to rose-purple bells atop slender stems. May/June. By August the plant is dormant. From the mountains of Europe and northern Asia.

Corydalis

Family: *Papaveraceae* (Poppy).

Common name: Fumitory. Golden Bleeding Heart.

Propagation: Sow in fall or stratify and place in refrigerator (prechill treatment) for spring sowing. Germination at 45 degrees, within 30 days,

Cortusa matthiolii

flowers, yellow tipped. All summer. Dry, rocky site. Self-sows readily.

Cotyledon

Family: *Crassulaceae* (Orpine).

Propagation: Sow with care, for the seed is very fine, in fall or spring, 50 to 60 degrees. Seed must be fresh.

Division in spring.

Cuttings in summer.

Culture: Shade. Gritty, sandy, limy soil with humus added.

Group plantings most effective.

Use: Rock garden. Rock wall. Container.

Species:

C. simplicifolia (syn. *CHIASTOPHYLLUM oppositifolia*): 6 inches. Fleshy, sedum-like leaves in rosettes. Pale to deeper yellow bells in drooping racemes. June/July. Not absolutely hardy in the North, but easily propagated.

is slow and erratic unless fresh seed is used.

Self-sows, but these seedlings are difficult to re-establish. Pot up and place in frame for a week or two before replanting to permanent spot.

Division in spring.

Cuttings in summer.

Culture: Sun or light shade. Well-drained, humusy soil. Space 8 inches apart in groups.

Use: Border. Rock garden. Naturalize.

Species:

C. aurea: 12 inches. Bright green, very divided leaves. Golden yellow flowers all summer. Prefers a sandy,

limy soil. Found from Manitoba to Minnesota.

C. cheilanthifolia: 9 inches. Fern-like foliage. Yellow flowers in spring.

C. lutea: 9 to 12 inches. Short-spurred, golden-yellow flowers bloom profusely from spring to frost. Attractive ferny, pale green, glaucous leaves. A treasure in my garden that never fails to attract attention. (See illustration, p. 29.)

C. ochroleuca: 9 inches. Rock plant with pale yellow flowers.

C. ophiocarpa: 1¼ feet. Grown mainly for its attractive foliage.

C. sempervirens: Biennial. 6 to 12 inches. Rosettes of finely divided, grey-green leaves. Clusters of pink

Corydalis lutea, Golden Bleeding Heart

Crocus

Family: *Iridaceae* (Iris).

Propagation: Seed sown in fall will germinate the following spring. Stratification and exposure to freezing temperature is required for spring sowing. Sow in large flats and allow to remain undisturbed for several seasons before setting out the (then large enough bulbs.

Corms purchased and planted in fall: fall-flowering types in August, spring-blooming types in September. Speed is imperative in setting out the fall-flowering species for they will bloom whether they are in the ground or not.

Culture: Sun or light shade. Well-drained sandy soil. These do well without fertilizer.

Plant in colonies, 3 to 4 inches deep (Dutch crocus, 2 inches deep), 2 to 4 inches apart. Allow the foliage to mature after the flowering season is over. The leaves appear in spring, ripen, and die down for the fall-flowering types, but they do not bloom until fall and do so without a reappearance of the foliage.

If it is necessary to transplant the corms, do it as the foliage withers: divide and replant immediately.

For winter-forced bloom, use the spring-flowering species. Plant 8 to 10 corms, 1 inch deep, in a 5 - or 6-inch pot. Place in cold frame (freezing conditions are necessary) ofr at least 6 weeks. Bring indoors anytime from January on, and top growth will start. Keep cool and out of the sun for the first week.

Use: Naturalize in the grass (do not mow until the leaves die down). Rock garden. Rock crevices. Beneath shrubs and evergreens. Containers. Indoor winter flower.

Species and varieties:

C. ancyrensis: Clusters of deep gold flowers. One of the earliest to bloom. March/April.

C. asturicus: Dark violet flowers in October.

C. aureus (syn. *C. flavus*, *C. moesicus*) Yellow Dutch Crocus: Flowers in bright yellow to orange-yellow shades. March/April.

C. balansae: Flowers of deep orange shade with brownish tinge on the outside. March.

C. biflorus (Scotch Crocus): White flowers, veined and feathered with purple markings, hairy yellow throat. March/April.

C. cancellatus: Fragrant white flowers in September.

C. chrysanthus: Fragrant, yellow-orange flowers. March/April. Hybrids and variants of this may be blue, yellow, and white, often with darker markings. The flowers are smaller than Dutch crocus but more free flowering.

C. Dutch Crocus: Flowers in shades of purple, blue, yellow, and white. March/April. These do better in more formal situations; they do not adapt well to naturalizing. "Blizzard"; "Early Perfec'-tion,' deep violet-blue; "Enchantress," pale blue; "Golden Goblet," are just a few of the named varieties.

C. etruscus: Lilac and cream flowers with yellow throats. March/April.

C. susianus (syn. *C. augustifolius*) Cloth of Gold: Starry, golden-yellow flowers, striped brown on outside of peals. March/April. Profuse flowering habit makes this a good naturalizer.

C. zonatus (syn. *C. kotschyanus*): Pale lilac to pinkish-lavender flowers with yellow throats. September.

Crucianella

Family: *Rubiaceae* (Madder).

Common name: Crosswort.

Propagation: Seed sown in spring at 65 degrees.

Division in spring.

Culture: Sun or light shade. Sandy soil.

Use: Rock garden. Trailer for dry bank. Carpet.

Species:

C. stylosa: 12 inches. Matting, prostrate habit. Hairy leaves arranged in whorls around the stem. Showy, small, rose flowers with prominent styles, in globose, terminal heads. July. Skunky odor. A native of Persia.

Crucianella stylosa, Crosswort

Curtonus

(see ANTHOLYZA) ....

Cyclamen

Family: *Primulaceae* (Primrose).

Propagation: Seed sown in warmth, 65 to 70 degrees. Fresh seed is necessary; it is preferable to sow as soon as possible after collection. It may take months to germinate otherwise and several years to flower. However, plants grown from seed are more free flowering than those obtained by division of the corms. Sow in a flat where they may be left undisturbed for several seasons, allowing the corms to grow on. Protection over winter will be necessary.

Division.

Corms ordered for late summer planting.

Culture: Shade. Very well drained, porous soil; add a goodly quantity of peat and leaf mold when planting. Fertilize in spring with bone meal and well-rotted manure. Set out in groups of three or more, flat-hollowed side up, 6 to 10 inches apart, and deep enough so that they are covered with 2 inches of soil. It is best to plant them when dormant, between June and August. Shallow rooted, so do not cultivate closely around these.

Use: Shady ground cover. Rockery. Woodland garden. Naturalize. Container. Cold greenhouse. (*C. europaeum*

and *C. neopolitanum* are the hardiest; the others will need protection.)

Species and varieties:

C. atkinsii: 3 inches. Basal, dark green leaves with silvery markings. Flowers resemble shooting stars, mostly red, but there are white and pink variations. January/March.

C. balearicum: Fragrant white flowers with rose throats.

C. cilicium: Dark green leaves, mottled and edged in silver. Fragrant, large flowers, pale pink or rose, deeper rose spots and purple throat. September/January.

C. coum (syn. *C. orbiculatum*): Deep green, roundish leaves. Red flowers with deeper red spots; also white, pink, or rose varieties. February/March.

C. europaeum: 4 to 5 inches. Bright green, white marbled, heart-shaped, evergreen leaves with purple undersides. Fragrant, red, rose-purple, purple, or white flowers. July/August. Native of the Swiss Alps.

C. neopolitanum: 3 to 6 inches. Very hardy and easiest of all to grow. Dormant from May to August, the leaves appear in autumn. Leaves are large, light green, marbled silver and white (longer than those of *C. europaeum*). Flowers are ¾ inch long, may be rose-pink, reddish-purple,

or white. August/September. Plant rather shallow, ½ inch soil covering corms.

C. repandum: 3 inches. Toothed leaves, silver marbled. Bright red flowers

with long narrow petals. April/June.

Cynoglossum

Family: *Boraginaceae* (Borage).

Common name: Chinese Forget-me-not. Hound's Tongue.

Propagation: Seed sown in spring at 50 degrees. Germination in 9 days.

Culture: Sun or partial shade. Average soil. Space 9 inches apart and plant in large groups (at least 10) as the flowers are not very large and are only showy when massed.

Use: Border. Naturalize.

Species and varieties:

C. amabile: Biennial. 2 feet. Masses of small, bright blue flowers in July. The flowering season is rather short.

Varieties: "Firmament" 1¼ feet, compact habit, indigo

Cynoglossum nervosum,
Chinese Forget-me-not

blue; "Pink Firmament," pink flowers, long season; "Snowbird," 2 feet, white.

C. caelestinum: 1½ feet. Blue and white flowers. Attractive to bees.

C. nervosum: 2 feet. Bright blue flowers in one-sided racemes. Blooms all summer. Originally from east Asia. Var. "*roseum*," 2 feet, rose-pink.

Cypripedium

Family: *Orchidaceae* (Orchid).

Common name: Lady's Slipper. Moccasin Flower.

Propagation: Germination is very poor. The seeds have no built-in food supply as most seeds do. There are 30,000 seeds or more in the walnut-sized seed capsules which split open when ripe, but very few (if any) ever sprout. I have never been able to germinate the seeds; however, if you wish to try, sow at 65 degrees, using well-rotted wood or if possible soil from a site where orchids are growing. It may very well be that a soil fungi is needed, as it is with some members of castilleja.

Seedling mix: equal parts of very old, decayed pine needles or rotting wood, peat and leaf mold, and sand. (See Chapter 1, orchid mixes on page 5.)

Division of crowns. Divide when dormant in fall or very early spring. The buds arise from the roots; there should

be at least one bud to a division.

Culture: Shade. Neutral to slightly acid, humusy soil, well drained. Enrich at time of planting with peat, leaf mold, and very well rotted manure. Moist in spring. Mulch annually with old pine needles, decaying wood, and leaf mold (they are shallow-rooted). Set out the plants so that the buds (eyes) are barely below the surface of the soil.

With care, this family may be moved with a large clump of soil even when in bloom if the site is prepared with conditions as close as possible to the natural environment; otherwise move in fall or early spring.

Use: Woodland garden.

Species and varieties:

C. acaule (Pink Lady. Pink or Stemless Lady's Slipper): 6 to 15 inches. Two large, prostrate, ribbed, oval, basal leaves. Solitary, large, bright purplish-pink slipper atop a leafless stem. May/June. Found in the evergreen woods of Canada and the northern states to as far south as North Carolina at elevations from 5,000 to 8,000 feet. Moisture requirements are easily met for the plant's natural habitat may be dry, sandy woods to actual bog, but they will not succeed in your garden except where you have already established other orchids. This is the most difficult to domesticate.

C. calceolus parviflorum (Small Yellow Lady Slipper): 10 to 18 inches. One to two flowers to a stem, to 5 inches

across, fragrant, shiny yellow with bronzy sepals and spiraled petals. May/June. This is a smaller plant than the Large Yellow Lady's Slipper; it also prefers a wetter site. Native to Canada and northeastern states.

Variety *C. c. pubescens* (often referred to as a seperate species): 1 to 2 feet. Hairy, oval leaves. Large yellow flowers, 1 to 3 to a stem, the pouch is pale yellow, the twisted sepals and petals may be yellow to purplish-brown. May/June. This will be happy under much drier conditions and neutral to limy soil. It is relatively easy to grow and divide. Native to Canada and the eastern states.

C. californicum: 1 to 1½ feet. Leafy stem carrying 6 to 12 flowers, brown-spotted, white to pinkish pouch, yellow petals and small, greenish-yellow to brown sepals. June/July. A bog plant. Do not disturb once it is established.

C. candidum (Small White Lady's Slipper): 6 to 10 inches. Solitary, small, white slippers. May/June. Prefers a limy soil, moist to boggy site, tolerant of sun. Native from New York to Minnesota.

C. montanum (Mountain Lady's Slipper): 1 to 2 feet. Long, hairy leaves. One to four flowers to a stem; white pouch, veined purple; petals and sepals oddly spiraled, bronze to purplish-brown hues. May/June. Indigenous to the Rocky Mountain forests up to 5,000 feet elevation. Not very difficult to transplant during the dry season of late summer when it is rather dormant.

C. reginae (Showy Lady's Slipper): 2 feet high, hairy, leafy stem carrying 1 to 4 flowers, 3 inches across; pouch varies from pink or rose to purplish-rose in color; sepals and petals are not spiraled and are usually white but may have a pinkish tinge. May/June. Found in the northeastern states. Neutral soil (peaty, but not acid), and constant moisture required; otherwise, it is another easy species to cultivate.

Dahlia

Family: *Compositae* (Daisy).

Propagation: Seed sown early in spring at 65 degrees. Germination in 4 days. Dwarf types like the Unwin hybrids flower as quickly from seed as from tubers or cuttings, and the plants tend to be more vigorous. They are easily transplanted; move outdoors in the same way and time as you would tomatoes (about the first of June in my area, which is 5,800 feet elevation.) For added insurance, I cover with Hotkaps for a week or so.

Tubers purchased for spring planting.

Cuttings in spring, bottom heat.

Cuttings in August, taken from nonflowering branches.

Division of clumps in spring, before setting out.

Culture: Sun. Well-drained, porous, fertile soil. Moist. Fertilize with phosphate but

gentian-blue flowers in open spikes. July to frost. This will bloom the first year if sown in April. I have found it to be very hardy and free of disease or insect pests. Western China.

D. zalil: 2½ feet. Thin spikes of yellow flowers. May/August. Asiatic origin.

Delphinum tatsienense, Tatsien Larkspur

Dianthus

Family: *Caryophyllaceae* (Pink).

Common name: Pinks.

Propagation: Germination is excellent with fresh seed collected and sown in late summer. With spring sowing, the various species require individual treatment.

D. alpinus and *D. arenarius* need cold to start, prechill in refrigerator before sowing. Germinate at 45 to 50 degrees. Time: within 2 weeks. Allwood of England suggests that his hybrids *D. "All-woodii"* and "Old Laced Pinks" be sown at 50 degrees. Germination in 5 days.

All the others will germinate well at 65 to 70 degrees in 2 weeks.

Division in spring (the only way to rid a clump of the worst pest of all—GRASS!)

Layering.

Cuttings with a heel, root quickly (about 3 weeks). Insert cutting in a damp rooting mix with gentle bottom heat, good air circulation, and cool air temperature; good light but not direct sunlight. Pot up to larger pots as necessary; these will die if root bound.

Culture: Sun. Well-drained, sandy, porous, limy soil. Space 4 inches apart for alpines, 6 to 8 inches apart for the others. Plant in masses for effect.

Use: Border. Rock garden. Cut flower. Edging or ground cover.

Species and varieties:

D. "Allwoodii" (Garden Carnation): A hybrid (*D. plumarius* x *D. caryophyllus*). 1 to 1½ feet. Flowers are usually double in shades of white to pink and very fragrant. July/August. Prefers sun but tolerates some shade. Gritty, limy soil. Do not pamper; they are completely hardy. (See illustration, p. 27.)

Dianthus allwoodii, Garden Carnation

D. alpinus (Alpine Pink):
4 inches. Tufted habit. Large,
flattish, rosy-pink flowers,
1½ inches across, with dark
eyes. June. A rock-garden
plant that prefers some shade,
loamy soil, and cool conditions. Var. "Little Joe" (*D.
plumarius* x *D. alpinus*),
single, crimson flowers.

D. arenarius (Sand Pink):
4 inches. Tufted habit. Blue-
green foliage. Flowers on 9-
inch stems, white with a
green spot and reddish beard.
Fragrant. June. From
Finland.

D. barbatus auriculaeflorus
(Auricula-eyed. Old
Fashioned Sweet William):
Biennial, but self-sows so
readily that the clumps appear
to be perennial. 1½ feet.
Small, phlox-like flowers in
clusters colored from white
with dark eyes to pink, red,
or deep wine with light
markings. Native from
Europe to Asia. Many
named varieties. (See
illustration, p. 27.)

Var. "Crimson Beauty";
"Giant White"; "Harlequin,"
several shadings of color all
in one cluster; "Indian Carpet," 6-inch dwarf, many
colors, auricula-eyed;
"Morello," crimson, dark
foliage; "*nigricana*," very dark
red flowers and dark purple
foliage; "Pink Beauty"
shades of salmon-pink;
"Scarlet Beauty," orange to
salmon-scarlet.

D. caesius (syn. *D. gratian-
opolitanus*) Cheddar Pink:
6 inches. Mat forming. Blue-
grey, glaucous foliage. Fragrant, small bright pink,
fringed flowers. June/July.
Var. "Rose Queen," double
rose.

D. carthusianorum giganteus:
2 to 3 feet. Small, terminal
clusters of rose to crimson
flowers sway on long naked
wands that rise out of the
clump of grassy leaves. Very
attractive and different.
July to frost. Hungarian.

D. deltoides (Maiden Pink.
Sops-in-wine): 6 inches.
Dwarf tufted habit. Small
rose-pink flowers, very free
flowering. June/July. Prefers
alkaline soil.

Varieties: "*alba*," white;
"*erectus*," crimson flowers in
short, erect spikes; "Brilliant,"
bright, psychadelic red
flowers completely hide the
grassy foliage.

D. fragrans: 12 inches. Very
fragrant white flowers.

D. knappii (Knapps Pink):
1½ feet. Clusters of yellow
flowers from June to frost.
Short-lived but comes true
from seed. A rare species
from southeast Europe.
Prefers sun and gritty,
porous soil.

D. neglectus (Ice Pink.
Glacier Pink): 2 to 6 inches.
Tufted cushions with cherry-
red flowers on 6-inch stems,
blue eyes and reverse of petals
a tannish hue. June.

D. "Old Laced Pinks": 1 to
1½ feet. Distinctive, parti-
colored, white and rose or
pink, fragrant flowers. Single
or semi-double. Sun and
alkaline soil. (See illustration, p. 27.)

D. plumarius (Cottage or
Grass Pink. Garden or Scotch
Pink): 12 inches. Flowers
fragrant and to 1½ inches
across. June/July. European.

Dianthus deltoides, Maiden
Pink "Brilliant"

Dianthus knappii, Knapps
Pink

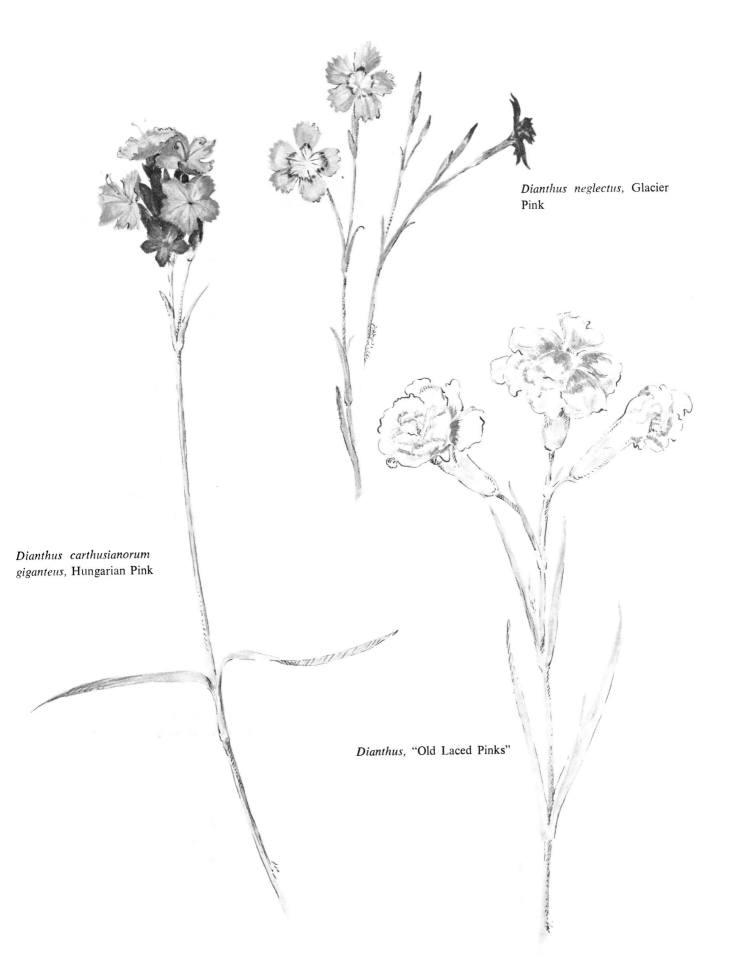

Dianthus neglectus, Glacier
Pink

*Dianthus carthusianorum
giganteus,* Hungarian Pink

Dianthus, "Old Laced Pinks"

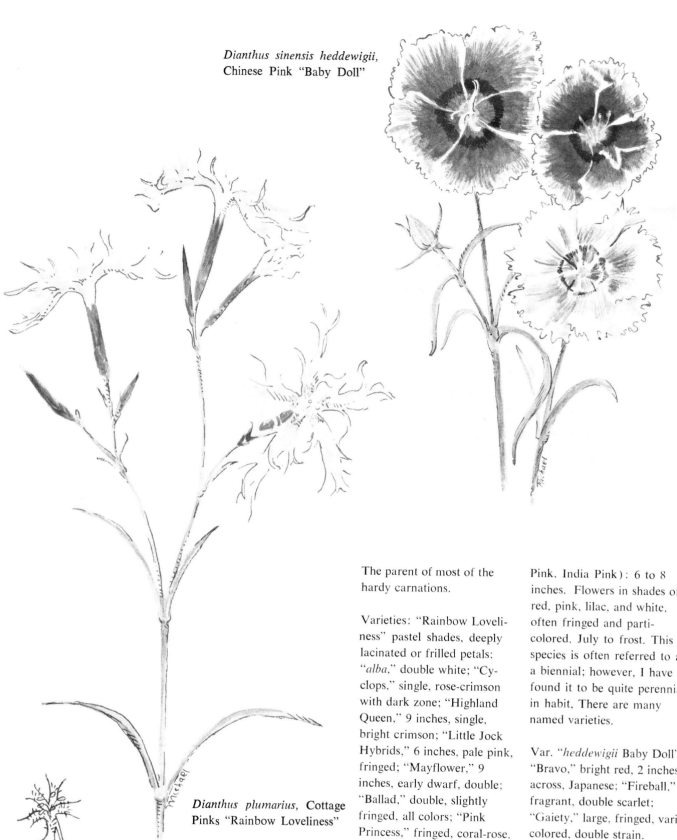

Dianthus sinensis heddewigii,
Chinese Pink "Baby Doll"

Dianthus plumarius, Cottage
Pinks "Rainbow Loveliness"

The parent of most of the hardy carnations.

Varieties: "Rainbow Loveliness" pastel shades, deeply lacinated or frilled petals; "*alba,*" double white; "Cyclops," single, rose-crimson with dark zone; "Highland Queen," 9 inches, single, bright crimson; "Little Jock Hybrids," 6 inches, pale pink, fringed; "Mayflower," 9 inches, early dwarf, double; "Ballad," double, slightly fringed, all colors; "Pink Princess," fringed, coral-rose. May. (This is a Cheyenne Horticultural Station introduction.)

D. sinensis (syn. *D. chinensis*) (Rainbow Pink. Chinese Pink. India Pink): 6 to 8 inches. Flowers in shades of red, pink, lilac, and white, often fringed and parti-colored. July to frost. This species is often referred to as a biennial; however, I have found it to be quite perennial in habit, There are many named varieties.

Var. "*heddewigii* Baby Doll"; "Bravo," bright red, 2 inches across, Japanese; "Fireball," fragrant, double scarlet; "Gaiety," large, fringed, vari-colored, double strain.

D. winteri: 9 inches. Large, single flowers in various colors. Very hardy.

Dicentra

Family: *Fumariaceae* (Bleeding Heart).

Common name: Bleeding Heart.

Propagation: Seed sown in late summer or fall. Prechilling is advised for spring sown seed (must actually freeze). Germination at 50 to 60 degrees. *D. eximia* germinates well if sown in summer.

Division of corms (*C. canadensis* and *C. cucullaria*) in early spring or after flowering in July.

Division of crown (*D. eximia*) or underground rhizomes (*D. formosa*) in April or July.

Root cuttings in early spring, 3 inches long, of *D. spectabilis*.

Culture: Shade. Neutral, well-drained, porous but humusy woodland soil. Add peat and well-rotted manure to garden soil when setting plants in the border. Set corms of *C. canadensis* and *C. cucullaria* 2 inches deep, 6 to 8 inches apart, anytime the plant is dormant.

Use: Shaded border. Rock garden. Woodland garden. Cut flower.

Species and varieties:

D. canadensis (Squirrel Corn): 6 to 12 inches. Feathery, grey-green foliage. Nodding, fragrant, spurred flowers in loose racemes, greenish-white, or often white, tinted purplish or pink. April. Many small tubers make up the root, resembling kernels of corn. Belonging to the open woods of northeastern Canada and the states as far west as Minnesota. Dormant by midsummer.

D. chrysantha (Golden Eardrops): 4 to 5 feet. Erect habit. Pale, bluish-grey, divided leaves. Hollow stems. Large panicles of short-spurred, golden-yellow flowers. A long tap root makes this difficult to transplant when mature. Mountains of California.

D. cucullaria (Dutchman's Breeches): 10 inches. Foliage very like *D. canadensis*, pale, bluish-grey, and fern-like. Small, nodding, white or pinkish flowers with yellow tips and wide-spread, plump spurs. April/June. White underground tubers. Becomes dormant after flowering when the weather turns hot and dry (which it always does!). A woodland species from New England to Missouri.

D. eximia (Plumy or Fringed Bleeding Heart): 12 to 18 inches high. Neat, bushy habit. Nonspreading. Very finely divided, grey-green, glaucous, basal leaves. Racemes of heart-shaped, nodding flowers, deep rose. pink to pink and white with short spurs. May/September. Most of the bloom is in June; given moisture, there is a scatter of bloom all summer. The parent of several named varieties. Native to the northeastern states. More tolerant of sun than the others and prefers a sandy soil. May be divided and moved anytime.

D. formosa (Western Bleeding Heart): 8 to 18 inches. Resembles *D. eximia*.

Blue-green foliage. Flowers in drooping clusters on naked stems, color varies from rose to white. April/June. Spreads by underground rhizomes. From the Pacific coastal ranges. Moist. Var. "Sweetheart," white, May/September.

D. oregana (syn. *D. glauca*): 8 inches. Very like a small *D. formosa*. Silvery-blue, divided leaves (foliage remains in good condition well into the fall). Flowers in dense panicles, nodding, cream with pinkish-tipped petals. May/July. Requires a porous, sandy to gravelly soil with peat added. From the Siskiyou Mountains of California and Oregon.

D. spectabilia (Bleeding Heart): 2 to 3 feet tall. The spreading, arching branches take up a space of 4 feet or more. If it is not matted down by a snowstorm in June or hail later on, the plant will not become dormant until September. Leafy stems with green, divided foliage, although not as finely cut as others of this family. Pendulous racemes of bright pink, heart-shaped flowers, 1 inch long, which hang from one side of the stem only. May/June. Native to Japan.

D. uniflora (Steershead): 2 to 4 inches. Solitary flower on a leafless stem, white or pink recurved petals and sack-like spurs (faintly resembles a steershead). Ferny basal leaves. Fleshy root. A tiny plant for the shaded rockery. From the western states, Wyoming to California.

Dictamnus

Family: *Rutaceae* (Rue).

Common name: Gas Plant. Burning Bush. Fraxinella. Dittany.

Propagation: Sow seed in fall as soon as ripe. For spring sowing, prechilling treatment in the refrigerator is necessary. Germinate at 45 to 50 degrees, 30 days or more. Seed is slow to sprout.

Culture: Sun. Good garden loam. Transplant when small (up to the third year), as it resents being disturbed. It will take 3 or 4 years to establish and bloom from seed. Space plants 12 to 18 inches apart.

Use: Border. Cut flower.

Species and varieties:

D. albus (syn. *D. fraxinella*): 2½ feet. Fragrant, dark green, pinnate leaves. White flowers in terminal racemes. June. Native from southern Europe to northern China. Var. "*purpureus*," rosy-purple flowers.

A combustible gas is given off by the leaves of a mature specimen. On a hot, still day, a lighted match held near a leaf will cause a brief flash but will not harm the plant.

Dierama

Family: *Iridaceae* (Iris).

Common name: Wand Flower. Angel's Fishing Rod.

Propagation: Seed sown in spring at 65 to 70 degrees. Germination slow, up to 3 months. Winter the seedlings the first season in a cold greenhouse or cold frame.

Division in early spring, or in fall if they are dug and stored over winter.

Culture: Sun. Average garden loam. Moist. Set corms 3 inches deep in early spring. Not dependably hardy; mulch for the winter or dig up and store over winter as you would gladiolus. When dividing clumps, allow several corms to a section.

Use: Border. Waterside garden.

Species:

D. pendula: 4 feet. Narrow leaves. Flowers, 1 inch long, in pale shades of lavender-pink to white. April/May.

D. pulcherrimum: 4 feet. Stiff, sword-like leaves to 2 feet long. Arching stems with terminal, nodding bells, 1½ inches long, purple to white in color. May/June. A native of South Africa.

Dietes

(see MORAEA). ....

Digitalis

Family: Scrophulariaceae (Figwort).

Common name: Foxglove.

Propagation: Seed sown in late summer produce flower-

ing plants the following year; or sow in spring at 65 degrees. Germination within 8 to 14 days. Important—this seed requires light to germinate—do not shade.

Self-sows.

Division in early spring.

Culture: Sun or light shade. Good garden loam, well drained. The sturdy stems do not require staking. Space 8 to 12 inches apart in groups.

Use: Border. Wild garden.

D. ambigua (syn. D. grandiflora) Yellow Foxglove: 2 to 3 feet. Hairy foliage. Flowering spikes, pale yellow, often marked brown, 2 inches long. June.

D. davisiana: 3 feet. Unusual bronzy flowers.

D. ferruginea (Rusty Foxglove): Biennial. 5 feet. Long, dense spikes, rusty-red, lower lip bearded. From southern Europe.

D. laevigata: 3 feet. Yellow, spotted purple flowers.

D. lanata (Grecian Foxglove): 2 to 3 feet. Flowers are white to creamy-yellow, veined, 1 inch long. July/August.

D. lutea (Straw Foxglove): 2 to 3 feet. Flowers yellow to white, ¾ inch long. Rare.

D. lutzi: 3 feet. Biennial. Salmon flowers. June/July.

D. mertonensis: 2 to 3 feet. Large, rose-pink flowers. June to frost. A tetraploid (D. ambigua x D. purpurea).

D. minor: 1½ feet. Deep purple flowers. Prefers shade.

D. nervosa: Long, dense racemes of small yellow flowers.

D. purpurea (Common Foxglove): Biennial. 3 to 4 feet. Flowers range from purple to pink and are usually spotted. Native to England. (See illustration, p. 28.)

Varieties: "alba," 3 feet, white; "Excelsior hybrids," 4 feet (the flowers are all around the stem and more upfacing); "Foxy," 2½ feet, dwarf (blooms 5 months from seed), spotted, brightly colored flowers in dense spikes; "gloxiniodes (gloxiniaeflora)," 3 feet, longer spikes and the large flowers are wider; "Shirley hybrids," have very large flowers; "monstrosa," 3 feet, rosette-topped; "maculata superba," heavily spotted flowers.

D. sibirica: Hairy foliage. Yellow flowers.

D. thapsi: 2 to 4 feet. Flowers in shades of pink to cream with purple or red dots. From Spain, but hardy.

Dispourm

Family: Liliaceae (Lily).

Common name: Fairy Bells.

Propagation: Seed collected in autumn; remove pulp and sow at once. A period of prechilling in the refrigerator will benefit spring sowing.

Division of underground rootstock in spring.

Culture: Shade. Neutral, humusy, woodland soil. Mo in spring. Similar in habit to solomon's seal but more tolerant of dry conditions. Space 6 to 8 inches apart, mass in colonies.

Use: Woodland garden.

D. lanuginosum (Yellow Mandarin): 1 to 3 feet. Stemless, oblong leaves. Nodding, greenish bells in upper leaf axils. May/June. Woodlands of Ohio south to Georgia.

D. oreganum: to 2 feet. Heart-shaped leaves. Flower creamy-white, about ½ inch long. April/June. Red-orang berries. Western states, Montana to Colorado.

D. smithi: to 3 feet. Whitish flowers, 1 inch long. Bright yellow berries. Another westerner.

D. trachycarpum: 1 to 2 feet Nodding bells, ½ inch long, white to greenish-yellow, are rather hidden by the leaves. April/June. Velvety, yellow-orange berries. Native to the Rocky Mountains, valley to 8,000 feet.

Dodecatheon

Family: Primulaceae (Primrose).

Common name: Shooting Star. American Cowslip.

Propagation: Seed sown whe ripe. Spring sowing requires prechilling treatment. Germination within 48 days at 45 degrees. Allow the seedlings to remain in the flat without disturbance for the first winter. Carry over with protection in cold frame or cold greenhouse. New growth will appear in March, and they may be transplanted into peat pots by mid-April for later transference to the garden. They take 3 years to bloom from seed.

Division of clumps when the foliage begins to die down, usually from August on. With the exception of potted plants in spring, transplanting must be done in August when dormant.

Root cuttings taken in late fall or early spring. Will bloom the second year.

Culture: Sun or shade. Well-drained, gritty soil with peat added. Moist in spring. Space 6 inches apart, always plant in groups.

Use: Rock garden. Border. Wild garden. Woodland garden.

Species:

D. clevelandi: 1½ feet. Rather small leaves. Purple flowers with yellow base and beak.

D. dentatum: 8 to 10 inches. Coarsely toothed, broad leaves. White flowers with purple bases. Rocky Mountains.

D. jefferyi: 18 inches. Larger and stouter than *D. pauci-* L *florum*. Leaves erect, to 12 inches long. Deep lavender-purple flowers. Rocky Mountains. This does not go into a summer dormancy and requires a humusy soil, shade and moist conditions.

D. latifolium (syn. *D. hendersonii*): 12 inches. Flowers are rose-purple to bright pink with deep purple beaks.

D. latilobum: 12 inches. Leaves to 10 inches long. Flowers in clusters, yellow-white with short beaks.

D. meadia: 2 feet. Flowers in umbels, variable in color, may be rose to rose-lilac, white, or purple. June. Must have a sunny position to flower. Natively from Pennsylvania to Wisconsin, this species has a longer blooming season than the westerners.

D. pauciflorum (syn. *D. pulchellum*, *D. cusickii*): 6 to 15 inches. Umbels of nodding flowers, pale lilac to rose-purple, yellow basal markings, flower to 1 inch long. May/July. Summer dormancy. Native to the Rockies.

D. radicatum: 6 to 16 inches. Flowers hang in terminal umbels, rose-red to rose-purple. The yellow fused stamens look like a bird's beak. Light green, basal leaves. The foliage dies down by late July here at 5,800 feet. Naturally the flowering season will be later at higher elevations. Native to the Rockies.

Doronicum

Family: *Compositae* (Daisy).

Common name: Leopard's Bane.

Propagation: Sow seed at 65 degrees. Germination is slow and erratic, within 4 weeks.

Division every other year in early fall when the plant is normally dormant.

Culture: Sun or light shade. Well-drained, good garden loam. Space 10 inches apart in groups of at least 6.

Use: Border. Cut flower. Wild garden. Rock garden.

D. caucasicum magnificum: 1½ feet. Basal, coarsely toothed, heart-shaped leaves. Solitary yellow flowers, 2 inches across. Late May/June. From southern Europe. Var. "Madam Mason," 2 feet.

D. cordatum: 9 inches. Dwarf, rock-garden type. Solitary, yellow flowers to 3 inches across. May/June.

D. pardalianches: 3 feet. Clusters of canary-yellow flower heads in June.

D. plantagineum (syn. *D. excelsum*): to 4 feet. Coarse leaves. Tuberous roots. Solitary yellow flowers, 2 to 4 inches across.

Doronicum caucasium magnificum, Leopard's Bane

Draba

Family: *Cruciferae* (Mustard).

Common name: Draba. Whitlow Grass.

Propagation: Seed collected and sown immediately; spring sowing requires a period of stratification and cold treatment. Germination at 50 to 60 degrees within 5 days.

Division in very early spring.

Culture: Sun. Stony, gritty soil. Absolutely perfect drainage. Moist during the growing season. Plant collection from the wild is not too difficult, providing the specimen is moved to a like environment.

Use: Excellent for rock garden or rock crevices. I thoroughly enjoy draba; it blooms gayly with the crocus even in the snow.

Species:

D. aizoides (Yellow Whitlow Grass): 3 to 4 inches. Dense rosettes of small, narrow, hairy-edged leaves. Fragrant, bright, sulphur-yellow flowers with conspicuous stamens in terminal racemes. April/May. An alpine species found on calcareous rock formations in the mountains of Europe.

D. pyrenaica (syn. *PETRO-CALLIS*) Rock Beauty: 2 to 4 inches. Small, dense rosettes of wedge-shaped leaves. Fragrant, white flowers fade to lilac or pinkish hues, 1 inch across. Alpine from the Pyrenees and Alps.

Dryas

Family: *Rosaceae* (Rose).

Common name: Dryad. Alpine or Mountain Avens.

Propagation: Seed (purchased or collected) sown in late summer or early spring. A period of cold is helpful in germinating spring-sown seeds. Germinate at 50 to 60 degrees.

Division of creeping rootstock.

Cuttings of mature wood.

Culture: Sun. Sandy, gritty, limy soil with perfect drainage. Rocky site is preferred. Moist during the growing season.

Use: Rock garden.

Species:

D. drummondi: 4 inches. Evergreen and mat forming. Hairy, oblong leaves with whitish-pink undersides, 1½ inch long. Solitary, nodding, shiny, cream-yellow flowers, ¾ inch across. The flowers never fully open. July/August. Northern Rockies.

D. hookeriana (syn. *D. octopetala*) Mountain Dryad: 6 inches. Creeping, mat-forming plant with woody stems. Evergreen, dark green, leathery leaves whose edges roll under, 1 inch long and with whitish undersides. Solitary, erect, strawberry-like, white flowers, 1 to 1½ inches across. July/August. This is a nitrogen-fixing plant. An alpine of the northern Rockies, 10,000- to 11,000-feet elevation.

D. suendermannii: A hybrid of *D. octopetalla* x *D. drummondi*. 6 inches high. Oblong leaves, 1 to 1½ inches long. Pale yellow buds open to large, nodding, shiny white flowers. June/July.

Echinacea

Family: *Compositae* (Daisy).

Common name: Cone flower.

Propagation: Sow in late summer or spring at 60 degrees. If the seed is fresh, germination occurs in 4 days. These do not reproduce true from seed.

Division in spring.

Root cuttings.

Culture: Sun. Average to limy soil. Dry. Transplanting is easy at anytime; move with a large ball of dirt. Space plants 2 feet apart. Division may be necessary every 3 or 4 years.

Use: Border. Wild garden. Excellent cut flower.

Species and varieties:

E. augustifolia: 18 inches. Flowers composed of dull purple to rose-purple rays and mahogany cones. Found from Saskatchewan to Texas.

E. pallida: 3 feet. Narrow leaves (not toothed). Rose-purple flowers to 5 inches across. Also a white form. June/July. Native from Nebraska to Texas.

E. purpurea (syn. *RUD-BECKIA purpurea*) Purple Cone Flower: 3 feet. Coarse, rough, toothed leaves. Solitary flowers, 4 to 5 inches across, having drooping, purple to reddish-purple rays, and high cones (disc florets) of dark purple. July/September. Native from Michigan to Georgia. The named cultivars are much superior to the species.

Varieties: "The King," 3 inches across, coral-red rays, brown cone, August; "White Lustre" or "White King," dullish white rays, greenish-brown cone; "Bright Star," very like "The King."

Echinops

Family: *Compositae* (Daisy).

Common name: Globe Thistle.

Propagation: Seed sown in spring at 65 degrees. Germination in 10 to 21 days.

Root cuttings.

Division of cultivars in spring, trim the long roots to about 6 inches long.

Culture: Sun or light shade. Well-drained soil on the porous, sandy side. Dry. Space 12 to 18 inches apart; these are robust growers but not invasive. Divide at least every fourth year.

Use: Border. Long-lasting cut flower. Wild garden. Everlasting bouquet. (Cut just before the flowers are fully opened.)

Species and varieties:

E. nivalis (syn. *E. humilis*): 4 feet. Whitish foliage, seemingly covered with cobwebs. White flower heads. July/August. Siberian.

The following two species are now throught to be selections but are still offered as separate species in catalogues.

E. ritro (Globe Thistle): 2 to 5 feet. Finely cut leaves. A neat appearing plant with globular, thistle-like flower heads of blue to violet-blue, 2 inches across. July/September.

E. sphaerocephalus: 4 feet. Prickly, deep-cut, thistle-like leaves, grey-green, with whitish undersides. Large blue flower heads. July/August. Variety "Taplow Blue" has flowers like steel-blue globes, 3 inches across.

Echium

Family: *Boraginaceae* (Borage).

Common name: Vipers Bugloss.

Propagation: Seed sown in spring at 45 to 50 degrees.

Culture: Sun. Average to poor soil, well drained. Dry. If the soil is too rich, the plant produces all leaves but no flowers.

Use: Border. Rock garden. Wild garden.

Species and varieties:

E. rubrum var. "Burgundy": Biennial, 3 feet. An English variety with long spikes of wine-red flowers. May/July.

E. vulgare (Blue Weed) var. "Blue Bedder": Biennial. 1 to 2½ feet. Coarse, hairy foliage. Long, dense spikes of bright blue, two-lipped flowers, pink buds opening blue. June/August. European.

Edraianthus

(see also WAHLEN-BERGIA)

Family: *Campanulaceae*.

Propagation: Seed sown from spring into summer at 60 degrees. Germination in 2 weeks.

Division in spring.

Culture: Sun. Well-drained, humus-enriched soil. Moist.

Use: Rock garden.

Species:

E. graminifolius: 3 inches. Upfacing, bells in shades of blue or violet in clusters at the tips of leafy stems which thrust out from the crown, like spokes on a wheel. June. Mediterranean. Resembles Wahlenbergia and is often classified as such.

Epilobium

Family: *Onagraceae* (Evening Primrose).

Common name: Fireweed. French Willow. Rose Bay. Great Willow Herb. Blooming Sally.

Propagation: Seed gathered in August and sown immedi-

ately. Seed sown in spring at 45 degrees. Germination in 5 days. Will bloom the first year.

Division in spring.

Underground rootstocks or runners.

Self-sows, but is not a pest.

Culture: Sun. Neutral, garden loam. Moisture in spring, otherwise may be dry. Space alpines 6 inches apart, others 8 to 10 inches in large groupings.

Use: Rock garden. Wild garden. Border. Open woodland.

Species:
E. augustifolium (syn. *CHAMAENERION augustifolium*): 3 to 6 feet. Rose to pink-lilac flowers to 1 inch across in long terminal spikes, the lower flowers blooming first. June/August. Var. "*album*," a white form. Narrow, willow-like leaves. Look for it on old forest burns in the Rockies, northern states, and Canada.

E. dodonaei (syn. *E. fleischeri*): 12 inches. Deep rose flowers. June/August.

E. latifolium (Broad-leaved Fireweed): 12 inches. A Rocky Mountain alpine, smaller than *E. augustifolium*

Fireweed
Epilobium augustifolium,

and has fleshy leaves that form a low mat. Leafy stems bear reddish-purple flowers resembling the evening primrose. Moist site.

E. nummularifolium (Creeping Willow Herb): 8 inches. Creeping habit. Round bronzy leaves. Small pink or white flowers, ¼ inch across. Rockery or ground cover. From New Zealand, this is of borderline hardiness and requires a winter mulch.

E. rosmarinifolium: 2 feet. Bright pink flowers. July/August.

Epipactis

(syn. *GOODYERA*)........ ....

Family: *Orchidaceae* (Orchid).

Common name: Rattlesnake Plantain.

Propagation: Seed sown on soil that orchids were growing in, or on damp sphagnum moss. Germinating temperature 60 to 65 degrees (see additional propagational advice for growing orchids Chapter 1, orchid mixes). Mix for seedlings: 1 part decayed leaf mold, 1 part chopped osmunda or tree fern fiber and sphagnum, and ½ part dried manure.

Division in spring or whenever transplanting is deemed necessary.

Culture: Sun or part shade. Rich, coniferous-woods soil on the acid side. Moist to boggy site preferable, but the plant is also quite drought resistant. Field collection:

move with a generous clump of earth and transplant to a site as much like the original as possible.

Use: Waterside garden.

Species:

E. gigantea: 1 to 3 feet. Distinctively veined, oval to lance-shaped leaves. Greenish, purple-veined flowers, 1 inch across, 3 to 10 on a stem. June/July. Spreads by creeping rootstock. Fairly easily cultivated for an orchid. Native from Washington to Utah, south to California.

E. palustris: 12 inches. Whitish flowers with red tints. Shady, boggy site.

Eranthis

Family: *Ranunculaceae* (Buttercup).

Common name: Winter Aconite.

Propagation: Stratifying and refrigerating the seed prior to spring sowing will improve germination, without cold treatment (or sowing in fall), these may not sprout until the second year.

Self-sows freely.

Division of tubers.

Tubers ordered for fall planting.

Culture: Sun or part shade. Well-drained, porous, enriched soil. Moist. Set out in colonies in August on into September, about 18 plants per square foot, 2 inches deep, 4 inches apart. When

dividing, separate by clumps, not single tubers.

Use: Rock garden. Border. Tree and shrub underplanting. Naturalize.

Species:

E. hyemalis: 3 to 6 inches. Bright green, basal leaves appear after the flowers. Up-facing, buttercup-like, bright yellow flowers, 1½ inches across, with a whorl of shiny, leafy bracts, like a collar, directly under the flower. Often blooms before the crocus. March/April. From southern Europe.

Eremurus

Family: *Liliaceae* (Lily).

Common name: Hardy Foxtail Lily. Desert Candle.

Propagation: Seed sown in fall; spring-sown seeds must be prechilled in the refrigerator. Germination temperature 50 to 60 degrees. This is quite difficult to propagate from seed.

Roots purchased for fall planting.

The root is fleshy and brittle but may be divided with care.

Culture: Sun. Light, sandy, humus enriched, limy soil. Perfect drainage very important. Moist while growing. After blooming, the plant becomes dormant. A mulch of coarse sand over the crown in winter is advised. Remove when danger of frost is over. These start growth very early in spring and with our erratic weather they would

be nipped. Do not hoe around the plant, for it has a very shallow root system. Plant in groups of 6 or more, 12 inches apart. Plant the roots in fall, 4 to 5 inches deep.

Species and varieties:

E. bungei (syn. *E. stenophyllus*): 2 to 4 feet. Basal, sword-like leaves and stout stems. Spikes of citron-yellow flowers with red stamens. June/July.

E. Highdown hybrids: 7 feet. Spikes of yellow, orange, or pink.

E. himalaicus: 3 feet. Spikes of white, bell-like flowers. June/July. Very hardy.

E. Olgae: 4 feet. Starry white flowers in July.

E. robustus: 5 to 8 feet. Rose to pink flowers in June.

E. Shelford: Very free flowering. Color is variable, but flowers are usually in shades of orange.

Erigeron

Family: *Copositae* (Daisy).

Common name: Fleabane. Cut leaf Daisy. Wild Daisy.

Propagation: Seed collected and sown in fall or sown in spring at 50 to 60 degrees; germination in 7 days.

Division in spring.

Culture: Sun. Light, sandy soil. Space the dwarfs 4 to 6 inches apart and the taller sorts 8 to 10 inches apart, setting out in groups.

Use: Border. Cut flower. Rock garden. Wild garden.

Species and varieties:

E. aurantiacus (Orange Fleabane. Orange or Double Orange Daisy): 9 to 12 inches. Double, orange to orange-yellow, daisy-like flowers, 2 inches across. June/August.

Varieties: "Azure Beauty," 1½ to 2 feet, lavender-blue; "Pink Jewel," 2 feet, 6 to 8 lilac-pink flowers on a stem (this is the first pink variety to reproduce true from seed).

E. caucasicus: 10 inches. Rose-lavender flowers. June/September.

E. compositus (Cut-leaf Daisy): 2 to 10 inches. Fern-like, wooly, grey, basal foliage. Small flowers are white, pale lavender, or bluish-pink. May/July. Native to the western states and Alaska. This should be planted where it will not be irrigated after it has ceased to bloom.

E. coulteri (Coulter's Daisy. Mountain Daisy): 4 to 20 inches. Lance-shaped, basal leaves (leaves and stem are hairy). White or lilac flowers from ¾ to 1½ inches across. July. Found in moist alpine meadows in the Rocky Mountains, Wyoming to New Mexico.

Erigeron aurantiacus, Fleabane "Azure Beauty"

E. glabellus (Smooth Wild Daisy): 6 to 20 inches. Narrow leaves. Violet-purple or white flowers, 1 to 3 large heads on a stem. July. Western states.

E. karvinskianus: 1½ feet. Alpine of trailing habit. Semi-double, white or pink flowers. August/September. Blooms the first year from seed. Suitable for the rock garden or rock walls.

E. macranthus (Rocky Mountain Daisy): Leafy, unbranching stems. Dull green, lance-shaped leaves with hairy margins. Flowers are lilac to bluish-purple shades with very numerous ray florets, to 2½ inches across, the several heads forming a flat-topped terminal cluster. Attractive wild flower, easily cultivated.

E. speciosis (syn. *E. stenactis*) Showy Fleabane. Oregon Wild Daisy: to 2½ feet. Clusters of rose or purple flowers, 1½ inches across, numerous narrow rays, yellow disc, up to 12 heads on a stem. June/July. Western states.

Erinus

Family: *Scrophulariaceae* (Figwort).

Common name: Crevice Plant. Alpine Balsam.

Propagation: Seed sown in spring at 60 to 65 degrees.

Self-sows.

Cuttings.

Culture: Partial shade. Well-drained, sandy, gritty soil.

Use: Rock garden. Rock-wall crevices. Container.

Species and varieties:

E. alpinus: 4 to 6 inches. Evergreen, dense tuft of sharp-toothed leaves. Reddish-purple, rose or pink flowers, ½ inch across in dense racemes. April/May. Native of the Alps. Var. "Abbotswood Pink"; "*albus*," white; "Dr. Hanell," deep pink. The varieties come true from seed.

Erinus alpinus, Crevice Plant "Dr. Hanel"

Eriogonum

Family: *Polygonaceae* (Buckwheat).

Common name: Umbrella Plant.

Propagation: Easily grown from seed sown in spring at 50 degrees. Sow rather thickly for the percentage of viable seed to any one lot seems low. *E. umbellatum* requires cold treatment prior to sowing; otherwise, sow seeds in fall. These are difficult to transplant except as young plants.

Self-sows readily.

Culture: Sun. Well-drained, porous, gravelly soils; actually very tolerant of environment. Moist in spring.

Use: Excellent rock-garden plant. Wild garden. Dried bouquet.

Species:

E. compositum: 5 to 16 inches. Wooly leaved. Flowers vary from cream and yellow to pink shades.

E. fasciculatum (California, Wild or Arroyo Buckwheat): 1 to 3 feet. Spreading clump. Wooly leaves to 1 inch long, whitish undersides. White to pink flowers in clusters. May/September. California and Nevada.

E. flavum piperi (Sulphur Flower. Piper Eriogonum): 6 to 8 inches. Long-stalked, erect, hairy leaves. Numerous flowering stems carrying umbels of hairy, yellow flowers, often tinged red at maturity. May/July. Rocky Mountains from Washington to Wyoming.

E. umbellatum (Sulphur-flowered Buckwheat): Basal, oval leaves, whitish underneath. Flowering stems, carrying umbels of showy, deep yellow flowers, rise from a branching, leafy, woody base. May/July. Rocky Mountains.

Eriophyllum

Family: Compositae (Daisy).

Common name: Oregon Sunshine.

Propagation: Seed sown in fall or spring at 45 to 50 degrees. Will bloom the first year.

Division in spring.

Culture: Sun. Well-drained garden loam. Dry. Plants may be collected in spring or fall; they are not difficult to move.

Use: Rock garden. Excellent for a dry site.

Species:

E. intergrifolium (Wooly Yellow Daisy. Small Oregon Sunshine): This is often referred to as a variety of E. lanatum. 4 to 24 inches high. Prostrate habit. The woody base may have 1 or more branching stems. White, wooly foliage. Flowers, ½ to ¾ inch across, yellow ray and disc florets. May/August. Rocky mountain area from dry foothills to 8,000 feet.

E. lanatum (syn. E. caespitosum) Oregon Sunshine: 12 to 18 inches. Spreading mound-like habit. Grey foliage. Very free flowering. Golden-yellow, daisy-like flowers. June/July.

Eritrichium

Family: Boraginaceae (Borage).

Common name: Alpine Forget-me-not.

Propagation: Seed collected and sown in fall, or subject to a period of freezing if sown in spring. E. nanum seed may be purchased. Seedlings are slow growing. Use a rock-chip mulch and avoid a

hot, humid atmosphere. These are difficult to cultivate, but every gardener who cherishes rock plants will try them.

Division in spring.

Culture: Sun. Porous, gravelly, well-drained soil. Moist during the growing season. There is a fair chance of success in collecting from the wild if the plant's native environment is duplicated as much as possible.

Use: Rock garden.

Species:

E. elongatum: 4-inch-high dwarf alpine. Leaves, covered with long white hairs, form cushions blanketed with numerous small, brilliant blue, yellow-eyed flowers, ¼ inch across. July/August. There are rare white forms. Search the rocky ridges at 9,000- to 12,000-feet elevation in the Rockies from Montana to New Mexico.

E. nanum: 6 inches. Brilliant blue flowers. Although found in Europe, this is now thought to be the same species as the American E. elongatum.

Erodium

Family: Geraniaceae (Geranium).

Common name: Heron's Bill.

Propagation: Sow in spring at 50 to 60 degrees. Germination will follow in 14 days.

Division in spring.

Culture: Sun. Sandy, well-drained, limy soil. Space 6 to 8 inches apart in groups.

Use: Border. Rock garden. Naturalize.

Species:

E. absinthioides amanum (syn. E. olympicum): 6 inches. Grey foliage. White flowers most of the summer.

E. chamaedryoides: 3 inches. Alpine plant. White flowers with rose veins. June/September. Var. "roseum," 2 inches, red-veined pink flowers.

E. cheilanthifolium: 4 inches. Ferny, silvery leaves. White flowers, rose veined, ¾ inch across. Hardy alpine from Spain.

E. corsicum: 6 inches. Rosettes of downy foliage. Pink flowers with rose veins from June on.

E. macradenum: 12 inches. Pale lavender flowers; the two upper petals are purple spotted.

E. manescavii: 1½ feet. Purplish-red flowers to 2 inches across. July to frost. Downy, dark green, deep-cut leaves. Seed pods supposedly resemble a heron's beak. European.

E. pelargoniflorum: 12 inches. White flowers with purple spots; color often variable.

E. trichomanefolium: 5 inches. Pink-veined, violet flowers.

Eryngium

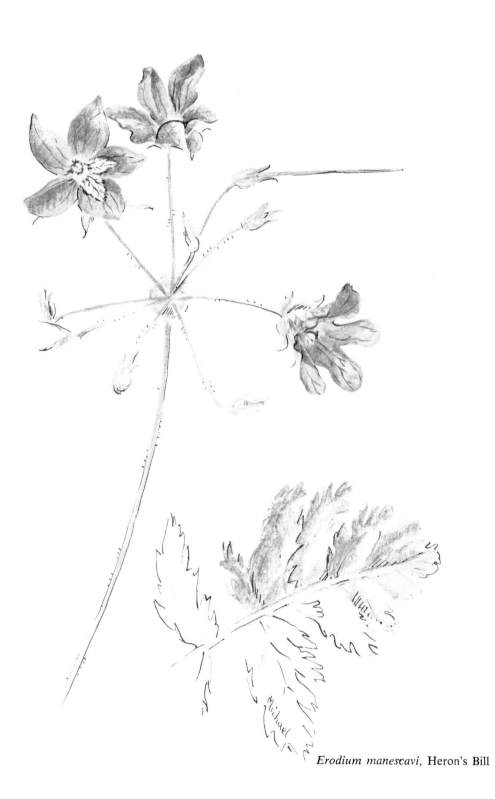

Erodium manescavi, Heron's Bill

Family: *Umbelliferae*
(Carrot).

Common name: Sea Holly.
Eryngo.

Propagation: Seed must be
fresh, evidenced by the fact
that seed collected and sown
when ripe in fall germinates
easily. Spring-sown seed
requires a period of pre-
chilling treatment in the
refrigerator. Germination at
50 to 60 degrees. Sprouting
should occur within 2 months;
however, they may not germinate until the second year no
matter what you do, so don't
discard the flat.

Division in early spring.

Root cuttings.

Culture: Sun. Light, sandy
soil. Dry. Stake taller species.
Set out the plants 10 to 12
inches apart, the tall sorts
2 feet apart.

Use: Specimen plant in the
border. Cut flower. Dried
winter bouquet. Rock garden.

Species and varieties:

E. *alpinum*: 1½ feet. Saucer-
like flower heads and upper
stems are a steel-blue color.
July/August. Var *"super-
bum,"* 2 feet, light blue,
tolerates shade.

E. *amethystinum*: 1½ feet.
Grey-green, holly-like leaves
with blue shadings. Stems and
flower bracts amythyst-blue.
July/September.

E. *bourgati*: 1½ feet. Greyish
leaves and blue stems. Globular, steel-blue flowers with

very unusual bracts. Mediterranean.

E. giganteum: 3 to 6 feet. The whole plant of bluish hue, the involucrum is ivory-white (the bracts surrounding the flower). It flowers once and then dies (monocarpic) but self-sows readily. August/September.

E. maritimum: 1½ feet. Broad, spiny, grey-blue leaves. Roundish flower heads of very pale blue surrounded by spiny bracts. July/August. European.

E. x oliverianum: 3 feet. Broad, highly cut, often blue leaves. Deep blue flowers, 1½ inches long, with very narrow stiff bracts. August/September.

E. planum: 2½ to 3 feet. Many branched plant with highly cut leaves. Pale blue globular flowers. July/August. Choice for the wild garden.

E. variefolium: 2 feet. Marbled leaves. Blue flowers in June/August.

E. wallichianium: 2 feet. Blue stemmed, small blue flowers.

Erysimum

Family: *Cruciferae* (Mustard).

Common name: Blister Cress. Dwarf Wallflower.

Propagation: Seed sown at 65 degrees. *E. asperum* sown in March will bloom the first year.

Division in spring.

Culture: Sun. Average to poor, sandy soil. Dry. Space about 10 inches apart. Mulch after the ground has frozen or give protection in the cold frame over winter.

Use: Rock garden. Border. Cut flower.

Species and varieties:

E. alpinum: 6 inches. Fragrant, sulphur-yellow flowers.

E. arkansanum: Biennial. 9 inches. Erect, bushy habit. Resembles a small wall flower. Scented, golden-yellow flowers. Var. "Golden Gem."

E. asperum (syn. *CHEIRAN-THUS allioni*) Siberian Wallflower: Perennial, but so short lived as to seem to be biennial. 9 to 24 inches. Low spreading growth habit. Clusters of yellow to orange flowers in June. Var. "Golden Bedder."

E. capitatum: Biennial. 1 to 3 feet. Erect, nonbranching habit. Narrow leaves. Dense racemes of bright yellow flowers, ½ inch long. Long, slender, four-angled seed pods. Indigenous to the western states and Rockies from valley to 9,000 feet. Very hardy, this requires no special winter care.

E. linifolium: 12 inches. Low clumps. Very free flowering. Masses of lilac-mauve flowers.

E. murale (Wallflower): Biennial. 1½ feet. Similar to *E. asperum*. Golden-yellow flowers in racemes.

Erythronium

Family: *Liliaceae* (Lily).

Common name: Dogtooth Violet. Fawn or Trout Lily.

Propagation: Seeds may be sown in July or when ripe; some germination occurs by fall, all by the following spring. (The first year a small bulb and one small narrow leaf develops.) Spring-sown seed require prechilling treatment. Keep the flat of seedlings moist and shaded. There is some bloom by the third year.

Corms: offsets removed in early spring or preferably during the late summer dormancy.

Underground stolons form offset bulbs in the eastern species. The westerners are usually propagated by seed.

Culture: Shade. Neutral, gritty soil, heavily enriched with leaf mold. Moist. Plant in masses, setting corms 3 to 6 inches deep and 4 to 6 inches apart. Place a rock under each bulb to keep this "oddball" from drawing itself too deeply into the earth to the point where it could not possibly bloom.

Transplanting collected plants from the wild will setback some of the species so they may not bloom for several years.

Use: Shaded rock garden. Woodland garden. Waterside.

Species and varieties:

E. albidum (White Trout Lily): Plain green leaves. Nodding, white lily-like flowers. Very tolerant of transplanting, it flowers soon after. From the midwestern woodlands.

Variety: "*mesochoreum*" white to lavender flowers. A prairie type from Iowa and Nebraska, it does not produce offsets.

E. americanum (Yellow or Eastern Trout Lily): 6 to 12 inches. Brown mottled leaves. Solitary, nodding, yellow, lily-like flowers with recurved petals. April/May. Most common in the eastern states. Produces many offsets. Transplanting bothers this species.

E. californicum (syn. *E. oregonum*, *E. revolutum praecox*): to 12 inches. Mottled leaves. Color of the flowers is variable but usually they have creamy-yellow petals with deeper yellow bases, several to a stem. Easily cultivated. From the open woodlands of Pacific coastal ranges.

Varieties. "*bicolor*," fragrant, white and yellow; "Pink Beauty"; "White Beauty."

E. citrinum: to 8 inches. Resembles *E. californicum* but smaller. White flowers with deep yellow or orange centers in April. May be successfully collected from the wild and domesticated. Mountains of Oregon and California.

E. dens-canis (Dog's Tooth Violet): 6 inches. Broad, mottled leaves. Color of flowers varies from pink to purplish-rose. 1 inch long. Found in Europe and Asia. Prefers a sunny spot. Increase is usually by offsets.

E. giganteum (syn. *E. watsoni*): 1½ feet. Mottled brown and green leaves. Large creamy-white flowers with maroon centers.

E. grandiflorum (Fawn or Glacier Lily): 9 to 24 inches. Two shiny, green, basal leaves. One to several flowers on a stem, large, bright yellow with orange bases, 2 inches long, recurved petals and sepals. April/May (the flowering season is extended into August, depending on elevation.) Var "*robustum*" is a larger type. Easily established mountain species of the Rockies and Cascades, found to 12,000 feet.

E. hartwegi (syn. *E. multiscapoideum*): to 6 inches. Mottled leaves. Resembles *E. californicum*, but the flowers are solitary and a deeper yellow. From the Sierra Nevadas, they also tolerate sun and heat better. These bloom the second year from seed.

E. howelli: Mottled leaves. Dark centered, yellow flowers that fade pink with maturity.

E. montanum (Avalanche Lily or Fritillaria): to 1½ feet. White flowers with orange bases and slightly recurved petals. An alpine found at timberline in Washington and Oregon, it is a difficult type to cultivate but very beautiful.

E. propullans: Narrow, mottled leaves. Solitary, small, pink flowers with yellow centers. A midwestern species that produces offsets.

E. purdyi: An easily cultivated species from the Sierra

Nevadas, having creamy-white flowers with lemon centers. Unlike other western types, this increases by offsets.

E. purpurascens: Leaves have ruffled edges. Yellow flowers with orange centers. Easily grown in western highland gardens, for this requires decomposing granite soils, good drainage, and our normally dry conditions of late summer and fall.

E. revoltum (Western Trout Lily. Mahogany Fawn Lily): 1 to 2 feet. Leaves mottled dark brown. Strong stems bear several flowers; large, deep pink, pale lavender, or white blossoms with yellow bases and reflexed petals. A Pacific coast species that tolerates quite boggy conditions.

Varieties: "Pink Beauty"; "Rose Beauty"; "Johnsoni," dark rose flowers; "Purdy's White."

E. tuolumnense: 12 to 15 inches. Plain green leaves. Robust growth. Flowers a deep golden-yellow with greenish bases.

Eupatorium

Family: *Compositae* (Daisy).

Common name: Boneset. Hardy or Perennial Ageratum. Thoroughwort.

Propagation: Seed sown in fall or early spring at 45 to 50 degrees.

Division in spring.

Culture: Sun or part shade. Average garden loam on the limy side and well drained. Space plants 12 to 15 inches apart. Divide as necessary or every third or fourth year.

Use: Border. Long-lasting cut flower. Wild garden. Woodland. Dried bouquet (cut just as the heads are opening, hang upside down to dry).

Species:

E. coelestinum (Mist Flower. Hardy Ageratum. Blue Boneset): 12 to 14 inches. Resembles the annual Ageratum. Coarse appearing, triangular-shaped, toothed leaves to 3 inches long. Dense clusters of blue to pale lavender flowers. August/October. Shallow rooted, so use care in cultivating. Spreads by underground stolons, but it is not weedy in the highlands for lack of moisture, and some winter kill. Native from New Jersey to Texas.

E. fraseri: 3 feet. Clusters of white flowers in June.

E. purpureum (Joe Pye Weed): 5 feet. Ovate, toothed leaves in whorls of 2 to 5 around the stem. Open clusters of purple to rose flowers. August/September. A coarse plant better used for naturalizing in a naturally wet spot. Found from New England to Minnesota and southward.

E. rugosum (syn. *E. ageratoides*) White Snakeroot: 2½ to 4 feet. Branching, bushy habit. Terminal, loose clusters of fluffy white flowers. August/September.

Excellent for woodland gardens, but keep in mind if you live on a ranch that this species is poisonous to cattle. Native from Saskatchewan to Texas and eastward.

Euphorbia

Family: *Euphorbiaceae* (Spurge).

Common name: Spurge. Milkwort.

Propagation: Sow seeds in fall when ripe (if collecting, bag the seed heads as they ripen, for these explode). Spring sowing at 45 degrees. Germination within 3 weeks. It is difficult to transplant, so place in its permanent position as a seedling.

Root cuttings in late fall or spring before growth starts.

Division of roots in spring.

Cuttings of basal shoots in July.

Culture: Sun. Light, gritty, well-drained soil. Space the dwarfs 4 to 6 inches apart, the others 12 to 18 inches apart in groups.

Use: Border. Rock garden. Wild garden. Cut flower (Char cut end with flame).

Species:

E. corollata (Flowering Spurge): 3 feet. Reddish leaves in fall. Flowers resemble baby's breath somewhat; clusters of tiny white flowers surrounded by petal-like bracts. July/August. Found from Minnesota to Texas.

E. griffithi: 2 feet. Sturdy, erect stems topped with bright yellow flowers in June.

E. myrsinites: 6 inches. Trailing, fleshy stems. Semi-evergreen, grey-blue leaves. Terminal yellow flower heads. May/June. Mediterranean. Rockery or rock wall plant; also said to repel moles.

E. polychroma (syn. *E. epitheymoides*) Yellow Spurge: 9 to 15 inches. Neat mound, very like a herbaceous bush. It is very attractive all summer, even when not in bloom. Yellow flowers are surrounded by showy yellow bracts. May/June. European. (See illustration, p. 30.)

E. sikkimensis: 3 feet. Brilliant red foliage in spring. Flower heads of greenish-yellow with yellow bracts through most of the summer.

E. wulfenii: 3 to 4 feet. Blue-green leaves. Conspicuous spikes of peculiar, spotted flowers with yellow bracts. May.

Ferula

Family: *Umbelliferae* (Parsley).

Common name: Common Giant Fennel.

Propagation: Seed sown in spring on into the summer, 65 to 70 degrees.

Culture: Sun or light shade. Average soil. Moist.

Use: Waterside background. Wild garden.

Species:

F. communis: 10 to 12 feet. Finely cut, ornamental leaves start growth very early in spring. Flat clusters of yellow flowers in June.

Filipendula

(syn. *SPIRAEA*) ....

Family: *Rosaceae* (Rose).

Common name: Meadow-sweet.

Propagation: Seed sown in fall germinates quite well in spring. Spring-sown seed must be stratified and exposed to cold. Germination occurs at 45 to 50 degrees and may stagger on over two seasons, so do not toss out the flat in disgust.

Division in spring.

Cuttings of creeping root-stock in summer.

Culture: Sun or light shade. Deep rich soil with peat and well-dried manure added. Moist (except for *F. hexa-petala*). Divide large clumps every four years. Space 1½ to 2½ feet apart, according to height of the species.

Use: Border. Cut flower. Woodland garden. Beside pool or stream. Good pot or tub plant.

Species and varieties:

F. camtschatica (Kamchatka Meadowsweet): 7 to 10 feet. Lobed leaves. Large white plumes in July. Native to northern Asia.

F. elegantissima: 4 feet. Feathery plumy heads of pink flowers.

F. gigantea: 6 feet. Large leaves and spreading heads of white flowers.

F. hexapetala (Dropwort): 2 to 3 feet. Tuberous root. Clusters of creamy-white flowers. June/August. Var. "*flore-plena*" is a double form. Sun and rather dry conditions.

F. multijuga: 6 inches. Basal leaves. Tiny heads of soft pink, rose. or white flowers in August. Japanese.

F. purpurea: 2 to 4 feet. Red-stemmed Japanese species. Pink or purple flowers in July. Needs winter protection. Var. "*alba*," white; "*elegans*," white flowers with conspicuous red stamens.

F. rubra (Queen of the Prairie): 4 to 6 feet. Creeping rootstock. Large, compound, pinnate leaves. Large, flattish, terminal clusters of deep pink flowers. June/July. To be found from Pennsylvania to Michigan. Var. "*venusta* Martha Washington Plume" is an improvement over the type, has fragrant, carmine-pink flowers. July/August.

F. ulmaria (Meadowsweet. Queen of the Meadow): 3 to 4 feet. Divided leaves with downy white undersides. White flowers, single or double, in dense clusters in June. From Europe to Asia.

Freesia

Family: *Iridaceae* (Iris).

Propagation: Sow at 65 to 70 degrees from March to May. It will often bloom by the next season. Remove to cooler place once germination occurs.

Corm offsets.

Culture: Sun. Loamy soil with peat and sand added. This is a half-hardy, topsy-turvy kind of plant for highlanders, for it will not bloom in summer. It would seem a poor choice to be included in this volume, and it is——unless you have a cold porch or greenhouse—— and then that winter bloom is surely appreciated. The warm house temperatures will not do; it must have about 50 degrees on the average. The plants benefit from being set out in the garden during the summer. Plant the corms 2 inches deep and 2 inches apart, and give them adequate moisture.

Indoor: Pot about 12 corms to an 8 inch bulb pan (point up), and store outdoors in the cold frame about late September into October, before real freezing occurs. Bring into the cool greenhouse and continue growing at 45 to 50 degrees, giving sun and moisture. Plant at intervals for continuous bloom. Dry off after flowering and store over summer in the pot or plant out into the garden.

Use: Winter flowers for greenhouse or cool porch.

Species:

It would appear that all that are offered at present are hybrids. These come in every color in the rainbow. Fragrant, tubular flowers, 2 inches long, in one-sided spikes on branching stems to 12 inches high. From South Africa.

Fritillaria

Family: *Liliaceae* (Lily).

Common name: Fritillary.

Propagation: Seed sown as soon as collected in mid-summer often starts in fall. Shade seedlings. This is not the easiest seed to germinate; I have struggled with it for years and have come to the conclusion that spring-sown seed requires a period of cold in the refrigerator, otherwise sprouting may not occur until the second season, if at all. Again do not give up, store the flat over winter in the cold frame or under the bench in the greenhouse, and in March bring it in to warmth and moisture.

Offsets from the bulb.

Bulbs ordered for fall planting.

Culture: Sun or light shade. Light, humusy soil. Moist, at least in spring. Set out bulbs in fall, 3 to 4 inches deep (depending on size) in large groups or colonies.

Use: Border. Rock garden. Naturalize in open woodland or wild garden.

Species:

F. acmopetala: 15 inches. Flowers are green outside, petals yellowish inside with purplish-brown streaks.

F. atropurpurea (Leopard Lily. Purple Fritillary): 8 to 30 inches. Grass-like leaves. Unbranching stem topped by 1 to 4 nodding, purplish-brown flowers with greenish-yellow spots; flowers are 1 inch across. May/June. Found in damp meadows and open woods of the western states.

F. gracilis: 15 inches. Wide-mouthed, bell-shaped flowers, purple with brown and yellow checkering.

F. graeca: 9 inches. Solitary, wine-colored bells.

F. imperialis (Crown Imperial): 3 feet. Stout, leafy stems, topped by whorls of drooping, lily-like, orange-pink, red, or yellow-red flowers. Ill-scented. May/June. Requires shade, manure-enriched loam, and moisture at least in spring. Protect from the wind; once it is established, do not disturb. Hardy, even though its home is Persia. It starts growth very early in spring.

F. lanceolata (Leopard Lily): 1½ feet. Lance-shaped leaves. Stems topped by 1 to 4 open bell-shaped, nodding flowers, greenish-yellow, mottled dark purple, to 2 inches across. May/June. Found in open dry woods (but moist in spring) in the Rocky Mountains.

F. messanensis: 1½ feet. Purplish-colored bells.

F. pallidiflora: 12 inches. Whitish flowers, red-purple inside.

F. persica: 3 feet. Deep violet-blue flowers.

F. pudica (Yellow or Golden Fritillary. Yellow Bell): 3 to 8 inches. Solitary, nodding, golden-yellow bell, fading to red. Very early in March to June depending on elevation. Rocky Mountain species preferring sun and sandy soil, dry in summer.

F. pyrenaica: 15 inches. Wine-purple flowers with spots.

F. recurva: 18 to 24 inches. Lily-like, orange and scarlet flowers. Look for this in the open, sun-spattered, dry forests of the western states.

F. roylei: 1½ feet. Flowers are yellow, green, and purple shades with purple inside. Himalayan.

F. tuntasia: 12 inches. Deep purple flowers.

Funkia

FUNKIA (See HOSTA) ......

Gaillardia

Family: *Compositae* (Daisy).

Common name: Blanket Flower.

Propagation: Seed sown at 50 to 60 degrees. Germination in 4 days. Named varieties may not come true from seed.

Gaillardia aristata, Blanket Flower "Goblin"

Division in spring; or in summer, cut around the perimeter of the plant (about 5 inches) with a sharp spade. New plants will grow from the severed roots.

Culture: Sun. Sandy, well-drained soil. Dry. Plant 8 inches apart in groups of 3 or more.

Use: Border. Rock garden. Cut flower. Wild garden. Being a native of this area, it is easily established.

Species and varieties:

G. aristata: 3 feet. Daisy-like flower, 2 to 4 inches across, golden rays and orange to purplish-red disc. June/August. Will bloom the first year from seed.

Varieties: "Burgundy," 2½ feet, coppery-scarlet; "Goblin," 12 inches, dwarf, bright yellow with deep red center; "Monarch strain"; "Tokaj," wine-red and tangerine combination; "Yellow Queen"; "Sun Dance," 8-inch dwarf, red with yellow edges, June to frost.

Galanthus

Family: Amaryllidaceae (Amaryllis).

Common name: Snowdrop.

Propagation: Seeds sown in fall or very early spring. Cool temperatures are needed to start. Germination is slow.

Self sows to some extent.

Division of offsets immediately after flowering. Bulbs purchased in fall.

Culture: Shade. Average to heavy soil with humus added. Cool and moist. Top dress with well-rotted manure in fall. Plant in masses in fall, at least by the dozen, 3 inches deep, 2 to 3 inches apart. Very hardy, the colonies will last forever. They resent being disturbed. Always allow the leaves to ripen thoroughly, or there will be no flowers the next year.

Use: Rock garden. Woodlands. Under trees and shrubs. Naturalize in lawns (don't mow until the leaves have withered).

Species and varieties:

G. elweissi (Giant Snowdrop): 6 to 12 inches. Very large, globular bells, 1½ inches long. March/April. Not always as completely hardy as G. nivalis. From Asia Minor.

G. nivalis (Common Snowdrop): 6 inches. Two or 3 basal, linear leaves to 10 inches long. Solitary, nodding, 1-inch-long, white bells. Very early. March/April. From Europe to western Asia. Var. "flora-pleno" is a double form.

G. plicatus: 6 inches. Variable. White flowers have green or yellow markings. Later flowering in April/May.

Galega

Family: Leguminosea (Pea).

Common name: Goat's Rue.

Propagation: Seed sown in spring at 65 degrees. Will bloom the first year.

Division in spring.

Culture: Sun. Average soil. Place where other plants will hide the bare spots these create, as they become dormant soon after flowering.

Use: Border. Cut flower.

Species and varieties:

G. officinalis: 3 feet. Bushy habit. Feathery foliage. Showy, pea-like flowers in dense racemes, lilac to rose-purple shades. June/July. From Europe and Asia.

Varieties: "alba," white; "carnea," rose: "Lady Wilson," blue and white flowers.

Galtonia

Family: Liliaceae (Lily).

Common name: Summer Hyacinth.

Propagation: Seed sown in spring at 65 degrees. Germination in 15 days. Some bloom the second year, all by the third.

Bulbs purchased for spring planting.

Culture: Sun. Well-drained, light, humus-enriched soil. More than normal moisture to produce flowers in our short season. Set bulbs 3 to 5 inches deep, 8 inches apart.

Many authorities recommend treating galtonia as you would gladiolus; however, I have found them to be much hardier. One fall, I neglected to dig a portion of the bed,

and they came up the following spring, blooming much earlier than those stored over winter and set out when danger of frost had passed. I would advise covering with a mulch though, if you are contemplating pushing your luck on this half-hardy bulb.

Use: Border; very striking when planted in groups of 10 or more.

Species:

G. candicans: Sturdy, erect, flowering stalks, 3 to 4 feet tall, rising from a basal clump of long, narrow leaves. Nodding, rather greenish-white bells along the upper half of the stem. August to frost. From South Africa.

Gaura

Family: Onagraceae (Evening Primrose).

Propagation: Seed sown in early spring at 65 degrees will bloom the first year if sown in April. Plant the seed with the fuzzy, pointed ends partially exposed.

Cuttings in midsummer.

Culture: Sun. Well-drained, sandy soil. Plant in groups of 3 or 4, spacing about 1½ feet apart.

Use: Border. Cut flower. Wild garden.

Species:

G. lindheimeri: 3 feet. Stalk-less leaves to 3 inches long in clumps from which rise branching flower spikes of star-like, pinkish-white

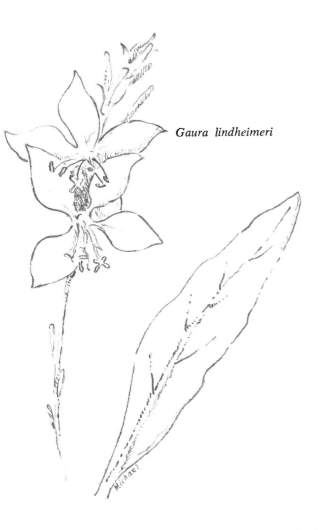

Gaura lindheimeri

flowers, 1 inch long. July/October. This is such a delightful plant that it should be better known. Native to the Southwest, this is often biennial in behavior; longevity is dependent on good drainage and winter mulch or constant snow cover.

Gentiana

Family: *Gentianaceae* (Gentian).

Common name: Gentian.

Propagation: Seed must be fresh for good results, collect in fall and sow immediately, or store cool and sow in spring following a pre-chilling period. Germination at 50 to 60 degrees, very slow, up to 5 weeks. Usually do not bloom until the third year. Be very careful not to overly disturb the roots when transplanting; this family does not tolerate much handling.

Careful division in early spring.

Stem cuttings in late spring.

Culture: Partial shade. Rich moist loam containing goodly amounts of peat and well-decayed manure. Good drainage is imperative. Irrigate well during the dry season. Top dress yearly with well-rotted manure and leaf mold. Do not disturb when once established. Plant in large groups, 6 to 8 inches apart.

Use: Rock garden. Border. Wild garden. Meadow or open woodland.

Species:

G. acaulis (Stemless or Spring Gentian): 3 to 4 inches. Clumps of broad, shiny, evergreen leaves. Huge blue, trumpet-like flowers. Native to the Alps. This is slow to germinate, tolerant of limy soils and some sun. It may be divided without injury.

G. altaica: 4 inches. Dense tufts. Trumpet-shaped, violet-blue flowers.

G. andrewsii (Closed or Bottle Gentian): 1½ to 2 feet. Deep blue to purple-blue flowers that never open in terminal and upper-leaf axil clusters. August/September. Var. "*alba*," a white form. Found natively from Quebec to Saskatchewan and northern states. Sun or shade, moist, neutral soil. Easiest of gentians to cultivate; mine are slowly forming a colony in the windbreak.

G. asclepiadea (Willow Gentian): 1½ to 2 feet. Erect habit. Willow-like leaves. Flowers, light to dark blue or deep violet, 1½ inches long, in leaf axils. White form, "*alba*." July/August. Self-sows. Prefers shade and deep, rich moist soil.

G. bigelovi: 12 inches. Spikes of numerous purple flowers. A Colorado species, excellent for the wild garden.

G. calycosa (Mountain Gentian): 4 to 12 inches. Solitary dark blue flowers, often spotted green. Late July/September. Rocky Mountains, 7,000 feet and above. Use a soil mix of sand, gravel. and humus. Moist.

G. crinita (Fringed Gentian): Biennial. 6 to 36 inches. Large, clear blue flowers, 2 inches long, fringed lobes. September/October. Found from Maine to Manitoba in sunny, naturally moist sites and neutral soil. Seeds ripening in October to November should be sown immediately. Sow the seed around the parent plants. Bacteria associated with the roots are necessary to the growth of the seedlings, or soil may be removed from near the established plants and the seed sown in this in flats as usual.

G. farreri: 3 inches. Prostrate stems are arranged wheel-like around the crown. The upfacing flowers, cambridge blue with white throats, are at the tips of the stems. Moist, cool, peaty soil.

G. gracilipes (syn. *G. purdomi*): 6 inches. Procumbent stems arch upward at their ends where are found the blue to violet-blue flowers. Chinese origin. Tolerant of sun and limy soil.

G. hascombensis: 2 feet. Spreading habit. Trusses of deep blue flowers.

G. lagodechiana: 12 inches. Solitary, deep blue to pale blue flowers. July/August. Sun or shade. Tolerant of soil. Easy from seed or cuttings.

G. linearis (Narrow-leaved Gentian): 1 to 2 feet. Terminal clusters of funnel-shaped blue flowers, rarely white. Bog plant found from Ontario to Minnesota.

G. lutea (Yellow Gentian):
3 to 4 feet. Pale yellow
flowers, 1 inch long, in dense
whorled cymes. The calyx
(outer floral leaves) resembles the spathe of jack-in-the-
pulpit. July/August.

G. makinoi: 1¼ feet. Terminal clusters of pale blue
flowers.

G. oregana (Western
Gentian): 18 to 24 inches.
Pale green foliage. Light blue
to darker blue flowers, 1½
inches long. Shade.

G. ornata: 4 inches. Procumbent habit. Solitary, pale blue
bells, 1 to 1½ inches long.
Moist, cool, peaty soil.

G. phlogifolia: 10 inches.
Flat-topped clusters of
clear blue.

G. porphyrio (syn. *G.
autumnalis*) Pine Barren
Gentian: 1½ feet. Linear
leaves on wiry stems. Brown-
spotted, light blue flowers,
2 inches long. August/Sep-
tember. Native to the sandy,
pine woods of New Jersey;
it prefers a light soil on the
acid side. It has deep tap root,
and so this is usually propagated by seed or root cuttings.

G. puberula: 12 to 18 inches.
Clusters of bright blue,
funnel-shaped flowers in
October. From the dry
prairies of South Dakota.

G. purpurea: 1½ feet.
Flowers are purplish-red,
yellow at the base.

G. quinquefolia (Ague Weed):
Biennial. 2 feet. Small,
tubular, light violet-blue
flowers in clusters. August/
October. From Maine to
Michigan.

G. rochelli: 2 to 3 feet. Semi-
evergreen. Trumpet-shaped,
blue flowers.

G. saponaria: 2½ feet.
Bottle-type flowers, pale blue
to white, 2 inches long. Moist
sites from New York to
Minnesota.

G. septemfida (Asian
Gentian): 8 to 26 inches.
Azure-blue, tubular flowers,
2 inches long, in clusters. July
to frost. Tolerant of soil, sun
or shade. Easy from seed
or cuttings.

G. sino-ornata (Chinese
Gentian): 6 to 7 inches.
Prostrate habit. Pale yellow-
ish-white flowers, dotted
purple. August/September.
Increase by stolons.

G. tibetica: 2 feet. Robust
plant with funnel-shaped,
greenish-white flowers.

G. veitchiorum: 4 inches.
Prostrate habit of growth.
Wide-mouthed, funnel-
shaped, deep blue flowers.

G. verna: 3 inches. Evergreen. Early flowering. Flat,
starry, blue flowers. Division
is possible, set out in shaded
frame to recuperate before
planting in new sites.

G. villosa: 10 to 20 inches.
Bottle type, flowers greenish-
white, 1½ inches long.
August/October. Native of
Pennsylvania.

Geranium

Family: *Geraniaceae*
(Geranium).

Common name: Cranesbill.

Propagation: Seed sown in
spring at 45 to 50 degrees.

Germination slow, about
2 months.

Division of crown in spring.

Root cuttings.

Culture: Sun or partial shade.
Average loam. Space 8 to 12
inches apart in groups of 3
or more.

Use: Border. Rock garden.
Wild or woodland garden.

Species and varieties:

G. argenteum: 2 to 5 inches.
Divided, silvery leaves. Large
pink flowers with dark lines.
June/July. Limy soil.

G. candidum: 6 inches. Rare
type with large white flowers,
having purple centers.

G. endressii: 12 inches. Rose-
flowers. June/July. Variety,
"Wargrave Pink." From
Pyrenees.

G. grandiflorum: 12 inches.
Deep-cut leaves turning red
in fall. Flowers pale lilac or
blue with red-purple veins.
Var. "*alpinum*" dwarf, large
blue flowers, 1½ inches
across. May/July.

G. maculatum (Wild Ger-
anium): Clusters of pale rose-
purple flowers. May/June.
From Maine to Manitoba.
Shady, moist, wild garden.

G. macrorrhizum: 12 to 18
inches. Spreading, mat-
forming plant with fragrant
leaves. Pink to deep red or
purple-red flowers. Southern
Europe. Good for holding
rocky slopes.

G. phaeum (Mourning
Widow): 2 feet. Flowers

almost black with a white
spot. May/June.

G. platypetalum (syn. *G.
ibericum platypetalum*): 1½
feet. Deep violet flowers with
reddish veins. July/August.
Var. "*album*," a white form.
The leaves turn orange-
crimson in fall.

G. pratense (Meadow Cranesbill): 2 to 3 feet. Lavender-
blue flowers, ½ inch across.
July/August. White variety,
"*album*."

G. psilostemon (syn. *G.
armenum*): 2½ feet.
Magenta-red flowers with
black spot at base of petals.
Free flowering. July/August.
Armenia.

G. renardii: 9 inches. Gray
foliage. White flowers with
violet-purple veins and
centers.

G. richardsonii (Richard's
Geranium): to 3 feet. Slender
growth. White flowers, pink
or rose veined. Same range as
G. viscosissimum.

G. robertianum (Herb
Robert): Biennial. 1½ feet.
Sprawling plant. Leaves turn
red in fall. Fragrant, red-
purple flowers. July/August.
A native American for the
shady, wild garden; too
weedy for the border.

G. sanguineum (Blood Geranium): 1½ feet. Color is
variable, but usually crimson
to blood red, 1½ inches
across. June/August. Var.
"*album*," white; "*lancast-
riense*," 6 to 9 inches, pale
pink to flesh color with purple
or red veins.

G. traversii: 12 inches. Grey-
green foliage. Single, pale
pink flowers.

Geranium platypetalum,
Cranesbill

G. viscosissimum (Sticky Geranium): to 3 feet. Hairy, palmate, five-lobed leaves, mostly basal. Flowers in loose clusters, purple to rose, rarely white, dark veins, 1 inch across. Rocky Mountains from 5,000 to 8,000 feet.

G. wallichianum (Late Cranesbill) "Buxton's Variety": 6 inches. Trailing habit. Finecut leaves. Violet-blue flowers with white eye, pale purple veins, 1¼ to 2 inches across. June/August. From the Himalayas, this is not completely hardy unless given a winter mulch.

Geum

Family: *Rosaceae* (Rose).

Common name: Avens.

Propagation: Sow in spring at 50 to 60 degrees. Germination is usually quite slow (about 4 weeks) and poor, therefore it is wise to sow rather thickly.

Division in early spring for selections or as necessary.

Culture: Sun. Light, well-drained, enriched soil. Moist. Dwarfs should be spaced 4 to 6 inches apart, 12 inches for the taller species. Group for effect.

Use: Rock garden. Border. Cut flower (pick when half open).

Species and varieties:

G. x Borisii (Boris Avens): 6 inches. Mound habit. Bright green, divided leaves. Small, rose-like flowers of yellow or orange-red hues.

June/August. A hybrid (*G. reptans* x *G. bulgaricum*). Sun or part shade. Not completely hardy in the highlands; mulch well or winter over in the cold frame.

G. bulgaricum: 2 feet. Yellow or orange flowers.

G. chiloense (Common Avens): 1 to 2 feet. Hairy foliage. Single or double scarlet flowers, 1½ inches across. June/July. From Chile, this is not reliably hardy here; winter in the frame or cold greenhouse.

Varieties: "Lady Stratheden," gold-yellow double; "Mrs. Bradshaw," double, scarlet to orange-scarlet, blooms from June on; "Prince of Orange"; "Fireball"; "Gold Ball."

G. coccineum: Single, red to orange-red flowers, 1 inch across. Var. "*flore-pleno*" is double. Asia Minor.

G. heldreichii: 12 inches. Orange-red flowers. This is a form of *G. montanum*.

G. montanum (Mountain Avens): 3 to 6 inches. Creeping habit. Short-stemmed, large, yellow flowers, 1½ inches across. June/July. Alpine. Sun or part shade, neutral to alkaline soil, moisture in summer.

G. pedki: 2 feet. Large yellow flowers, 1 inch across. Resembles *G. montanum* but not so tolerant besides being much taller and having larger leaves. Moist soil tending toward the acid. Mountains of New Hampshire.

G. reptans: 6 to 9 inches. Mat forming, spreading by runners. Large yellow flowers, 1½ inches across. Ferny foliage. A true alpine, it will not tolerate hot, humid conditions. Requires a rocky site and very good drainage of soil and air.

G. rivale (Water Avens): 9 inches. Nodding, red or pink flowers with orange shadings. Sun or part shade. Moist; this is a wet meadow plant.

G. rossii: A Rocky Mountain species, resembling *G. triflorum*, but the flowers are yellow and the seed heads are not feathery. Ferny leaves turn reddish-purple in fall. Open shade.

G. triflorum (syn. *G. ciliatum*) Old Man's Whiskers. Long Plumed Avens. Apache Plum: 6 to 12 inches. Fernlike, hairy leaves, mostly basal. Purple or pinkish, nodding flowers; sepals and bracts are pink. May/July. Feathery seed heads. Dry sites to 8,000 feet in the Rockies and northern states.

Gilia

Family: *Polemoniaceae* (Phlox).

Common name: Skyrocket. Standing Cypress.

Propagation: Sow in early spring at 45 to 50 degrees. Germination follows in 10 to 20 days. This will bloom the first year if started in March.

Self-sows readily.

Culture: Sun. light, sandy soil. Dry. Space 8 inches apart

in groups; they stand like sentinels in the border. I allow the seedlings to come up where they will; it is easy to recognize the ferny foliage and with care to avoid hoeing them up.

Use: Border. Easily naturalized (scatter the seeds in late fall or as they ripen).

Species:

G. rubra: Biennial. 3 feet. Solitary, tall, erect spike, covered over half its length by brilliant red, tubular flowers. August to frost. A native American. The humming birds fight over territorial rights to gilia, and it's my favorite too(but not for the same reason). It offers a striking contrast to the shasta daisy which blooms at the same time. (See illustration, p. 29.)

Gillenia

Family: *Rosaceae* (Rose).

Common name: Bowman's Root. Indian Physic.

Propagation: Seed sown in fall or spring at 50 to 60 degrees.

Division in spring.

Culture: Shade. Slightly acid, peaty soil. Moist. Plant in masses for effect.

Use: Border. Rockery. Woodland garden.

Species:

G. trifoliata: 2 to 3 feet. Ornamental, cut foliage; the pointed leaves are divided

into three leaflets. Flowers in loose panicles, range from red and rose, to white. May/June. Found from the mountain woodlands of Ontario south to Kentucky.

Gladiolus

Family: *Iridaceae* (Iris).

Common name: Gladiolus.

Propagation: Seed sown in early spring at 45 to 50 degrees germinates quite readily. Growing from seed is often the simplest or only way of obtaining the various species.
Corms of nemed varieties purchased for spring.
Cormels (the tiny corms that surround the large corm by fall): Store in slightly moist sand or vermiculite over winter, set out in rows for growing on in spring, 2 inches deep and 1 to 2 inches apart.

Culture: Sun. Humus-enriched, light, sandy soil. Mix superphosphate in the soil bed before planting. Additional all purpose fertilizer should be hoed and watered in beside the plants during the growing season. Adequate moisture at all times.

Being half hardy, the corms may be set outdoors when the soil is prepared in spring. Plant at least 6 to a group, 3 to 4 inches deep, 4 to 6 inches apart. Before planting, treat with Ceresan (1 ounce to 3 gallons of water), soak in this solution for 15 minutes, or you may use Lysol (1 tablespoon to 1 gallon of water) for 3 hours. Placing the corms in net

sacks for dipping simplifies the task, making it less difficult to keep the varieties separated. Save your net onion sacks for this or make your own out of netting. Drip dry and plant immediately.

Dig in fall when frost has killed the foliage, cut off the tops, dry and clean, store in frost-free place.

Use: Border. Cut flower (cut when lowest buds begin to open). Containers.

Species and varieties:

The Baby types (not the Miniatures, which are quite different) are not suited for the western highlands unless you are fortunate enough to have a greenhouse. They are very tender and bloom in winter.

G. Butterfly hybrids: 2 feet. Flowers are small to medium size, slightly ruffled, with various color combinations, all with dark markings in the throat.

G. byzantinus: 2 feet. Flowers in loose spikes, usually red.

G. communis: 1½ feet. Large flower in rose or white.

G. gandavensis: 2 feet. Flowers bright red with yellow markings. August/September.

G. palustris: 1¼ feet. Flowers usually purple-red. July/August.

G. tristis: 1½ to 2 feet. Flowers are especially fragrant at night, yellowish-white, often tinged red, 2½ to 3 inches across.

Hybrids and named horticultural varieties are too numerous to begin to mention. They come in every color and size imaginable. I listed the Butterfly hybrids because they do so well in the border, seldom demanding attention.

Glaucium

Family: *Papaveraceae* (Poppy).

Common name: Horned Poppy. Sea Poppy.

Propagation: Sow in spring at 45 to 50 degrees. Germination in 16 days. Cold frame the first winter, set in permanent places the following spring. This often does not bloom until the third year.

Culture: Sun. Light, sandy soil. Space plants 8 to 10 inches apart.

Use: Border. Rock garden.

Species:

G. flavum: 1½ feet. Orange-scarlet to orange-yellow, poppy-like flowers, to 3 inches across, on branching stems from July on. Very attractive, deeply cut, silvery-white leaves, mostly basal. Very odd seed pods, 8 to 9 inches long and thin. I have found this to be slow growing but hardy. It is not long lived and often dies out by the fourth year. Gather the seed and sow in flats, as this does not naturally self-sow to any degree. (See illustration, p. 29.)

Glaucium flavum, Horned Poppy

Globularia

Family: *Selanginaceae* or *Globulariaceae*.

Common name: Globe Daisy.

Propagation: Seed sown in fall or early spring at 45 to 50 degrees. Sow thickly, percentage of viable seed is low.

Cuttings.

Division after flowering.

Culture: Sun. Sandy, gritty, limy soil and rocks on which to spread out.

Use: Rock garden.

Species: All originate in the mountains of southern Europe and Asia.

G. cordifolia (Blue Globe Daisy): 4 inches. Prostrate subshrub, matting habit. Woody stemmed. Leaves notched only at their tips. Numerous globular, blue flower heads, ½ inch across.

G. nudicaulis: 9 inches. Similar to *G. trichosantha* but larger flowers, deep blue,

1 inch across, atop naked stems.

G. pindatus: 9 inches. Neat, compact dwarf with small blue flowers.

G. trichosantha (Globe Daisy): 9 inches. Tufted habit. Toothed leaves, 1 inch long. Small, pale steel-blue, fluffy, globular flower heads, ½ inch across, on leafy stems.

G. vulgaris (syn. *G. willkommii*): 12 inches. Fluffy blue balls in May. There is a white form of this. From the Caucasus.

Goodyeara

(see EPIPACTIS) ....

Gunnera

Family: *Haloragidaceae*.

Propagation: Seed sown in spring in warmth, 60 to 70 degrees. Difficult to germinate, but often the only method of obtaining this plant, for it is seldom offered by nurseries.

Culture: Partial shade. Deep, enriched soil. Moist. Fertilize heavily during the growing season. Needs a sheltered spot. Not completely hardy, mulch for winter or dig and store the rhizomes as you would dahlias.

Use: Bold background for the water garden.

Species:

G. *chilensis*: 3 to 5 feet. Huge leaves, 4 to 5 feet across, lobed, toothed, and rather frilled. Numerous reddish flowers in cob-like clusters, growing close to the ground, followed by tiny red fruits.

G. *manicata*: 6 feet. Leaves 4 to 6 feet across, red ribbed, with spiny, prickly hairs on the leaf stalks. Reddish-green flowers on a tapering spike to 3 feet tall.

Gypsophila

Family: *Caryophyllaceae* (Pinks).

Common name: Baby's Breath.

Propagation: Seed sown from spring to midsummer. Germination at 60 to 70 degrees in 7 to 14 days.

Midsummer cuttings of G. *repens*.

Division in spring.

Culture: Sun. Average garden loam on the limy side, well drained. Dry. Transplant when young. Does not like to be disturbed when once established. Give enough room to the tall sorts, 2 feet apart at least.

Use: Border. Rock garden (dwarfs). Cut flower (cut before blooms are fully open). Dried bouquet.

Species and varieties:

G. *acutifolia*: 2 feet. Flowers are larger than G. *paniculata* and lilac pink in color. August. From the Caucusus.

G. *cerastioides* (Mouse Ear): 3 to 4 inches. Creeping habit, forms a dense mat of downy white foliage. Quite large white flowers, ⅔ inch across, petals are veined pink or purple. May/June. Prefers a soil on the acid side.

G. *manginii*: 3½ feet. Small panicles of white flowers with a pinkish cast. Mongolian.

G. *oldhamiana*: 2½ to 3 feet. Rather sprawling habit of growth. Large dense clusters of bright flesh-pink flowers. July/October. From Korea. Var. "Flamingo" is double.

G. *pacifica*: 3 to 4 feet. Loose, graceful habit. Flowers pale rose to pale purple. Siberian.

G. *paniculata*: 2 to 3 feet high and as wide across. Branching clusters of airy masses of tiny white flowers in July. I prefer the double varieties; they are much more showy for the space this plant occupies.

Varieties: "*compacta*," 1½ foot compact dwarf; "*flore pleno*, Snow White," 3 feet, double white flowers; "Snowflake," double white; "Bristol Fairy" 1½ feet.

G. *repens* (Creeping Baby's Breath): 6 inches. Trailing, spreading habit. Prostrate stems to 18 inches long. White flowers in June. Alpine origin.

Var. "*rosea*," 4 inches, cushion type, pink to rose flowers, May/June; "Rosy Veil," 18 inches, double pink or white, June/August; of upright growth, it would fit in the border as well; "Bodgeri," 12 inches, white or pink double flowers.

Habenaria

Family: *Orchidaceae* (Orchid).

Common name: Bog Candle. Fringed or Rain Orchid.

Propagation: Commercial sources of seed or plants are sometimes available, otherwise collection from the field is necessary (see Cypripedium).

Division of tuberous root.

Seedling transplant mix: equal parts soil, peat and coarse sand.

Culture: Partial shade or sunny, moist site. Naturally heavy, moist soil (as is found in a wet meadow or alongside pond or stream); however good drainage is imperative.

Create a sandy, gravely base if necessary, adding generous amounts of peat to increase acidity. Set roots 1 inch deep, using care because the fleshy root is quite brittle. Difficult, but not impossible, to cultivate.

Use: Naturalized in moist, open woodland, meadow, or stream side.

Species:

H. *chlorantha* (Butterfly Orchid): 15 inches. Fragrant white flowers.

H. *ciliaris* (Yellow Fringed Orchid) to 2½ feet. Spikes of large orange-yellow flowers with long, deeply cut, fringed lips. July/August. Northeastern states.

H. *dilatata* (White Bog Orchid): 1 to 2 feet. Flowers on the upper portion of the stem, bright green, linear, 6-inch-long leaves on the lower. Dense spikes of waxy white flowers, spurred at base of lip. June/August, depending on elevation. Naturally wet sites from valley to 10,000 feet, common to the western half of North America.

H. *fimbriata* (Large Purple Fringed Orchid): to 4 feet. Easily transplanted species of the northeastern states. Fragrant, rose-purple, lilac, or white flowers with toothed petals and deeply fringed lips. May/June.

H. psycodes (Small Purple Orchid): 1 to 2½ feet. Fragrant, purple flowers, fringed-lipped. August. Most easily grown of all the species. Found from Quebec to Minnesota.

Hacquetia

Family: *Umbelliferae* (Carrot).

Propagation: Seed sown in spring at 45 to 50 degrees.

Culture: Partial shade. Well-drained, humusy soil.

Use: Rock garden. Woodland garden.

Species:

H. epipactis: 4 to 10 inches. Rare species from the open woodlands of the Alps and Carpathian Mountains. Palmately lobed leaves. Yellow flowers in small circular umbels. April.

Hedysarum

Family: *Leguminosae* (Pea).

Common name: French Honeysuckle. Sulla Clover.

Propagation: Sow seed at 60 degrees. Germination in 6 days. Transplant as seedlings, as these have very long roots.

Division in spring; but it is not easy.

Culture: Sun. Light, humusy soil, well drained. Adequate moisture during the dry season.

Use: Herbaceous shrub. Rock garden.

Species:

H. coronarium: 3 feet high and as wide (give it enough room). Pinnate leaved, long, willowy, arching branches with small terminal spikes of fragrant, red, pea-like flowers. July/August. I have not found this to be long lived ——three years at the most.

H. obscurum: 12 inches. Red-violet flowers in long loose racemes. Rock-garden type.

Helenium

Family: *Compositae* (Daisy).

Common name: Sneezeweed. Helen's Flower. False Sunflower. Yellow Star.

Propagation: Sow seed at 60 degrees. Germination in 7 days. Seed saved from cultivars (named varieties) does not always reproduce true to type.

Division in early spring, usually needed every third year.

Culture: Sun. Average, well-drained soil. Moist. Tall sorts may be pinched back as with mums to induce branching and neater habit. Do this no later than June. Space plants 2 feet apart.

Use: Border. Cut flower. Wild garden.

Species and varieties:

H. autumnale: 4 feet. Coarse, branching habit. Daisy-like flowers, rays brown to red, gold, or yellow, with shading darker at the base, and yellow disc. August on. A native American. (see illustration, p. 29.)

Varieties: "Riverton Gem," 3 feet, yellow with center blotch of brownish-red; rays have a crinkly, crepe-paper texture, June to frost if faded flowers are removed; "Riverton Beauty," yellow, dark purplish center; "Moerheim Beauty" flowers maroon or brownish-red; "Bruno," dark red.

H. bigelovii (Western Sneezeweed): 2 feet. Deep yellow rays, black to brownish disc. From California, this prefers a sunny, moist site in the wild garden.

H. hoopesii (Orange Sneezeweed): 1½ feet. Large

Helenium autumnale, Helen's Flower "Riverton Gem"

flowers to 3 inches across, solitary or several to a stem, ray florets yellow to orange-yellow and with 2 to 3 indents at the tips, discs are yellow fading brown. May/June. Rocky Mountains.

H. nudiflorum: Yellow drooping rays, brown to purple discs. For the moist wild garden.

Helianthemum

Family: *Cistaceae* (Rock Rose).

Common name: Rock or Sun Rose.

Propagation: Seed sown in spring or summer at 70 degrees. Some bloom the second year.

Cuttings taken with a heel in August.

Softwood cuttings in June.

Culture: Sun. Well-drained, sandy, limy soil. Dry. This does not transplant well; set in permanent place when young. Allow 18 to 20 inches for the plant to spread. Prune after flowering or they become quite straggly. Winter mulch is advised in open winters.

Use: Rock garden. Border. Ground cover.

Species and varieties:

H. mummularium (syn. *H. chamaecistus*, *H. vulgare*): 6 to 12 inches high. Woody stemmed, dwarf evergreen shrub that eventually spreads to 2 feet or more. Yellow,

cup-shaped flowers, 1 inch across, in terminal loose racemes, last but a day. July/September. From southeastern Europe.

Varieties: "*alba*," 9 inches, white; "primrose," 9 inches high, pink; "*croftianum*," silvery foliage and apricot-yellow flowers; "Ben Heckla," brick red; "Ben Alder," flowers a brownish-red with deeper red centers.

H. mutabile: 12 inches. Dwarf evergreen. Flowers may be pink, red, purple, yellow, copper, or white. June/September.

H. tuberaria: 12 inches. Differs in that it is a herbaceous perennial (not woody). Clusters of yellow flowers, 1½ inches across. July/September.

Heliopsis

Family: *Compositae* (Daisy).

Common name: Oxeye. Rough Oxeye. False or Orange Sunflower.

Propagation: Seed sown at 65 degrees; germination in 10 days. Blooms the first year from seed if started in March. Reproduces true to type from seed.

Division in spring; usually a necessity every third year.

Culture: Sun. Average soil. Dry. Space plants 12 to 15 inches apart; mass for gorgeous color, like a bit of the sun fallen.

Use: Border. Cut flower. Wild garden.

Species and varieties:

H. helianthoides pitcheriana (syn. *H. laevis*): 2 feet. Profuse flowering habit. Deep yellow rays, flat dark disc. July/September. Found from Minnesota to Illinois.

H. scabra vitellina: 3 feet. Large double golden-yellow flowers. July to frost. Native from Maine to Arkansas.

Var. "*gigantea*," 3 feet, extra large golden-yellow; "Light of London"; "*patula*," new hybrid with very large orange flowers, double row of rays.

Hemerocallis

Family: *Liliaceae* (Lily).

Common name: Day Lily.

Propagation: Method 1: Plant seeds in November in flats, stack flats one on top of another outdoors (cold frame is a good place), bring into the greenhouse in February to germinate. Keep actively growing all winter, and they will often flower by next fall or the following summer.

Heliopsis scabra vitellina, Wxeye

Method 2: Seed sown in spring at 45 degrees; germination will follow in 23 days. Grow on in the flats or bulb pans until time to transplant into the garden. Fertilize 3 or 4 times during the growing season. Some will bloom the second year, all the third.

Cultivars are best purchased, because seed of the named varieties will not reproduce true. This is not to infer, however, that the results would not be as pleasing and charming as their parents.

Division in spring or fall. Dig up the clump, cut back the roots half way and the tops to 2 inches, and divide the crown as desired.

Culture: Sun or light shade. Average soil with humus added. Adequate moisture during the dry season. Space 12 inches apart in groups of three or more. Allow about 2 feet around the perimeter of the group for spreading. Set the crown at soil level. Very easily transplanted at any time, but the top growth must always be cut back by half.

Use: Border. Rock garden. Wild garden. Cut flower: pick just as the buds are about to open; the bloom lasts but a day.

Species: There are hundreds of named varieties, too numerous to mention.

H. aurantiaca (Golden Summer Day Lily): Resembles *H. fulva* but is smaller and paler in color. July.

H. citrina (Citron Day Lily): Night blooming. Fragrant, pale yellow flowers.

H. dumortieri (Narrow Dwarf Day Lily): 2 feet. Orange flowers in clusters in May.

H. flava (Common Yellow or Lemon Day Lily): 2 to 3 feet. Fragrant, lemon-yellow, medium-sized blooms. May/June.

H. fulva (Fulvous Day Lily. Tawny or Common Orange Day Lily): 3 to 4 feet. Flowers in soft orange to reddish hues. July. A rapid spreader, this is better suited to the wild garden. Japanese.

H. gracilis: 2 feet. Small lemon-yellow flowers. May/June. Rock garden or naturalize.

H. middendorfi (Amur Day Lily): 3 feet. Pale orange flowers to 3 inches across, in clusters. Siberian.

H. thunbergi (Late Yellow Day Lily): 3 feet. Flowers a clear lemon-yellow with greenish insides. July.

Hepatica

Family: *Ranunculaceae* (Buttercup).

Common name: Liverleaf. Liverwort. Mayflower.

Propagation: Seed sown in spring. It must be fresh. Slow to germinate; most will not germinate until second year.

Self-sows readily (if collecting, tie a small bag over the seed head to catch the dispersing seed).

Division of fibrous-rooted clumps after flowering. Leaves die down after

blooming period for a short time and then are renewed.

Transplants easily, even in bloom.

Culture: Shade. Well-drained, sandy, humus-enriched, neutral soil. Dry. Benefits from applications of well-rotted manure. *H. americana* prefers more acid conditions; incorporate goodly quantities of peat and pine needles into the soil when planting. Plant in masses for effect.

Use: Woodland or open-shaded garden (some sun is required when flowering in early spring). Ground cover; all of the species have attractive evergreen leaves.

Species:

H. americana (Round-lobed Hepatica): 6 inches. Basal leaves, thickish, with 3 to 5 rounded lobes. Earliest of spring flowers, usually pale blue, some rose or white, 1 inch across. Native to states east of the Mississippi from Canada to Georgia.

H. angulosa (*H. transsilvanica*): Hungarian species with leaves having 3 to 5 lobes, toothed at the tips. Flowers in early spring, 1¼ inches across.

H. acutiloba (Sharp-lobed Hepatica): Long, hairy stemmed, evergreen leaves having 3 pointed lobes. Pale flowers ranging from pale blues and lavender to pink and white. Deeper hues and doubled flowers are often found. May. Very tolerant of limy soils. Found natively from Canada to the southernmost states east of the Mississippi.

H. nobilis (*H. triloba*): 16 inches. Very like *H. americana* but having larger and often double flowers with showy stamens. European.

Herniaria

Family: *Caryophyllaceae* (Pinks).

Common name: Rupture Wort.

Propagation: Seed sown in early spring at 45 to 50 degrees. Germination in 5 days.

Division in spring.

Culture: Sun or light shade. Light, sandy soil.

Use: Rock garden. Ground cover.

Species:

H. glabra: 4 inches. Evergreen trailer forming mats of moss-like foliage that turns bronzy-red in winter. Fast growing.

Hesperis

Family: *Cruciferae* (Mustard).

Common name: Sweet Rocket.

Propagation: Seed sown in March at 60 to 65 degrees.

Self-sows readily.

Culture: Sun. Average garden loam.

Use: Border. Cut flower. Wild garden.

Species and varieties:

H. matronalis (Dame's
Violet): Perennial but not
long lived. 2 feet. Erect
branching habit of growth.
Pyramidal flowering spikes
resemble *Phlox paniculata*.
Flowers are ½ inch across
in shades of white, rose, or
mauve to purple. May/
August. Very fragrant, especially in the evening.

Var. "*alba*," white form;
"*purpurea*," violet flowers.

Heuchera

Family: *Saxifrageae*
(Saxifrage).

Common name: Coral Bells.
Alumroot.

Propagation: Sow in spring at
50 to 60 degrees. Germination in 20 days.

Division in spring. This
should be done every third
year, or the clump
eventually dies.

Cuttings in July, any leaf
with stem or part of a basal
shoot will root.

Culture: Sun. Rich, well-
drained soil. Space plants 6
inches apart in groups. Set
the crown a bit below the
soil level, as it has a tendency
to work up in winter, leaving
the roots exposed.

Use: Border. Rock garden.
Ground cover. Edging for
walk or terrace. Cut flower.
Wild garden.

Species and varieties:

Heuchera sanguinea, Coral
Bells "Bressingham hybrid"

H. americana: to 3 feet.
Leaves mottled reddish-
bronze. Greenish-white
flowers in panicles. April/
June. A better choice for the
wild flower garden, this
prefers shade and a limy soil.
Native from Connecticut to
Michigan.

H. brizoides: 2½ feet. A
free-flowering pale pink
hybrid.

H. cylindrica: 1½ feet.
Heart-shaped leaves.
Yellowish-green flowers.

H. ovalifolia (Oval leaf
Alumroot): 4 to 24 inches.

Tufts of sticky-haired, oval
leaves. Spike-like cluster of
yellowish bells. Rocky Mountain species found in aspen
groves or sunny dry sites
from Alberta to Colorado.
For the wild garden.

H. sanguinea: 1½ feet. Red
to pink flowers. June/July.
From the southwestern states.
(See illustration, p. 28.)

Varieties: "Bressingham
Hybrids," 2 feet, wiry slender
stems carrying tiny bells in
shades of white, pink, or red,
July/August; "Edgehill,"
bright crimson; "Snowflake"
and "June Bride," white
forms; "Freedom," rose
pink; "Fire Sprite," red.

H. tiarelloides (syn.
HEUCHERELLA *tiarel-
loides*): A cross between
Heuchera and *Tiarella
cordifolia*. 12 inches. Pink,
red, or white flowers in May.

H. villosa: Profuse flowering
woodland plant for the wild
garden. Tiny white bells in
August/September.

Heucherella

(see HEUCHERA
tiarelloides)

Hibiscus

Family: *Malvaceae* (Mallow).

Common name: Rose Mallow.

Propagation: Collected seeds
sown anytime. Germination at
60 to 65 degrees in 3 days;
usually excellent.

Division in spring, not easy
with a mature plant.

Cuttings in August.

Culture: Sun or part shade. Rich, humusy loam. Moist (originally marsh plants). Shelter from the wind. Space 2 feet apart in spring, setting the eyes 4 inches below soil level. Slow to start in spring, so stake the site and use caution when hoeing.

Use: Sentinel of the border. Singly as a specimen. Natural moist site beside water.

Species and varieties:

H. moscheutos: to 8 feet. Robust habit. Thick sturdy stems. Large creamy-white flowers with dark red centers. The parent of many cultivars. Native from Ohio to Indiana.

Var. "Giant Mallow Marvels" (*H. palustris* x *H. moscheutos*), 3 feet or more high, has large flowers of crimson, rose, pink, or white, August/ September; "Southern Belle," new hybrid with huge flowers to 11 inches across, red, white with red centers, or shades of pink.

H. grandiflorus: 5 to 6 feet. Very large pale pink flowers. There are white "*albus*," rose "*roseus*," and red "*ruber*" varieties of this species.

H. palustris (Swamp Rose Mallow): 3 to 6 feet. Very large pink flowers, 4 to 6 inches across, in terminal clusters. There are also red and white forms. August/ September. Slow growing, but it eventually makes a large clump. Long lived in moist, neutral soil. Parent of commonly offered garden cultivars. Native from Massachusetts to Indiana.

Hippeastrum

Family: *Amaryllidaceae* (Amaryllis).

Common name: Amaryllis. Barbados Lily.

Propagation: Sow at 70 degrees. Germination within 14 days. Blooms in 3 years from seed.

Bulb offsets.

Culture: Shade. Light, sandy soil with humus added. A half-hardy bulb, plant outside when danger of frost is over. Dig and store in sand for the winter.

Indoor: for winter bloom, pot with upper half of bulb exposed, water sparingly until growth appears. Prefers temperature of 65 degrees. Often blooms before leaves appear. After flowering period, allow leaves to mature and set the plant out in the garden for the summer when weather permits.

Use: Protected garden bed or planter. Container or pot plant.

Species and varieties:

H. Dutch hybrids: 18 to 24 inches. Clump of large, strap-like leaves to 24 inches long. Flowers come in all colors; may be red, salmon, orange, pink, or white. The lily-like flowers, projecting horizontally outward like the spokes of a wheel, are in umbels atop sturdy hollow stems.

Hosta

(syn. FUNKIA) ....

Family: *Liliaceae* (Lily).

Common name. Plantain Lily.

Propagation: Seed sown in fall, or stratify and expose to freezing conditions for several weeks prior to spring sowing. Cool temperatures, shade, and even moisture is required to sprout the seed (see *Hemerocallis*). It takes 2 to 3 years to flower from seed, and this genus does not reproduce true from seed. The variegated types revert to plain green.

Division of (young) clumps in spring only.

Creeping root or stolon of *H. decorata.*

Culture: Sun or partial shade. Well-drained, rich, humusy soil. Moist. Annual dressing of well-rotted manure or compost, and superphosphate in spring. When setting out plants, dig a good-sized hole and use generous amounts of peat, mixing well with the soil. Plant in groups of not less than 3, 6 to 8 inches apart. Very long lived, they do not require transplanting or dividing.

Use: Border. Rock garden. Edging of walk or drive. Container. Cut flower.

Species and varieties:

H. albomarginata: Similar to *H. lancifolia*, but the leaves are white-edged. Lavender flowers in September.

H. decorata (syn. Thomas Hogg) Blunt-leaved Plantain Lily: 2 feet. Oval, blunt-tipped leaves, 6 inches long, white margins. Purple flowers, 2 inches long, in August. Spreads by stolons.

H. fortunei (Tall-cluster Plantain Lily): 2 to 3 feet. Large glaucous, blue-green leaves. Flowers vary from lavender-blue to white, 1½ inches long. May/July.

H. glauca (syn. *H. sieboldiana*) Blue-leaved Plantain Lily: 1½ feet. Leaves blue-grey to greyish-green, to 12 inches long, having a rough-appearing textured surface due to heavy veining. Grown for the foliage, the flowers are pale lilac to white and do not show much above the leaves.

H. japonica (syn. *H. lancifolia*) Japanese or Narrow-leaved Plantain Lily: 2 feet. Resembles *H. caerulea*, but the flowers are more lavender in color, 2 inches long, blooming in August. Slender, lanceolate, dark green leaves, 6 inches long.

H. plantaginea (syn. *H. subcordata*, *H. grandiflora*) Fragrant Plantain Lily: 2½ feet. Large, pale green, heart-shaped, deeply ridged leaves. Lily-like, fragrant, white flowers, 4 inches long. August/September.

H. rectifolia: 1½ feet. Large, green leaves held erect. Dark lilac flowers.

H. undulata (syn. *H. media picta*, *H. variegata*) Wavy-leaved Plantain Lily: 1½ to 3 feet. Leaves have wavy margins and are variegated, white on green. Clusters of bell-shaped, pale lavender flowers in July. This species increases quite rapidly.

H. ventricosa (syn. *H. ovata, H. caerulea*) Blue Plantain Lily: 2 to 3 feet. Deep green, heart-shaped leaves with prominent ribs and twisted tips. Blue flowers in loose racemes. July/September. From eastern Asia.

Hyacinthus

Family: *Liliaceae* (Lily)

Common name: Hyacinth.

Propagation: Sow seed from spring into summer at 65 to 70 degrees.

Bulbs purchased for fall planting.

Culture: Sun. Well-drained, sandy soil with humus added. If a large bed is prepared, well-rotted manure may be incorporated into the soil, but do not allow the fertilizer to come in actual contact with the bulbs. In subsequent fertilizing of the hardy bulbs, use fertilizers high in phosphorous and potash but low in nitrogen.

Plant bulbs in fall, 6 inches deep (bulb should be covered with 3 to 4 inches of soil), 5 to 6 inches apart. Water well so that the root system is established before a hard frost.

Winter forcing for indoor bloom: Plant medium-sized bulb in 4-inch pot, 2 to a 5-inch pot, or 3 to a 6-inch pot, the top half of the bulb remaining uncovered. Use a soil mix of equal parts soil,

peat, and sand. Place in a dark place (about 50 degrees) for 2 months, bring into room temperature and shade with a paper cone until the flower shoots begin to grow. For a longer flowering period, keep out of bright sun and find a cooler temperature at night. There are on the market specially prepared bulbs for forcing and lovely glass containers for starting these, as well as for crocus.

Use: Border. Rock garden. Cut flower. Containers. Shrub or tree underplanting. Naturalizing in the lawn (do not cut the grass until the leaves have died down.) Winter forcing.

Species and varieties:

H. amethystinus: 6 inches. Nodding small flowers in loose spikes, clear light to deep blue shades. Spain. There is a white variation *"alba."*

H. azureus (syn. *H. ciliatus* or *MUSCARI azureum*): 3 to 8 inches. Flowers range from china blue to darker blue. March/April.

H. orientalis (Common Hyacinth): 6 to 12 inches. Linear-lanceolate, bright green leaves. Funnel or bell-shaped flowers to 1 inch long in shades of blue, purple, or white in terminal, cylindrical spikes. Native to the eastern Mediterranean and western Asia.

Parent of the Dutch Hyacinth (most commonly grown) whose flowers have a larger range of color, including shades of pink, red, salmon, and cream as well as the original blues.

Hydro-phyllum

Family: *Hydrophyllaceae* (Waterleaf).

Common name: Waterleaf. Cat's Britches.

Propagation: Seed or plants must be collected from the field. (I have never discovered a commercial source.) Seed collected and sown in August. Transplanting anytime if care is given so that the fleshy root is not injured; dormant period of early fall is best.

Division in spring.

Culture: Part shade. Fairly rich, humusy soil. Moist.

Use: Attractive underplanting for shrubs. Woodland garden. A native plant that should be better known.

Species:

H. capitatum (Ballhead Waterleaf): 4 to 16 inches. Long-stalked, mostly basal, fleshy, hairy, divided leaves. Rain water caught in the leaf gives the plant its common name. Dense, globular flowering heads made up of white to purplish-blue bells (which supposedly resemble a cat's paw, although I fail to see a comparison, the long stamens being the claws). The flowers are partially hidden, for the stems are shorter than the leaf stalks. May/June. After seeding, the plant goes dormant; the thick, fleshy root carries it through the dry season. A Rocky Mountain species, valley to 9,000 feet elevation.

Hymeno-callis

(syn. *ISMENE*)

Family: *Amaryllidaceae* (Amaryllis)

Common name: Peruvian Daffodil. Spider Lily.

Propagation: Seed sown in spring at 70 degrees. Germination follows in 16 days.

Bulbs purchased for spring planting.

Culture: Sun or half shade. Well-drained, enriched, sandy, limy soil. Set bulbs 3 to 4 inches deep, 6 inches apart in garden bed in spring after the soil has warmed. Fertilize with well-rotted manure. Handle in the same manner as gladiolus. Lift before frost and store in vermiculite in fairly warm (50 degrees) place. Do not remove the roots, but prune back slightly before replanting.

Use: Border. Container. Force for winter bloom.

Species and varieties:

H. calathina: 2 feet. Dark green, strap-like leaves. Large fragrant, white, trumpet-shaped, spidery flowers, 4 inches long, 4 to 5 flowers on a stem. It blooms soon after planting.

Varieties: "Sulphur Queen," yellow; "Festalis," very reflexed outer petals; "Advance," larger than type, white with green striped throat.

H. ovata (syn. *H. fragrans*)
Mediterranean Lily. Sea
Daffodil: 12 inches. Fragrant,
sea-green flowers in July.

Iberis

Family: *Cruciferae* (Mustard).

Common name: Candytuft.

Propagation: Sow in spring
at 65 degrees.

Root divisions in spring.

Cuttings in midsummer.

Self-sows readily.

Culture: Sun. Light, well-
drained soil. Remove spent
flowers when bloom is over
and shape to retain neat habit.
As with dianthus, grass
should never be allowed to
infiltrate these plants; the
only solution is to dig up the
whole clump and remove the
grass——every single bit of it.

Use: Edge of border (too
spreading for the rock
garden).

Species:

I. gibraltarica (Giberalter
Candytuft): 12 inches.
Procumbent habit. Rather
variable from seed. Flattish
clusters of flowers, white
with tints of lilac. May/June.
Not as hardy as *I. sempervirens*. Spain

I. sempervirens (Edging or
Evergreen Candytuft): 12
inches high but spreads to 2
feet across in mounds. Not
evergreen in the highlands.
Dark green leaves. Raceme-
like clusters of white flowers
completely cover the plant

from May to June. The
blooming season seems rather
short. There are several
named varieties. Southern
Europe origin.

Iliamna

(syn. *SPHAERALCEA*) .... ..

Family: *Malvaceae* (Mallow).

Common name: Mountain
Hollyhock. Maple Mallow.
Globemallow.

Propagation: Seed collected
from August on (an indi-
genous wild flower; no
commercial source of seed
that I know of). Sow in fall
or early spring.

Division of plants in
spring or fall.

Culture: Sun or part shade.
Average garden loam.
Natively, often found near
natural sources of water.

Use: Border. Wild flower
garden.

Species:

I. rivularis: 3 to 4 feet.
Resembles a miniature hollyhock. Flowering spikes in
light pink to rose-lavender
shades. June/July. Rocky
Mountains, 5,000 to
9,000 feet.

Incarvillea

Family: *Bignoniaceae*
(Bignonia).

Common name: Hardy
Gloxinia. Trumpet Flower.

Incarvillea delavayi, Hardy
Gloxinia "Bees Pink"

109

Propagation: Sow in spring at 45 to 50 degrees. Germination in 8 to 14 days.

Root division in spring; however, this is not easy as it has a fleshy root.

Culture: Sun. Light, porous, humus-enriched soil. Space 8 inches apart in groups of 6 or more. Slow to appear in spring, so mark their sites. I have found both species to be completely hardy.

Use: Border. Rock garden.

Species and varieties:

I. delavayi: 1½ feet. Large pinnate leaves. Rose-purple, gloxinia-like flowers. Var. "Bee's Pink" flower scapes have 1 to 12 large pale pink trumpets, 2 inches across. July/August.

I. grandiflora brivipes: 6 to 12 inches. Large trumpet-shaped, crimson-rose flowers in terminal racemes in June. Chinese.

Inula

Family: *Compositae* (Daisy).

Common name: Caucasian Inula.

Propagation: Sow seed at 65 degrees; germination follows in 8 days.

Division in early spring.

Culture: Sun. Average soil. Moist. Division every three years. Space plants 12 inches apart in masses.

Use: Border. Cut flower. Wild garden.

Species:

I. ensifolia: 9 inches. Erect habit. Hairless leaves. Medium-sized yellow flowers to 1½ inches across. July/August.

I. helenium (Elecampane): 5 feet. Leaves have velvety undersurfaces. Flower heads made up of numerous narrow yellow ray florets. July/September. European species better used in the wild garden.

I. orientalis (syn. *I. glandulosa*): 2 feet. Large, hairy, bright green leaves. Solitary, fringed, orange-yellow flowers, 4 to 5 inches across. July to frost. Himalayan.

I. royaleana: 2 feet. Orange-yellow flowers to 4 inches across. July/August.

Iris

Family: *Iridaceae* (Iris).

Common name: Iris.

Propagation: Collect seeds when pod is dry, store dry and cool, sow in flats from spring into early summer. If there is no germination during the summer, wait until the temperatures fall to 40 degrees or less before bringing in for the winter. Germination may be induced by using pre-freezing treatment. Half-fill refrigerator tray with water, placing 2 or 3 seeds in a cube, freeze. Fill the rest of the tray with water and freeze for a week. Thaw out the cubes and plant in flats. Germinate at 50 to 60 degrees. (Do not use pre-freezing treatment for

Louisiana iris.) Spring-sown seed will bloom the third year.

Fall sowing: Sow flat and leave outside to cold, freezing conditions before bringing into the greenhouse; germination should begin immediately. Carry through the winter actively growing, transplant to cold frame or garden in the spring and these will usually flower by the second year.

The iris is not difficult to raise from seed, and this is often the only method of obtaining some of the really delightful species which reproduce true from seed. The flower is not self-fertilizing; insects or man are the pollinators.

Division of rhizomes in August, one section to one fan of leaves; cut the leaves back to about 6 inches long before replanting.

Division of stolons of *I. cristata*.

Culture: Bearded (pogon) type: Sun. Neutral, sandy, well-drained soil. Late summer dormancy is the time to divide the clumps, and this should really be undertaken every 3 to 4 years. Water well for new growth before frost.

Beardless (apogon) type: Tolerates partial shade; sun during part of the day is necessary, however. Rich humusy to heavy soils, even to marshy conditions. Frequent division is not necessary, but if required, should also be done in fall.

Fall or reblooming types: Do not go dormant in summer, so treat as you would any

perennial; feed and water at regular intervals. These are rather rare.

Space all types 16 to 18 inches apart, setting the roots shallow so that not over 1 to 2 inches of soil covers the rhizome. Place in groups of 4 to 6, allowing a 3-foot perimeter around the groupings.

Use: Bearded type: Border or very effective when massed by themselves in a separate bed. Beardless type: waterside ornamentals. Long-lasting cut flower.

Species and varieties:

I. arenaria: 4 inches. Dwarf bearded form with bright yellow flowers, orange beards.

I. aurea (syn. *I. crocea*): 3 to 4 feet. Spuria type from Kashmir. Golden-yellow flowers. June/July.

I. bucharica: Flowers have small white standards, deep yellow falls, and waved golden crest. Turkestan.

I. chamaeiris: 12 inches. Bearded. Parent of most garden cultivars. Colors vary from white to yellow or blue. April/May. Native to southern France and northern Italy.

I. chrysographes: 1½ feet. Fibrous-rooted Chinese species with deep violet-blue flowers, gold markings on the falls. Var. "*rubella*" deep reddish-purple. Requires light shade, moist, peaty soil.

I. clarkei: 2 feet. Resembles *I. sibirica*, the color being variable ranging from blue to shades of red.

I. delavayi: 3½ feet. Flowers are a deep violet with a small white blotch.

I. dichotoma (Vesper Iris): 2 to 3½ feet. Beardless. Flowers in clusters on branching stems, color is variable. The small flowers may be white with purplish tints to greenish-white and a lavender tinge. Blooms open late in the afternoon and last but a day. Siberian.

I. douglasiana: 1½ to 2 feet. Several flowers to a stem may be creamy-white, yellow, lilac, rose, or reddish-purple. Very tolerant of harsh conditions. Native of California and Oregon.

I. Dutch hybrids: Orchid-like flowers of great color range, white, yellow, orange, mauve, blue, deep purple, and bicolored. May/June. Prefers sun and well-drained soil. Long-lasting cut flower.

I. ensata: 1½ to 3 feet. Chinese species with bluish-purple to lavender and white flowers in July.

I. foetidissima (Gladwin Iris): 1 to 2 feet. Grey-blue flowers in May. Sometimes grown mainly for the attractive seed pods. Very hardy.

I forrestii: 15 inches. Fibrous-rooted. Brownish-purple veined yellow flowers. June. Chinese. Part shade and moist slightly acid soil.

I. fulva (Copper Iris): 2 to 2½ feet. Beardless. Color of the 2 or 3 terminal flowers varies from red or pink to yellow but is usually a copper hue. Native to the Gulf coast but is hardy in the North. Neutral soil and constant moisture required.

I. germanica (Common or German Iris): 2 to 3 feet. Bearded. Flowers may be white, yellow, rose, red, or purple and combinations of all. May/June. Flowers are 6 petaled, consisting of 3 upright (standards) and 3 drooping petals (falls), the beard is about halfway down the falls. As it has a rather short season of bloom, I set them off in a bed by themselves. There are hundreds of named varieties.

I. gracilipes (Slender or Crested Japanese Iris): 8 to 12 inches. Rock-garden dwarf. Slender leaves give it a fragile appearance. Several flattish flowers on arching, branched stems, pale lavender-pink, white veins and yellow centers. May/June. Must have shade, soil enriched with leaf mold and peat.

I. Higo: Japanese species with single or double flowers, colors ranging from lavender-pink to blue or white, 8 inches across; 6 petaled, but some varieties have only 3 large petals. Moist site. This does not set seed except when aided by hand pollinization.

I. innominata: 9 inches. Grassy foliage. Flowers may be blue-purple, lilac, golden-yellow, or yellow with brown stripes. Hybrids of this have a larger range of color——purple, pink, cream, and yellow shades. A fibrous-rooted species suitable for the rock garden or woodland. From the mountains of Oregon and northern California.

I. kaempferi (Japanese Iris): 2½ to 4 feet. Beardless. Fibrous rooted, this requires a rich, humusy soil on the acid side and moist. One or more flattish, saucer-like flowers, 4 to 6 inches across, to a stem. Velvety, deep colors of red, wine-red, rose, purple, lavender, blue, and white with mottled and veined variations; there are even double - and triple-petaled varieties. June/July.

I. kerneriana: 3 feet. Spuria type with yellow flowers.

I. mellita: Bearded and rhizomatous. Red-edged, dull green leaves. Large reddish flowers with white beards in June. It often blooms again in fall if there isn't an early freeze.

I. minuta: An almost stemless Japanese dwarf for the rock garden. Small yellow flowers. April/May.

I. missouriensis (Rocky Mountain Iris or Flag): 1 to 3 feet. One to 4 flowers to a stem, pale to violet-blue, dark veined, 2 to 3 inches long. May/July. Found from valley to 10,000 feet elevation in the Rockies; in fact, it is the only Iris native to this area. Tolerant of moist or dry sites as long as there is spring moisture.

I. nepalensis (syn. *I. decora*): 9 inches. A rare form having pale to deep lilac flowers.

I. ochroleuca (syn. *I. orientalis, I. gigantea*) Yellow Iris: 3 to 4 feet. Beardless, spuria type. Flowers a creamy-yellow with deep yellow marking on the falls. June/July. Robust habit. Long-lasting cut flower. Requires a rich, moist soil.

I. pseudacorus (Water Iris. Yellow or Water Flag): to 3 feet. Bright yellow flowers in clusters (rarely, purple-veined). June. The flowers shine like fog lights in the shade and against the green. Happy in boggy sites near water, but equally able to adapt to rich, humusy, shaded areas in the garden and the north sides of buildings or walls. Originally from Europe and North Africa, it is now naturalized over much of North America.

I. pumila (Dwarf Iris): 5 - to 6-inch dwarf for the rock garden or front of border. Bearded and rhizomatous. Spreading habit; this requires frequent division. Short-stemmed, small purple, reddish-purple, blue, yellow or white flowers in April. Many named varieties.

I. reticulata (Fragrant or Violet-scented Iris): Bulbous. 6 - to 8-inch rock-garden species. Bluish-green, four-sided leaves appear after the flowers. Fragrant flowers, 2 inches across, rich violet-purple edged with gold. A long-lasting cut flower. May be potted and forced for winter bloom (6 to 8 bulbs to a 4 - or 5-inch pot). This is not an easy species to maintain.

I. setosa: 15 inches. Variable species from Alaska. Flowers are usually purple but may also be lavender or reddish-purple.

I. sibirica (Siberian Iris): 2 to 3 feet. Beardless. Narrow grass-like leaves. Small to medium-sized flowers may be purple, lilac, blue, dark red, or white. June. Var. "Perry's

Blue," very large, pale blue; "Snow Queen." A good cut flower. Prefers sun and a neutral to slightly acid, heavy, rich, moist soil.

I. sintenesii: 9 inches. White flowers, purple-blue veins and markings.

I. tectorum (Roof Iris): 9 inches. Rather broad foliage. Netted, pale blue flowers. Not very happy with a cold, dry environment. Needs shade and a moist, rich, slightly acid soil.

I. tenax (Oregon Iris): 6 to 12 inches. Fibrous-rooted. Resembles a small Japanese iris. Grassy leaves. Flowers are greyish-lavender, purple to reddish-purple; midridge of falls is yellow. Woodland or rock-garden type. Sun or shade, sandy, well-drained site. From Washington and Oregon.

I. tingitana fontanesii: 2 feet. Flowers having dark standards, orange throat, and pale falls with dark markings. Morocco.

I. verna (Vernal Iris): A dwarf having only 3-inch-high flowering stems. Leaves are 6 to 8 inches long. Solitary flower, erect standards of lavender-blue, yellow centers, a wide band of yellow-orange down each fall. April/May. A woodland type from Pennsylvania and southward that prefers a rather moist, acid soil. Does not transplant well.

I. versicolor (Large Blue Flag): 1½ to 3 feet. Violet-blue flowers. May/July. Var. "*kermesina*" has wine-purple flowers. Neutral soil. Forms colonies in a moist, wild garden. Northern states and Canada.

I. xiphioides (English Iris): 1½ feet. Bulbous. Resembles outwardly a Japanese iris. Flowers may be purple, purple-red, or deep blue with gold blotch on the falls. June. Var. "*alba*," white form. Needs a cool, moist, rather acid soil. Set out bulbs in fall, 3 to 4 inches deep and 4 inches apart. In spite of the common name, this is a native of Spain and may not always exhibit the hardiness of the other species.

I. xiphium (Spanish Iris): 1½ to 2 feet. Small violet-purple flowers in June. Parent of many varieties, including the Dutch hybrids. Spain and northern Africa.

Ismene

(see HYMENOCALLIS) ......

Ixiolirion

Family: *Amaryllidaceae* (Amaryllis).

Common name: Siberian Bluebells.

Propagation: Sow seeds from spring into summer at 65 to 70 degrees.

Offsets.

Culture: Sun. Light, fairly rich soil. Requires excellent drainage. Set bulbs 3 inches deep and 6 inches apart. Mulch lightly for winter or dig and store as for gladiolus — with good drainage, however, these should be hardy.

Use: Rock garden.

Species:

I. montanum (syn. *I. ledebourii*): 1½ feet. Narrow, grey-green leaves. Blue to lilac-blue, starry flowers, 2 inches across, in loose clusters. May/June. A rare, hardy bulb from central Asia.

Jasione

Family: *Campanulaceae* (Bellflower).

Common name: Sheep's Scabious. Sheep's Bit. Shepherd's Scabious.

Propagation: Seeds sown at 65 degrees. Germination in 16 days.

Division in spring.

Culture: Sun or light shade. Loamy but porous soil. Moist. Space 6 inches apart in groups of at least 10 to make a show. Natively, this is an alpine meadow plant.

Use: Rock garden. Border. Cut flower.

Species:

J. humilis: 9 inches. Blue flowers to ½ inch across. From the Pyrenees.

J. montana major: Biennial. 12 inches. Pale blue flower heads, 1 inch across.

J. perennis: 6 to 12 inches. Tufted rosette habit. Globular flower heads made up of many tiny, light blue bells, 1 to 2 inches across. July to frost. Southern Europe.

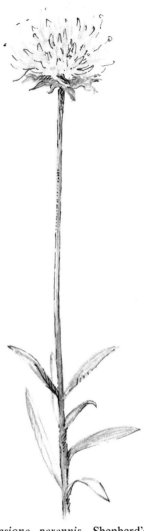

Jasione perennis, Shepherd's Scabious

Jeffersonia

Family: *Berberidaceae* (Barberry).

Common name: Twin Leaf.

Propagation: Seed sown in fall or very early spring. Germinates at cool temperatures; very slow, may take to 2 years.

Divide in early spring or fall after foliage dies down.

Culture: Partial shade. Neutral to slightly acid,

sandy peat or woodland soil. Easily domesticated.

Use: Woodland garden.

Species:

J. diphylla: 6 inches. Leaves are mostly basal, deeply divided into two leaflets. Solitary white flowers, 1 inch across, yellow stamens; blooms last but a day; May. Seed capsule maturing in August is shaped like a jug; the top opening is shaped like a lid. Native from Ontario to Iowa and eastward.

J. dubia: 4 inches. Heart-shaped leaves, glaucous underneath. Larger pale blue flowers. May/June. Japanese.

Kentranthus or Centranthus

Family: *Valerianaceae* (Valerian).

Common name: Pretty Betsy. Red Valerian. Jupiter's Beard.

Propagation: Sow at 50 to 60 degrees from spring into summer. Do not shade with paper, they need light to sprout. Germination within 15 days. Blooms the first year from seed if started in March.

Division in spring.

Culture: Sun. Average garden loam. Space 10 to 12 inches apart.

Use: Border. Wild garden.

Species:

K. ruber: 1½ to 2 feet. Flowers in dense, terminal clusters; small red flowers from June to frost. Var. "*albus*," a white form. Europe to southwestern Asia.

Kniphofia

Family: *Liliaceae* (Lily).

Common name: Tritoma. Red Hot Poker. Torch Lily.

Propagation: Seed sown in spring at 50 to 60 degrees. Germination in 17 to 20 days. Cold frame for the first winter and set out to permanent places the following spring. It blooms well by the third year when started from seed.

Division in early spring, usually necessary every third year, otherwise the clumps will gradually die.

Culture: Sun. Sandy, well-drained soil. Phosphate dressing in spring. Although often referred to as a tender sort, I have found it to be completely hardy, and it receives no special attention in my garden. Good drainage is probably the pertinent factor. The tall thick stems withstand our winds without staking. Space plants 18 inches apart, setting the crown at surface level.

Use: Border. Cut flower.

Species:

K. caulescens: 4 feet. Glaucous, grey-blue leaves. Flowers, red-salmon fading to yellowish-white. June on.

Kniphofia uvaria, Red Hot Poker

K. foliosa: 2 to 3 feet. Racemes of small yellow to reddish-yellow flowers. May/June.

K. galpinii: 2 feet. Tiny racemes of yellow-buff flowers, tinted salmon-orange. July on.

K. rufa: 2 feet. Very narrow leaves. Yellow flowers.

K. tubergenii: Cream-yellow flowers. The parent of the pastel and white varieties.

K. uvaria (syn. *K. pfitzeri*, *K. aloides*): 3 to 4 feet. Spikes of orange-yellow, red, or yellow. August. The source of most of the common garden varieties. (See illustration, p. 29.)

Lapeyrousia

(syn. *ANOMATHECA*) ......

Family: *Iridaceae* (Iris).

Propagation: Seed sown in spring at 65 to 70 degrees.

Cormels and bulbs increase quite rapidly.

Culture: Sun. Light soil. May not require digging and storing over winter if given a site with excellent drainage and some winter protection; otherwise treat as you would gladiolus.

Forcing for winter bloom: pot and store in cold frame or cold cellar. Pack damp sand or peat around the pots. (Hardy and half-hardy bulbs need a period of cold for root growth.) Bring into warmth when roots start to grow out of the drainage holes (about 6 weeks) and

before really cold weather begins. Give light and water.

Use. Border. Rock garden. Container. Winter forcing.

Species:

L. cruenta: 1 to 1½ feet. Long narrow leaves. Freesia-like, red flowers in one-sided spikes. Flowers may also be white, violet, or rose shades. July. A half-hardy species from South Africa.

Lavandula

Family: *Labiatae* (Mint).

Common name: Lavender.

Propagation: Seed sown at 65 degrees. Germination in 15 to 20 days.

Cuttings in June/July, tip or heel.

Culture: Sun. Light, sandy, limy soil; must be well drained. Dry. Prune after flowering. Space 12 inches apart.

Transplant in early spring before new growth starts.

Use: Rock garden. Border. Untrimmed dwarf hedge. Dried flower petals for sachets.

Species and varieties:

L. spica (syn. *L. officinalis*, *L. vera*) Common or True Lavender: A woody perennial or subshrub. 3 feet. Very fragrant spikes of lavender flowers, ½ inch across. July/August. Mediterranean.

Varieties: "Munstead," 12 inches, dwarf, compact, blue flowers; *"nana alba"* 6 inches, dwarf with silvery-white foliage; *"nana atropurpurea* Hidcote," 12 inches, grey-green leaves, deep purple-blue flowers, July to frost.

Leon-topodium

Family: *Compositae* (Daisy).

Common name: Edelweiss.

Propagation: Sow in fall or stratify and refrigerate prior to spring sowing. Germination in 11 days at 45 to 50 degrees. Best grown from seed, because division is not very successful.

Culture: Sun. Sandy, gritty, well-drained soil. Moist.

Use: Rock garden. Container.

Species:

L. alpinum: 4 to 12 inches. Tufted habit. White, wooly, basal foliage. Terminal flower heads, the flowers in star-like clusters (the true flower is inconspicuous, being enveloped in wooly bracts). June/July. Native of the European Alps and mountains of central Asia.

L. sibiricum: 12 inches. Mound habit. Flowers like silvery, wooly stars. A Russian species, this withstands more heat than does alpinum.

Leontopodium alpinum, Edelweiss

Lewisia

Family: *Portulaceae* (Portulaca).

Common name: Bitter Root.

Propagation: Seed collected or purchased and sown in fall; it must be fresh. Spring sowing requires a period of stratification at cold temperatures. Germination will occur at cool (45 to 50) temperatures. It often takes 2 years to sprout.

In collecting seed, tie a small plastic sack well down on the stem, over the seed head until it ripens, or it will break off and blow away before you are aware.

Spring division of the fleshy crown. Dust the cut surface with a fungicide.

Culture: Sun. Gritty, gravelly soil. Moist in spring, dry in summer. I have successfully transplanted them even when in full bloom, although as a general rule it is better done in spring or when dormant in late summer. Spectacular when set out in masses. A rock chip mulch will prevent rotting of the crown.

Use: Rock garden. Sunny wall crevices. Wild garden.

Species:

L. columbiana: 6 to 9 inches. Rosette of narrow evergreen leaves. Flowers in branched clusters, white to pale pink, often with darker stripes. Var. "*roseum*," deep rose.

L. cotyledon: Very free flowering. Variable color, ranging from waxy to white with pink veins or pink. May/June. Alpine. Shade and adequate moisture all summer.

L. howelli: 9 inches. Ovate, evergreen leaves, edges waved and often red tinted. Flowers in clusters, usually pink with purple veins, white margins, to 1 inch across. There are hybrids of this species. From the mountains of northern California and Oregon, 1,000 to 8,000 feet.

L. rediviva (Live Forever. Bitter Root): Narrow, fleshy leaves, 1 to 2 inches long, form rosettes which usually disappear by the time the plant blooms. Thick fleshy roots, but not very long. One to 3 flowers to a very short stem, white or pink, to 2 inches across, rather resemble a small water lily. Flowers open in the morning and close at night. May/July. Summer

dormancy. Common from gravelly dry valleys to 8,000 feet, Montana to Colorado.

L. tweedyi: A West Coast species from the mountains of central Washington. 4 to 6 inches. Fleshy, broad, evergreen leaves to 4 inches long. One to 3 flowers to a stem, pale salmon-pink, 2 inches across. May/June. This requires at least 18 inches of space.

Liatris

Family: *Compositae* (Daisy).

Common name: Gay Feather. Blazing Star.

Propagation: Sow in fall, or in spring at 45 to 50 degrees. Spring sowing should be preceeded by a period of prechilling in the refrigerator. Germination takes 15 days or more. Reproduces quite true from seed.

Division in spring, usually every fourth year.

Cuttings of basal leaf with heel in August (merely pull away).

Culture: Sun. Sandy, well-drained soil. Dry. Tall sorts may need staking. Mass for effective display, spacing 8 to 10 inches apart.

Use: Border. Cut flower. Excellent in the wild garden.

Species and varieties:

L. callilepsis: 2 feet. Fluffy appearing spikes of purple flowers. August to frost. Var. "Kobold," deep purple.

L. graminifolia (Grass leaved Blazing Star): 2 to 3 feet. Small corms. Grass-like leaves. Narrow spikes of purple flowers in August. Flowering stems are often branched. Found in dry, open woods of New Jersey.

L. ligulistylis: 12 inches. Rose-purple flowers in flattened clusters.

L. punctata (Dwarf Gay-feather): 1 to 2 feet. Dense spikes of rose-purple flowers. July/September. Leafy stem and linear leaves covered with translucent dots. From the prairies and foothills of Manitoba south to New Mexico.

L. pycnostachya (Kansas or Cattail Gay Feather): 2 to 5 feet. Long racemes of lavender to rose-purple flowers that open from the top of the spike downward. August/September. Found from Minnesota to Nebraska.

L. scariosa (Button Blazing Star): 2 feet. Flowers, rose-purple to bluish-purple (rarely white) in looser racemes——the flower heads are more separated on the stem. August to frost. Dry woods of Pennsylvania westward to North Dakota.

Varieties: "Snow White"; "White Spire"; "Silver Tips," lavender flowers with a silvery cast; "September Glory," purple, unusual in that all the flowers open at one time.

L. spicata (Spiked Gay Feather): 2 feet or more. Long, dense spikes of distinctive fluffy flower heads of rose-purple. July/September. Moist site. New York to

Michigan. Var. "*montana*," a dwarf with shorter spikes.

Lilium

Family: *Liliaceae* (Lily).

Common name: Lily.

Propagation: Sow seed in fall or very early spring. There is considerable variation according to species as to time and type of germination. *L. humboldii* requires 3 months of stratification prior to spring sowing.

The following species are sown in spring (sprouting will occur in 2 to 5 months, but no top growth will appear until the second year): *L. auratum, canadense, japonicum, kelloggii,* and *martagon.*

Sow the following in March or April (germination in 3 to 5 weeks, transplant to flats and carry over the first year in the cold frame): *L. aurelian* hybrids, *cernuum, concolor, dauricum, tsingtanense, davidii, formosanum, henryi, leichtinii, maxwell,* and *medeoloides.*

Sow *L. giganteum* in fall; germination and top growth will appear the second spring.

Another method by which you may be able to fool the recalcitrant types is by sowing seeds when ripe in containers of moist vermiculite at 70 degrees; within 6 to 8 weeks, tiny bulbs will often have formed. Store in cool (to 35 degrees) place until spring, plant in flat

115

until large enough to set
out in the nursery.

Bulbils: Some species produce
tiny bulbils in the leaf axils.
Remove in August and plant
about 1 inch deep.

Division: Lift clump in
spring or early fall (after
flowering), shake off the
dirt and separate the bulbs,
trying not to rip off the
roots. When stems are too
close together and flowers
are small and few, it is time
to divide, usually every
3 or 4 years.

Scales: Remove from the
parent bulb after the flowering period is over, dust with
a fungicide, and set 2 inches
deep in a sterile medium such
as vermiculite; carry over
winter in cold frame or
greenhouse.

Bulbs ordered for fall
planting.

Culture: Sun. Average garden
soil with peat and leaf mold
added. Good drainage
imperative. Summer mulch
is beneficial in keeping the
roots cool. Give them plenty
of water when coming into
bloom. Potted lilies may be
moved anytime; otherwise,
fall planting is preferable.
Set out the Madonnas earlier
(September), all others later
(October or November).
Plant bulbs 4 inches deep for
dwarfs, 6 inches deep for the
taller sorts, 8 to 12 inches
apart, depending on the
height. I like to put a handful
of sand under each bulb.
Stake the taller types. Remove
seed pods unles you wish to
save some.

Use: Border. Rock garden
(dwarfs). Woodland garden.

Naturalize (especially *L.
canadense* and *superbum*).
Container. Cut flower (cut
just as buds swell).

Species and varieties:

L. amabile: 3 feet. Red
flowers, spotted black.

L. auratum (Gold Banded
Lily): 4 feet. Very large
flowers, to 10 inches across,
fragrant, bowl-shaped with
flaring trumpet, white with
gold stripes and crimson or
maroon spots. August.
Requires a peat-enriched soil.
Stem rooting——plant 8 to
10 inches deep. Of Japanese
origin, this is the parent of
many garden hybrids. Var.
"*platyphyllum*," 6 feet, large
and vigorous type, flowers to
12 inches across, gold banded
and spotted brown or red;
"*rubrum*," red striped instead
of gold.

L. aurelian hybrids: 6 feet.
(Resembles most the parent
L. henryi). Variable flower
types, some having reflexed
petals and others trumpet
shaped, may be yellow,
orange, cream, or white with
yellow to orange centers.
August. Prefers partial shade.
Var. "Thunderbolt" has
melon-colored flowers.

L. Bellingham hybrids: 6 feet.
Orange-yellow to orange-red
flowers, spotted mahogany,
recurved petals. Pacific
coast origin. Var. "Buttercup" multiplies rapidly.

L. bolanderi (Thimble Lily):
2 to 3 feet. Bell-shaped
flowers, purplish-red, spotted
purple, often having green
throats. July. From Cali-
fornia. A stem rooter; set
bulbs 8 inches deep.

L. bulbiferum croceum
(Orange Lily): 3 to 4 feet.
Erect blossoms of tangerine-
orange, spotted purple. June.
European. Stem rooting; plant
6 inches deep.

L. canadense (Meadow or
Canada Lily): 3 to 4 feet.
Nodding, rather small, open
bell-shaped flowers, yellow to
orange-red, spotted purplish-
brown inside. June/July. Best
adapted to light, high shade.
Var. "*flavum*," pendant,
yellow flowers. Found in
moist meadows of north-
eastern America.

L. candidum (Madonna Lily):
2 to 4 feet. Fragrant, waxy,
white flowers, like short,
broad-mouthed trumpets.
June. From southern Europe
and southwestern Asia. Var.
"*Salonikae*," earlier and larger
flowers; "Cascade strain,"
very vigorous type. Divide or
set out bulbs in August and
September, shallow, just
beneath the soil surface, as
this roots at the base of the
bulb (2 to 3 inches deep).

L. cernuum: 1½ feet. Fragrant, nodding flowers of pale
pink, reddish-purple spots.
June/July. Asiatic origin.

L. columbianum (Columbia
Lily): 2 feet. Pendant flowers
with reflexed petals and
sepals, bright golden-yellow
to red-orange in color with
purple spots. A Rocky Mountain species, usually found on
the west slope. Requires soil
more on the acid side and
light shade. A base rooter;
set bulbs 6 or 7 inches deep.

L. cordatum: 5½ feet. Rare
type. Large trumpets opening
greenish-white and maturing
pure white, conspicuous
golden-yellow anthers.

L. davidii: 3½ feet. Variable
from seed. A Chinese species
usually found in orange-red
shades with black spots.
Stem-rooting type; plant 6
inches deep.

L. formosanum: 3 feet. Long,
narrow, white trumpets,
petals tinged rose-purple on
the outside. The latest to
flower(if not cut down by
frost first) September/
October. Var. "Little Snow
White," 8- to 10-inch dwarf
with huge white flowers
(blooms in 18 months from
seed); "Priceii," 2½ feet,
white with deep red or purple
markings on the outside.

L. giganteum: 8 to 12 feet.
Largest of all lilies. Fragrant,
long tubular, white trumpets,
6 inches long, striped red
inside and tinged green on
outside. Roots from the base
of the bulb; plant shallow,
about 5 or 6 inches deep.
High shade, protection
from wind and stake.
Himalayan.

L. Golden Harvest hybrida:
5½ feet. Large flowers with
slightly recurved petals,
varies from white to yellow
and orange hues, all with deep
green throats. August.

L. hansonii (Japanese Turks-
cap): 3½ to 4 feet. Pendant,
orange-yellow flowers,
spotted brown of Turk's cap
type. June/July. From Japan
and Korea. Roots along the
stem; set 6 inches deep,
in light shade.

L. henryi: 4 to 6 feet. Chinese
species with recurved petals,
golden-orange to soft yellow-
orange shades, brown spots.
August. Willowy stemmed;
needs staking, high shade.
Stem rooting; plant 9 or 10
inches deep.

L. humboldtii magnificum (Orange Humboldts Lily): 4 feet. Red-orange flowers with maroon spots. A Californian, it prefers peaty soil and open woods. Base rooting; set 6 inches deep.

L. japonicum: 2 to 3 feet. Not completely hardy but worth a try. A rare Japanese species with rose-pink, broad, funnel-shaped trumpets. Peaty soil. Stem rooting; plant bulbs 6 to 8 inches deep.

L. kelloggii: 3 feet. From California. Fragrant flowers of pink to pink-mauve, maroon spots, and yellow bands. Base rooting; set bulbs 6 inches deep. Light shade, sandy, peaty soil.

L. leucanthum centifolium (syn. *L. centifolium*) Chinese White Lily: 5 to 8 feet. Long, funnel-shaped, white flowers, pale yellow throats, rose-purple keel; colors will often vary into pink or yellow shades. From China, not completely hardy. Stem rooting; plant 9 inches deep or more.

L. longifolium praecox "White Queen": 2 to 3 feet. Easy to raise from seed, flowers in 12 months. Early flowering, nodding, extra long, white flowers.

L. mackliniae: 1½ feet. Nodding, bell-shaped flowers, white inside, rose-purple on the outside.

L. martagon (Turban or Turk's Cap Lily): 4 feet. Drooping flowers in tiers along the stem, recurved petals, shades ranging from soft waxy pink to purplish-rose, spotted black. Var. "*album*," June flowers of waxy white; "*cattaniae*," glossy, fleshy-petaled, wine-colored flowers; "*dalmaticum*," 6 feet, deep purplish-black. Needs full sun. Very permanent type. Stem rooting; set bulbs 4 to 5 inches deep.

L. michiganense (Michigan Lily): 2 feet. Similar to *L. canadense*, red-orange flowers, reflexed petals, spotted. June/July. Spreads by horizontal rhizome; is better used for naturalizing in the wild garden. Found from Manitoba to Arkansas and eastward.

L. Mid-Century hybrids: 2 to 4 feet. Erect and out-facing cups of yellow, red, to maroon shades. June/July. Vigorous, easily cultivated. Do not require staking.

L. nepalense: 2½ feet. Fragrant, funnel-shaped flowers of greenish-yellow, deep reddish-purple throat. Var. "*robusta*," large, pendant, green flowers with purple centers. Rare.

L. nobilissimum: 1½ to 2 feet. Rare Asiatic species. Fragrant, open-funnel-shaped, white flowers with distinctive dark brown anthers. July.

L. Olympic hybrids: Resemble *L. regale* but are creamy-white with green or bronze on reverse of petals. July.

L. pardalinum (Panther or Leopard Lily): 5 feet. Nodding, bright orange-red flowers, lighter orange centers, and dark red spots, reflexed petals. From California and Oregon, needs a moist, peaty soil. Rhizomatous type, dictates shallow planting.

L. pyrenaicum (Yellow Turk's Cap Lily): 3 feet. Easily grown species from the Pyrenees. Flowers are yellow to greenish-yellow with purplish-black spots. Roots from the base of the bulb; plant 4 or 5 inches deep.

L. regale (Regale Lily): 3½ to 5 feet. Long trumpets in large terminal clusters that are fragrant, ivory-white, pink tinged on the outside, yellow throats. July. Hardy and easily raised species from China (often blooms the second year from seed). Var. "G. C. Creelman," very large flowers. Stem rooting; plant 9 to 10 inches deep.

L. rubellum: 2 feet. Rose flowers shading to pale pink, golden anthers. Earliest to bloom, May/June. Rare species from Japan. Rock-garden type. Gritty soil and light shade. Stem rooting; plant 4 to 6 inches deep.

L. rubescens (Lilac, Redwood, or Chaparral Lily): Medium-sized, flaring trumpets, white with purple markings. From California and Oregon, prefers soil on the acid side. Base rooter; set bulbs 5 or 6 inches deep.

L. sargentiae: 3½ feet. Similar to *L. regale* but outside of flowers tinged brown, brown anthers.

L. speciosum magnificum (Japanese Lily): 2½ feet. Slightly drooping flowers, recurved petals, rose background with red streaks and purple spots. August/September. Var. "*rubrum* Red Champion and White Champion." Stem rooting; set bulbs 9 to 10 inches deep.

L. Sulphur hybrids: 5 feet. Very large trumpets varying in shades from pale yellow to deep sulphur yellow.

L. superbum (American Turk's Cap Lily): 4 to 6 feet. Large pendant flowers, reflexed petals, orange to crimson, spotted brown, brown stamens. A stem rooter (the bulb also forms rhizomes); set 8 or 9 inches deep. Easily established if conditions are met. This is a bog plant needing peaty, moderately acid soil. Originally found in wet meadows from New York to Minnesota.

L. szovitsianum (syn. *L. monadelphum*): 5 feet. Flowers are canary yellow, often having purple spots. Caucasus. Partial shade preferred. Roots from base of bulb; set 6 to 7 inches deep.

L. tenuifolium (syn. *L. pumilum*) Coral or Siberian Lily: 1¼ to 2 feet. Turk's Cap type flower, nodding, reflexed petals, waxy red. June. Grass-like leaves. Easy from seed. A good dwarf for the rock garden. Stem rooting; plant 4 inches deep. Var. "Golden Gleam," orange-yellow.

L. tigrinum (Tiger Lily): 3 to 5 inches. Orange-red, reflexed flowers, brown or black spots. August. Stem rooting; set bulbs 7 to 8 inches deep. Better used for naturalizing. Originally from Asia.

L. tsingtauense: 2 to 3 feet. Star-shaped, waxy, bright orange flowers, petals rather fleshy, 4 to 5 inches across. June/July. Foliage in whorls around the stem. Eastern China.

117

L. umbellatum syn. L. hollandicum, L. montanum)
Western Orange Cup Lily.
Western or Wood Lily: 1 to
2 feet. Red-orange, cup-shaped flowers, spotted purple, from 1 to 3 per stem.
June/July. Stem rooting; set
5 or 6 inches deep. Found in
moist, often wooded sites
from the mid-western plains
throughout the Rocky
Mountains.

Limonium

(syn. STATICE)........ ....

Family: Plumbaginaceae
(Plumbago).

Common name: Sea Lavender. Hardy Statice.

Propagation: Seed sown in
fall, or soak seed for 2 hours
in tepid water and sow in
spring at 50 to 60 degrees.
It seldom flowers before
the third year.

Division in spring.

Culture: Sun. Light, sandy,
well-drained soil. A long tap
root discourages transplanting of mature plants. Set out
12 to 18 inches apart. Does
not like to be disturbed; it
takes 3 to 4 years to establish
itself.

Use: Border. Rock garden
(dwarfs). Cut flower. Winter
bouquet.

Species and varieties:

L. bellidifolium (syn. L.
caspia): 9 to 12 inches. Blue
to pale lilac flowers.
July/August.

L. bonduellii: Biennial. 1 to 2
feet. Deeply lobed, basal
leaves. Tiny yellow flowers in
airy clusters. August/October.

L. dumosum: 20 to 24 inches.
Huge heads of small silvery,
greyish-lavender flowers.
August/September. Give
these at least 2 to 3 feet
of space.

L. incanum nanum: 6 inch
dwarf. "album," white flowered; "roseum," rose flowers.

L. latifolium or latifolia:
2 to 2½ feet. Dark green,
leathery leaves to 10 inches
long. Great panicles, 1½ to
2 feet across, made up of
myriads of tiny lavender-blue to purple flowers. July/
August. The most spectacular
as well as the hardiest. Space
2 to 3 feet apart; a mature
plant will spread to as much
as 3 feet wide. Var. "Collier's
Pink"; "Violetta."

L. minutum: 6-inch dwarf
with violet to reddish-purple
flowers. Rock plant.

L. tataricum (syn. L. goniolimon): 1 to 1½ feet. White
flowers. This is the best
species for dyeing the flowers.
Var. "nanum," 9-inch dwarf
with pink flowers in August.
An improvement over
the type.

Linum

Family: Linaceae (Flax).

Common name: Flax.

Propagation: Seed sown at 65
degrees, germinates in 11 days
or so. Often blooms the first
year if sown in March.

Self-sows, but not as much
as you would expect.

Division in spring.

Stem cuttings in August of
L. salsoloides.

Culture: Sun. Light soil.
Tolerates aridity. Transplant
when young, as these do not
move well. Space taller sorts
8 to 10 inches apart, dwarfs
4 to 6 inches apart.

Use: Border. Rock garden.
Wild garden.

Species and varieties:

L. alpinum (Alpine Flax):
6 to 10 inches. Small greyish
leaves. Pale china-blue
flowers. May/June. Rock
garden dwarf.

L. capitatum: 1½ feet.
Golden-yellow flowers in
June.

L. flavum (Yellow Flax):
12 inches. Transparent
yellow flowers, ¾ inch
across, on stiff leafy stems.
July/August. Var. "compactum" 6-inch dwarf with large
yellow flowers. (See
illustration p. 29.)

L. kingii: to 12 inches.
Yellow flowers with distinctive styles. Found throughout
the Rocky Mountain area.

L. lewisii (Blue Flax. Lewis
or Prairie Flax): 8 to 24
inches. Sky-blue flowers, ½
to 1 inch across, on very thin
arching stems. June/August.
From valley to 8,000 feet,
Alaska to Mexico. One of the
most desirable and easily
grown wild flowers in the
highlands, I have had several
clumps in the garden
for years.

Linum flavum, Yellow Flax

L. monogynum: 1½ feet.
White flowers to 1 inch
across. Native of New Zealand and not completely
hardy.

Linum narbonense, Flax
"Heavenly Blue"

118

L. narbonense: 2 feet. Sky-blue flowers with white eye and white stamens. Var. "Heavenly Blue," larger in form and flower than *L. perenne*, luminous ultra-marine flowers from June on. (See illustration, p. 28.)

L. perenne (Blue Perennial Flax): 1½ to 2 feet. The bright blue flowers open but one day, shatter, and are gone by afternoon. Constant display from June/August. European. I have tried the white variation "*album*" but found it to be not nearly so attractive as the blue.

L. salsoloides (Eyed Flax): 6 inches. Trailing or matting habit. Needle-like leaves. Large pearly-white flowers with purple-blue centers. July. Rock plant.

Liriope

Family: *Liliaceae* (Lily).

Common name: Creeping Lily-turf.

Propagation: Sow seeds in fall. For spring sowing, soak seeds overnight in tepid water. Germination within 4 weeks at 50 to 60 degrees.

Division in spring.

Culture: Sun or part shade. Average, well-drained garden loam. Space plants 4 to 6 inches apart in colonies.

Use: Rock garden. Edging. Ground cover. Erosion control of banks.

Species:

L. graminifolia (syn. *L. spicata*): 9 inches. Terminal racemes of tiny, deep violet-blue or pink bells rising from semi-evergreen clumps of grassy leaves. July/August. Black berries in fall. Spreads by underground runners. Originally from Asia.

L. muscari (Blue Lily-turf): 1½ feet. Semi-evergreen, grassy leaves. Racemes (like grape hyacinth) of deep lilac-blue flowers. August/September. Japanese.

Litho-spermum

(syn. *MOLTKIA*) ....

Family: *Boraginaceae* (Borage).

Common name: Gromwell.

Propagation: Seed sown in spring at 50 to 60 degrees. Germination within 7 weeks ——very slow.

Culture: Sun or high filtered shade. Rich, humusy (add peat), well-drained soil. Mulch with stone chips, roots must be kept cool.

Use: Sheltered spot in rock garden or border edge.

Species:

L. graminifolium (syn. *L. suffruticosa*): 9 inches. Narrow leaves, semi-evergreen if snow covered. Soft pale blue flowers. July/August. European.

L. intermedium: 10 to 12 inches. Shrubby. Spreading heads of bright blue flowers.

L. purpureo-caeruleum: 1 to 2 feet. Trailing stems. Flowers opening reddish and then turning blue.

Lunaria

Family: *Cruciferae* (Mustard).

Common name: Honesty. Satin Flower. Moonwort. Money Plant. St. Peter's Penny.

Propagation: Seed sown from spring into summer, 50 to 65 degrees, usually sprouting in 10 days.

Self-sows.

Culture: Sun or light shade. Average garden loam.

Use: Border. Cut flower. Winter bouquet; cut when the green fades out of the seed pods, remove the outer husk.

Species and varieties:

L. annua (syn. *L. biennis*): Biennial. 2½ feet. Erect, branching plant with single, fragrant violet flowers. May. Heart-shaped leaves. Most often grown for its ornamental silvery, papery seed pods, 2 inches long and as wide.

Varieties: "*alba*," white flowers; "Munstead Purple," 3 feet, lilac to purple flowers; "*variegata*," 3 feet, crimson flowers, and variegated foliage.

L. rediviva: 2 feet. Leaves more sharply toothed. Flowers white with violet markings. Seed pods are

longer and taper sharply at the ends. This species is more perennial in habit than the above.

Lupinus

Family: *Leguminosae* (pea).

Common name: Lupine.

Propagation: Seed collected when mature, usually from early August into late fall. Sow in spring, nicking the seeds and soaking in water overnight beforehand. I also advise using an inoculant for nitrogen-fixing bacteria (wet the seed and roll in the inoculant before planting). I have found this results in a more robust seedling. Sow at 45 to 50 degrees in March, germination in 7 to 21 days. To avoid difficulty later on, transplant the seedling to peat pots or sow directly in the pot, and there will be no setback when transferring to the garden. The hybrids are variable, and do not always reproduce true to color from seed.

Division in spring, but not easy (in fact almost impossible).

Cuttings just as new growth starts; each cutting must have a portion of the yellow crown. Shade.

Culture: Sun. Light, well-drained, slightly acid to neutral soil. Add peat and superphosphate when planting. Moist. The Rocky Mountain species enjoy a rock chip mulch and rocky sites in general. Space 10 inches apart with the exception of the shrubby types which need more room. If you must transplant, do it in early spring just as new growth starts. Many of this genus are poisonous to livestock at some time during the growth cycle. None of them are weedy.

Use: Border. Rock garden. Wild garden.

Species and varieties:
L. arboreus (Tree Lupine): 4 feet. Sprawling, branching, woody stems. Erect sulphur-yellow racemes, 6 to 12 inches long. From California and not completely hardy.

Var. "*paynei*," variable in color, blue, purple, pink, or white; "Golden Spire," 5 feet, long golden-yellow spikes; "Mauve Queen," rosy-mauve; "Snow Queen"; "Yellow Boy."

L. argenteus: 2 to 3 feet. Silver leaves. Rose, white, or violet flowers. Western states.

L. caespitosus: Rocky Mountain species. The basal leaves are as long as the stems.

L. caudatus (Silver or Tailcup Lupine): 1 to 2 feet. Pubescent foliage, leaves hairy on both sides. Downy racemes of blue, violet, or white flowers, to ½ inch long. Indigenous to the Rockies.

L. cytisoides (syn. *L. latifolius*) Canyon Lupine. Blue Bush Lupine: 4 feet. Blue to pinkish-lavender shades. California.

L. laxiflorus (Looseflower Lupine): Rocky Mountain species which differs in that the upper leaf surfaces are not hairy and the flowers are farther apart, more loosely arranged on the stem. Flowers may be blue, lilac, yellow, or white.

L. parviflorus (Lodgepole Lupine): 1 to 2 feet. Terminal racemes of tiny light blue to whitish flowers, less than ¼ inch long. Bright green, palmately compound leaves, 5 to 11 leaflets. Rocky Mountains.

L. perennis (Blue, Sun Dial or Wild Lupine. Quaker Bonnets): 1 to 2 feet. Downy leaves. Flowers usually blue, but there are also pink or white forms. June/July. From eastern states, this prefers a sandy, slightly acid soil.

L. polyphyllus "Dwarf Minarette": 1½ feet. Dwarf form of the Russell hybrids, they are more tolerant of limy soils, and I have found these to be more adaptive to highland conditions. Will bloom in August if started in March. Mixed colors of blue, rose, yellow, or red, often bicolored. May/June.

L. polyphyllus "Russell Hybrids": 1½ to 3 feet. Often does not bloom until the third year from seed. "Day Dream," salmon-pink with touch of yellow; "Monkgate," 1½ feet, deep blue and white, June/July; "Lady Gay," 3 feet, canary yellow; "Venus," salmon-pink shading to red; "Gardsman," orange-red.

L. sericeus (Bluebonnet): 1½ feet. Small flowers of light blue to white in dense terminal racemes.

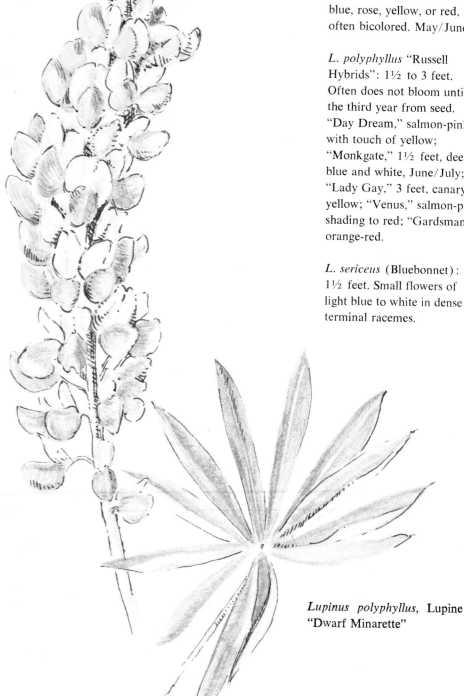

Lupinus polyphyllus, Lupine "Dwarf Minarette"

Lychnis

Family: *Caryophyllacae* (Pink).

Common name: Maltese Cross.

Propagation: Seed sown from spring into summer at 60 to 65 degrees. Germination in 7 days.

Division in spring.

Culture: Sun. (*L.* x *haageana* prefers some shade) Sandy, well-drained soil. Dry. Divide every third year or as necessary. Place dwarf forms 6 inches apart, taller forms 10 to 12 inches apart, planting in masses for effect.

Use: Border. Rock garden.

L. alpina (syn. *VISCARIA alpina*) Arctic or Red Campion: 4 to 9 inches. Dwarf tufted habit. Narrow leaves. Dense terminal racemes of rose or red-purple flowers, ½ inch across. May/July. Also red or white forms.

L. chalcedonia (Maltese Cross. Jerusalem Cross. Scarlet Lightning): 1½ to 3 feet. Terminal clusters of bright red flowers, 1 inch across, with clefted petals. June/July. Native to Russia.

Varieties: "*salmonea*," unusual pastel salmon shade, July/August; "*alba*," white; "*plena*," double form.

L. coronaria (Mullein Pink. Rose Campion. Dusty Miller): 2 feet. Wooly, silvery foliage. Solitary, rather maroon colored flowers, 1 inch or more across. June on. From

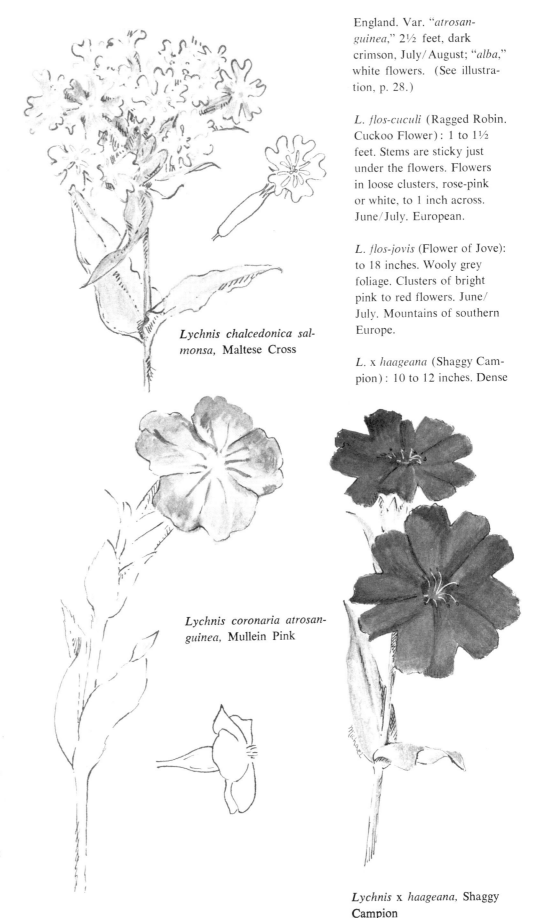

Lychnis chalcedonica salmonsa, Maltese Cross

Lychnis coronaria atrosanguinea, Mullein Pink

Lychnis x *haageana,* Shaggy Campion

England. Var. "*atrosanguinea*," 2½ feet, dark crimson, July/August; "*alba*," white flowers. (See illustration, p. 28.)

L. flos-cuculi (Ragged Robin. Cuckoo Flower): 1 to 1½ feet. Stems are sticky just under the flowers. Flowers in loose clusters, rose-pink or white, to 1 inch across. June/July. European.

L. flos-jovis (Flower of Jove): to 18 inches. Wooly grey foliage. Clusters of bright pink to red flowers. June/July. Mountains of southern Europe.

L. x *haageana* (Shaggy Campion): 10 to 12 inches. Dense

heads to 2 inches across in salmon, orange-red, and scarlet hues. June/July. A hybrid (*L. fulgens* x *L. coronata sieboldii*) but reproduces true to type from seed. Often blooms the first year. Prefers partial shade.

L. pyrenaica: Small rock-garden species with pink and white flowers.

L. viscaria (see VISCARIA).

Lysichitum

Family: *Araceae* (Arum).

Common name: Yellow Skunk Cabbage.

Propagation: Seed sown in August or spring at 45 degrees ·(see directions for *Caltha*).

Small plants dug in spring.

Culture: Sun or part shade. Boggy, marshy site. Space at least 3 feet apart, clumps are large.

Use: Bog garden. Waterside. A rare specimen that is well worth the effort if you can match its natural habitat.

Species:

L. americanum: Very large leaves to 5 feet long by 15 inches across in basal clusters. Blooms before the leaves appear. Calla-like flowers consist of a spadix and spathe, bright yellow, on 8 - to 12-inch high stems. This does not have the unpleasant odor of the true skunk cabbage (*Symplocarpus foetidus*) which is an eastern species.

Natively found in wet woodlands and marches of the Rockies.

Lysimachia

Family: *Primulaceae* (Primrose).

Common name: Loose Strife.

Propagation: Seed sown in spring at 45 to 50 degrees.

Division in spring.

Rooting stems (*L. nummularia*). Cover trailing stem at intervals with soil; new plants will arise and may be detached and transplanted elsewhere.

Culture: Partial shade. Humusy loam. Moist. Set *L. nummularia* 12 to 18 inches apart when using as a shady ground cover. It is also excellent in containers and hanging baskets.

Use: Border. Water or wild garden. Woodland. Ground cover. Cut flower.

Species and varieties:

L. clethroides: 3 feet. Terminal spikes of white flowers, the spike being bent like a goose's neck. July/August. From China and Japan.

L. nummularia (Creeping Jenny or Charley. Moneywort): Evergreen. Creeping, matting habit. Prostrate stems to 2 feet long, root at the joints. Round leaves. Numerous, fragrant, small, solitary yellow flowers, 1 inch across. June/August. Var. "*aurea*," golden-yellow leaves which

are of good color if grown in the sun. European.

This could be a pest in areas of plentiful rainfall. Since we cannot lay claim to that requirement, the plant is useful and controllable.

L. punctata (Yellow Loose Strife): 1½ to 3 feet. Bright yellow flowers in axillary whorls. June/July. From eastern Europe. Tolerates sun.

L. vulgaris (Golden Loose Strife. Willow-wort): 2½ feet. Erect habit. Willow-like leaves. Phlox-like, terminal panicles of orange-dotted, yellow flowers. June/July. Requires a shady, moist site.

Lythrum

Family: *Lythraceae* (Loosestrife).

Common name: Purple Loosestrife. Willow Herb.

Propagation: Seeds sown in fall or early spring at 45 degrees. Germination in 15 days.

Softwood cuttings in summer (when growth firms).

Culture: Sun or part shade. Average, well-drained soil. Moist. Difficult to transplant except as seedlings. Plant in groups of three or more, 1½ to 2 feet apart.

Use: Border. Cut flower. Wild garden. Water garden.

Species and varieties:

L. salicaria: 3 feet. Woody, upright plant with lanceolate leaves and tiny magenta to purplish-red flowers, ¾ inch

across. August. This has become a weed in the East; in our arid country, it is advisable to use as a stream or pond side ornamental. For the garden border, it is preferable by far to use the following varieties: "*roseum superbum*" 3 feet, wand-like dense, terminal spikes of carmine-rose; "Morden's Pink," 3 to 4 feet, pink sterile flowers, very tolerant; "Morden's Rose"; "Morden's Gleam," deep red.

Maiamthemum

Family: *Liliaceae* (Lily).

Common name: False or Wild Lily-of-the-Valley. Canadian Mayflower.

Propagation: Berries sown in fall.

Culture: Shade. Average garden loam with peat added. Moist but not wet. Easily transplanted if a large soil ball is taken.

Use: Ground cover. Woodland garden.

Species:

M. bifolium (syn. *M. canadense*): 6 to 7 inches. Creeping, matting habit. Sparsely leaved, 2 to 3 mostly basal, oval leaves. Flowers resemble lily-of-the-valley. Erect, terminal racemes of small white bells in May. Clusters of pale red berries in fall. Related to Smilacina. Found in the northern hemisphere. *M. canadense* is sometimes considered to be a separate species and indigenous to northeastern America alone.

Macleaya

(see BOCCONIA) ....

Malva

Family: *Malvaceae* (Mallow).

Common name: Musk Mallow. Musk Rose.

Propagation: Seed sown at 65 degrees with germination in 4 days.

Division in spring.

Root cuttings.

Culture: Sun. Average, well-drained soil. Dry. Divide every third year. Space plants 18 inches apart.

Use: Border. Wild garden. Open woodland.

Species:

M. alcea fastigiata: 2 to 3 feet high and as wide. Spreading, bushy habit. Bright rose, mallow-like flowers in terminal clusters. July/August. European.

M. moschata (Musk Mallow): 2 to 3 feet. Clusters of flowers in upper leaf axils, light pink to red, to 2 inches across. There is at times a white variant. June/August. European. Will tolerate quite moist locations.

M. setosa hybrida: 6 feet. Hollyhock-like flowers in shades ranging from red to white.

Malva alcea fastigiata,
Musk Mallow

Matricaria *parthenium*

(see CHRYSANTHEMUM

Meconopsis

Family: *Papaveraceae* (Poppy).

Propagation: Seed must be fresh. Sow in fall or spring. Spring sowing must follow a period of freezing, either in cold frame or freezer. Remove to warmth, about 50 to 60 degrees. Germination within 4 weeks. Pot up seedlings and frame for the first year,

setting out in the garden the second spring.

Culture: Partial shade. Enriched, humusy soil (add peat and leaf mold) but well drained. Moist. Shelter from wind which would shatter the flowers. Cool. Once established, they dislike being disturbed. Plant in colonies, 8 to 10 inches apart.

Use: Naturally moist shaded area. Ideal beside pool or stream.
Species and varieties:

M. betonicifolia (syn. *M. baileyi*) Himalayan Blue Poppy: 2½ feet. Sky-blue flowers, to 3 inches across, with bright gold anthers. June/August. Var. *"alba,"* white. Native to Tibet.

M. cambrica (Welsh Poppy): 1 to 1½ feet. Finely cut leaves, silvery underneath. Solitary, pale yellow to orange flowers, to 3 inches across. European. Var. *"aurantiaca,"* deep buff or orange; also a double form. Short-lived; encourage self-sowing habit.

M. grandis: 3 feet. Rich violet flowers to 4 or 5 inches across.

M. integrifolia (Yellow Chinese Poppy): Biennial. 1½ to 3 feet. Long narrow leaves. Clusters of primrose flowers, 4 to 6 inches across.

M. napaulensis (syn. *M. wallichii*) Satin Poppy: 4 feet. Color variable, red to purple-blue or purple-red and yellow. Finely cut, silvery foliage.

M. quintuplinervia (Hairbell Poppy): 12 inches. Bluish-purple flowers.

M. regia: 3 feet. Attractive silver leaves in flat rosettes. Large yellow flowers.

M. simplicifolia: 2½ feet. Solitary, nodding, sky-blue to purple flowers. Nepal.

M. superba: 3 feet. Solitary, white flowers, 2½ inches across, in leaf axils, distinctive gold anthers.

Megasea

(see BERGENIA) ....

Mertensia

Family: *Boraginaceae* (Borage).

Common name: Bluebells. Lungworts. Languid Ladies.

Propagation: Seed sown in fall or spring at 45 degrees.

Division during fall or late summer dormant period.

Root cuttings, 2 inches long, in fall; give winter protection and set in permanent position in early spring.

Culture: Part shade. Neutral, enriched, humusy soil. Moist during the growing season, but dry later in summer. Transplant in very early spring or when dormant, spacing plants 6 to 8 inches apart.

Use: Rock garden. Shaded border. Woodland garden.

Species:

M. ciliata (Mountain Bluebell): 1 to 5 feet. Hollow-stemmed. Gray-green, alternate, lance-shaped, smooth surfaced but hairy edged leaves. Flowers in loose terminal clusters. Pink buds open to nodding, tubular, light blue flowers, ¾ inch long. June/August, from 5,000 to 12,000 feet. Look for it in open woodland, damp meadow, or streamside in the Rockies from Montana to New Mexico. If given a moist location, it will not die down in late summer.

M. longiflora (Western Lungwort): 3 to 12 inches. Short roots. Pale green leaves. Sky-blue bells, ½ to 1 inch long. April/May. Dormant by June. Montana to California.

M. pulchella (Small Bluebells): 3 to 8 inches. Tuberous rooted. Egg-shaped, fleshy leaves, ¾ to 4 inches long with rough margins. Flowers in dense terminal clusters of 10 to 20, red in bud, opening a deep-sky blue, tubular, ¾ inch long. April/July. Sunny or shady sites in the Rocky Mountain region from 2,000 to 8,000 feet.

M. sibirica: 12 inches. Purple to light blue flowers rarely white) in long racemes. East Asia.

M. virginica (Virginia Cowslip or Bluebells): 1 to 2 feet. Glaucous, mostly basal leaves. Flowers in nodding clusters, pink and blue buds open as light blue bells, fading pink again as they mature, 1 inch long. May. Dormant by late summer. New York to Minnesota and southward.

Mimulus

Family: *Scrophulariaceae* (Figwort).

Common name: Monkey Flower.

Propagation: Plants easily domesticated when shifted from the wilds to the garden, or seed collected in August. Spring sowing at 65 degrees; germination in 5 days. Blooms the first year, but may not be perennial if conditions are not met. In fact, I have found this to be very poorly equipped to withstand any amount of dryness.

Culture: Sun or part shade. Neutral, humusy, moist soil. Space 4 to 6 inches apart in masses.

Use: Ideal for the naturally wet spot by pond or stream. Potted for house or greenhouse.

Species and varieties:

M. aurantiacus (Bush Mimulus): 4 feet. Shrubby. Apricot or yellow flowers. Better placed in the wild garden.

M. cardinalis: 1 to 2 feet. Sticky, hairy leaves. Flowers, red or red and yellow combined. June/August. Likely to be short lived. Indigenous to the Rockies.

M. cupreus: to 12 inches. Color variable. The leaf reminds me of lettuce in form and texture. June/August.

Varieties: "Red Emperor," 6 inches, color varies from scarlet to rather faded rose shades; "Monarch Strain,"

12 inches, very large flowers, all spotted or blotched; "Whitecroft Scarlet," 4 inches, orange-scarlet.

M. guttatus (syn. *M. langsdorfi*) Yellow Monkeyflower. Wild Lettuce: to 1½ feet. Deep yellow flowers with red spotted throat. Rocky Mountain native. Often confused with *M. luteus*.

M. lewisii (Red or Lewis Monkeyflower): 1 to 2½ feet. Rose-red flowers with yellow throats (rare white form). Found in the Rockies, naturally wet sites, 5,00 to 10,000 feet. Partial shade. Tolerates drier conditions.

M. luteus (Golden Monkeyflower. Monkey Musk): 1½ feet. Prostrate habit. Yellow flowers, spotted red or purple. Prefers shade. Var. "*guttatus*," 9 inches, yellow flowers, spotted purple or brown.

M. moschatus (Common Musk): 4 to 9 inches. Spreading dwarf. White hairy leaves. Small pale yellow flowers with brown dots. Native to the Columbia River, Washington.

M. ringens: 2 feet. Single lavender or white flowers in upper leaf axils. Eastern states.

M. variegatus: 12 inches. Large blotched flowers. Variety "Bonfire," 9 inches, orange-red to red.

Mitchella

Family: *Rubiaceae* (Madder).

Common name: Partridge Berry. Squaw or Twin Berry.

Propagation: Berries sown in peat in fall. Germination is slow and erratic.

Division in spring.

Softwood cuttings in August, root in moist sand and peat mix.

Stem rootings; prostrate stems will root wherever they touch the ground. Help nature along by covering stem at intervals with soil. When roots have formed, detach stem from parent plant.

Culture: Shade. Soil on the acid side (this will not do well in extremely alkaline areas). There is fair success in neutral soils that have large amounts of leaf mold, decaying pine needles, and peat added. Transplanting may be accomplished by taking a large square of sod with the plants. Set plants 6 to 18 inches apart in colonies.

Use: Shady ground cover, fine under evergreens. Woodland garden. Rock garden. Container (glass bowl terrarium).

Species:

M. repens: Evergreen. Trailing, matting habit; roots along the stem. Paired leaves, dark green, shiny, roundish, to ¾ inch long. Fragrant, trumpet-like twin flowers (united at their bases), waxy white, ½ inch long. June/July. Red berries remain all winter (bird food). Found in dry coniferous woods from Minnesota to Texas and eastward.

Mitella

Family: *Saxifragaceae* (Saxifrage).

Common name: Bishop's Cap. Mitrewort.

Propagation: Seed sown as soon as it is ripe; germinates quickly. Purchased seed is sown in fall, or stratify and sow in early spring; often does not germinate until the following spring.

Self-sows.

Division in spring.

Softwood cuttings in summer.

Culture: Shade. Well-drained, neutral soil——preferably a wood soil, but if not, add generous quantities of leaf mold and peat. Moist. Set out in colonies.

Use: Woodland garden.

Species:

M. breweri: 6 inches. A dainty plant with basal heart-shaped leaves and white to greenish flowers. Western states.

M. diphylla: 3 to 8 inches. Many heart-shaped leaves. The whole plant is hairy. Slender, terminal, loose racemes of small white flowers. April/June. Found from Minnesota to Missouri and eastward.

Moltkia

(see LITHOSPERMUM) ....

Monarda

Family: *Labiatae* (Mint).

Common name: Beebalm. Bergamot. Oswego Tea.

Propagation: Seed collected in fall (October on). Sow at 65 degrees. Germination in 9 days.

Division every third year in spring.

Culture: Sun or light shade. Average soil. Moist. Space plants 10 to 15 inches apart in groups.

Use: Border. Cut flower. Wild garden. Attractive to bees, hummingbirds, and seed-eating birds.

Species and varieties:

M. didyma (Oswego tea or Beebalm): 2 to 3 feet. Shaggy red flowers. July/August. Prefers shade and moist conditions. Native to the eastern states and Canada.

Many varieties: "*alba*," white; "Cambridge Scarlet"; "Adam," scarlet flowers and longer season than Cambridge; "Croftway Pink," rose-pink; "Granite Pink; "Mahogany," wine-colored;

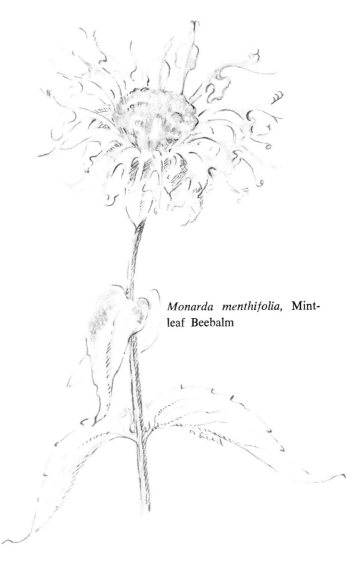

Monarda menthifolia, Mint-leaf Beebalm

"Sunset," purple; "Salmon Queen."

M. fistula (Wild Bergamot): 2 feet. Shaggy flowers, 1½ inches across, may be purple, lavender, pink, or white. July/August. Tolerant of poor, dry conditions. Found in eastern states from Maine to Florida. Good for naturalizing in the sunny wild garden.

M. menthifolia (Mintleaf Beebalm. Lemon Mint. Horsemint): 2 feet. Similar to mint, but the flowers are in terminal clusters. Rose to bluish-purple, 1 to 3 inches across. June/August. Hairy foliage. Native to the western states and Canada.

Montbretia

(see TRITONIA) ....

Moraea

(syn. DIETES) ....

Family: *Iridaceae* (Iris).

Common name: African Iris. Fortnight Lily.

Propagation: Seed sown in warmth, 65 to 70 degrees. Germination in 4 weeks.

Division of corms or rootstocks.

Culture: Sun. Light, sandy soil. Adequate moisture. (Flowers last but a day.) Not hardy; winter care as for gladiolus.

Indoor forcing: pot up and expose to fairly cold tempera-

tures (but not freezing) before bringing indoors.

Use: Border. Forcing for winter bloom.

Species and varieties:

M. bicolor: 2 feet. Light lemon-yellow flowers, 2 inches across, having brown spots and maroon blotches.

M. iridioides: 1½ to 3 feet. Resembles a small iris. White, waxy flowers, 3 inches across, with yellow-orange or brown spots. Var. "Johnsoni," 2 feet, more robust than the type and blooms several times during the summer, white with lavender and orange markings.

M. pavonia: 1 to 2 feet. Red flowers with blue or greenish-black markings at the base of each petal. Var. "*lutea*" is yellow; "*villosa*," a purple form.

M. robinsoniana: to 8 feet. Australian species with loose clusters of white flowers, red and yellow spotted.

M. spathacea: 12 inches. Fragrant, bright yellow flowers.

Muscari

Family: *Liliaceae* (Lily).

Common name: Grape Hyacinth.

Propagation: Seed sown when ripe, or stratify and refrigerate for several weeks and sow in spring. Cool temperatures needed for germination.

Self-sows readily.

Offsets.

Purchase bulbs for fall planting.

Culture: Sun or shade. Average light soil. Plant in masses, 4 inches deep, setting bulb so 1 inch of soil covers the tip.

Forcing for winter bloom: in early November, plant 3 bulbs to a 3-inch pan and leave outdoors for 12 weeks, either buried in a trench or in cold frame.

Use: Rock garden. Naturalize in grass. Woodlands. Beneath trees and shrubs. Cut flower. Winter forcing.

Species and varieties:

M. armeniacum: 6 to 12 inches. Spikes of fragrant, azure to purplish-blue flowers. May. Var. "*cantab*," light blue; "Blue Spike," miniature 5 or 6 inches high; "Early Giant," is the easiest to force.

M. azureum (syn. *HYACINTHUS ciliatus*).

M. botryoides coeruleum (Common Blue Grape Hyacinth): 6 to 12 inches. Very free flowering type. Bead-like flowers of deep bright blue. Var. "*album*," white form; "Heavenly Blue" is larger than type.

M. comosum (Fringe or Tassel Hyacinth): 15 inches. An oddity from Europe and southern Russia having bluish-purple, sterile flowers in long, loose racemes and also bearing the brown fertile flowers on the same spike. Var. "*plumosum or monstro-

sum*" (Plume or Feathered Hyacinth) 7 inches, sterile, violet to reddish-purple flowers having unusual lacinated petals (like feathered plumes). May. An excellent cut flower.

M. paradoxum: 9 inches. Bluish-black flowers in dense racemes. From the Caucasus.

M. tubergenianum: 6 inches. Free-flowering sort with spikes of true blue flowers, darker blue toward the top of the spike and growing lighter at the bottom. April.

Myosotis

Family: *Boraginaceac* (Borage).

Common name: Forget-me-not.

Propagation: Seed sown at 65 degrees, germination in 10 days. *M. palustris* blooms in 3 months from seed.

Division in spring or fall.

Cuttings.

Culture: Sun or partial shade. Light, humusy soil. Moist. Will tolerate quite boggy conditions. Set out plants in large groups or colonies, spacing 6 inches apart.

Use: Border. Rockery. Naturalize in open woodland or at edge of stream or pond. Long-lasting cut flower.

Species and varieties:

M. alpestris (syn. *M. sylvatica*) Wood Forget-me-not: 9 inches. Erect branching

Myosotis palustris semper-florens, Forget-me-not

plant, tufted habit of growth. Small blue flowers from May to frost. Prefers shade. Self-sows readily. European. (This is not as hardy as *M. palustris.*)

M. palustris semperflorens (syn. *M. scorpiodes*) Scorpion Grass: 6 inches. Semi-prostrate habit. Racemes of small, jewel-like, bright blue flowers with a golden eye. May to frost. Native from Europe to Asia. Quite happy at north side of buildings or beneath trees if moisture is applied whenever the plant shows signs of wilting. When

well established, I have found this species to be quite tolerant of our dry summers.

Two plants to a 10-inch basket make a charming display in the green house or on a porch.

Myrrhis

Family: *Umbelliferae* (Parsley).

Common name: Sweet Cicely. Myrrh.

Propagation: Sow seed in fall or stratify for a month or two at cold and freezing temperatures and sow in spring. Germination is often delayed until the following spring.

Division in spring.

Culture: Partial shade. Average garden soil.

Use: Border. Leaves used for flavoring.

Species:

M. odorata: 2½ to 3 feet. The whole plant is aromatic. Hairy, finely cut leaves. Compound umbels (to 2 inches across) of white flowers. May/June. Odd beaked fruits. Native to the mountains of Europe.

Narcissus

Family: *Amaryllidaceae* (Amaryllis).

Common name: Daffodils.

Propagation: Seed sown as soon after gathering as possible, or in early spring, in which case it will not often germinate until the following spring. Stratifying and exposing to cold and freezing temperatures prior to sowing in spring will sometimes encourage sprouting. Sow in flats where the tiny bulbs can remain and enlarge without disturbance for at least a year.

Division: dig up when leaves begin to dry, separate, and replant at once.

Bulbs purchased for fall planting. Order in August for September planting.

Culture: Sun or light shade. Light sandy to deep rich loam. Not at all fussy, but it must have a well-drained site. If possible, mix bonemeal into the bed before planting. Daffodils are not heavy feeders.

The flowers always face the sun; choose the site accordingly. Set out in natural-appearing groups. Small bulbs 4 to 6 inches deep, average size bulbs 6 to 8 inches deep and 6 to 8 inches apart. If autumn is dry, it is advisable to irrigate so that rooting is well under way before a hard freeze. Foliage must be allowed to ripen and die down naturally, or there will be no flowers next season.

Winter forcing: as with all hardy bulbs, pot up with just the tips of the bulbs showing and place in trench or cold frame. Bring inside in December or January when well rooted. Keep cool and out of strong light until top growth turns green.

Use: Border. Rock garden. Cut flower (cut when half open). Water garden. Naturalize in grass and under trees. Forced winter bloom.

Species and varieties:

N. barri: Hybrid. Solitary flowers having white or yellow perianths (outer petals) and red or yellow cup. The cup being less than ⅓ the length of the perianth. Var. "Firetail"; "Red Bird."

N. bulbocodium (Hooped or Petticoat Narcissus): 6 inches. Very variable. Rush-like foliage. Solitary flowers, usually the up-facing trumpet type, white or yellow with inconspicuous petals. Origin, southern Europe and North Africa. Var. "*citrinus,*" pale yellow; "*conspicuus,*" golden yellow.

N. campernelli (syn. *N. odorus*) Campernelle: (Often referred to as Jonquilla hybrids) very fragrant, golden-yellow flowers, 2 to 6 to a stem. There is a double form.

N. canaliculatus: 6 inches. Bluish-green foliage. A polyanthus type having 3 to 4 fragrant flowers to a stem. Globular golden cups and white perianth.

N. cyclamineus: 6 inches. A rare species from Portugal. Drooping flowers resemble cyclamen blossoms having long, narrow, tubular cups, ½ inch wide with slightly frilled edges and very reflexed perianth. Usually lemon to orange-yellow shades.

N. incomparalis: Flowers having yellow or white perianth and yellow or red cup, ¾ as long as the perianth. From Europe. Var. "Gracilis"; "Tenuior"; "Sir Watkin."

N. jonquilla (Jonquil): Hollow, rush-like leaves. Fragrant, short-cupped, bright yellow flowers in clusters, 2 to 6 on a stem. April. Originally from southern Europe and Algeria. There is a double form; hybrids of this are available.

N. juncifolius: 6 inches. Bright yellow flowers in April. Prefers shade and sandy soil.

N. leedsi: A hybrid having white petals and short yellow cup. Var. "White Lady"; "Southern Gem"; "Queen of the North."

N. minimus: 3 to 6 inches. Tiny yellow trumpet ½ inch long.

N. minor: 6 inches. Scented, nodding flowers of soft yellow hues.

N. poetaz: Hybrid (*N. tazetta* x *N. poeticus*). The hardiness of the poeticus parent is dominant. Flowers in clusters, 6 to a stem. Very shallow, open cups. Var. "Yellow Cheerfulness"; "Innocence," white petals and shallow orange cups; "Scarlet Gem," yellow perianth, reddish-orange cups.

N. poeticus (Poet's Narcissus): Fragrant, solitary flowers with white perianth and shallow, saucer-like, yellow cups edged in red. Very free flowering and wonderful for naturalizing. South Europe and Mediterranean origins. Var. "*recurvus*" (Pheasant's Eye), often 2 flowers to a stem, recurved petals; "*albo*

pleno odorata" (Gardenia Narcissus), a double white form.

N. pseudo-narcissus (Trumpet Daffodil): 12 inches. Variable. Showy, fragrant, solitary, drooping yellow flowers with long trumpets (the trumpet as long or longer than the perianth). European origin. Many hybrids have been created from this species. "King Alfred," "Mt. Hood," and "Spring Glory" are just a few.

N. triandrus (Angel's Tears): 6 inches. Small drooping white flowers, in clusters of 1 to 6 per stem. From Spain, this prefers shade and a light gritty soil. Var. "*calathinus*," pale yellow; "*albus*," creamy-white flowers formed rather like a cyclamen, having globular cups and recurved petals.

Nepeta

Family: *Labiatae* (Mint).

Common name: Catmint.

Propagation: Seeds sown at 65 degrees, germinating in 8 days.

Division in spring.

Cuttings in midsummer of half-ripened wood.

Culture: Sun. Light, sandy to poor soil. Dry. Division every third or fourth year. Shear lightly after flowering season is over. Space 6 to 12 inches apart, depending on height.

Use: Border. Edging. Cut flower.

Species and varieties:

N. cataria (True Catnip): 2 feet. Pale downy foliage. Mint-like, pale lavender to white flowers in spikes to 5 inches long. Odor is supposedly attractive to cats. My cats evidently do not run true to form, for they pay no attention to the plant.

N. x *faassenii*: 12 inches. Pungent grey foliage. Purple-blue flowers. May/August. A hybrid (*N. nepetella* x *N. mussinii*) that seldom sets seed.

N. hederacea (Creeping Jenny. Gound Ivy. Gill-over-the-ground): Creeping, mat-forming habit. Small spikes

Nepeta, Catmint "Souv. d'Andre Chaudron"

of light blue flowers in May. Excellent ground cover in sun or shade. Var. "*variegata*" has vari-colored leaves.

N. macrantha (Giant Flowered Catnip): 1 to 2 feet. Large violet, mint-like flowers.

N. mussinii (Dwarf Catnip): 1 to 2 feet. Spreading habit. Downy grey foliage. Flowers, pale to dark blue in long racemes. May/June. This has a shorter flowering season than *N. x faassenii*. An excellent ground cover.

N. nervosa: 12 inches. Light blue flowers. July/August. Himalayan.

N. nuda: 1 to 3 feet. Erect habit. Green leaves. Panicles of violet or white flowers spotted purple. South Europe.

N. Souv. d'Andre Chaudron (a hybrid, the American name is "Blue Beauty"): 1 to 1½ feet. Upright habit. Aromatic, dark grey-green foliage. Flat-sided, squared stems. Spikes of large dark purple-blue flowers. June/July. Matures into a fine hardy, herbaceous hedge.

N. wilsoni: to 2½ feet. Hairy leaves. Dark blue flowers in widely separated clusters.

Oenothera

Family: *Onagraceae* (Evening Primrose).

Common name: Sundrops. Evening Primrose.

Propagation: Seed sown at 65 degrees, germination in 5

days. If sown in April, will bloom the first year. Transplant when small, for these have long fleshy roots.

Culture: Sun. Light, gravelly, well-drained soil. Dry. Space 8 inches apart except for the spreading kinds; those need about 12 inches. Plant in groups.

Use: Border. Rock garden. Wild flower garden.

Species and varieties:

O. acaulis (syn. *O. taraxifolia*) Biennial Sundrop. Dandelion Leaf Sundrop: 6 to 12 inches. Prostrate, trailing habit. Greyish, dandelion-like

leaves. A short-lived plant with day-opening white flowers, to 4 inches across, fades to rose in maturity. July/August. From Chile.

O. biennis (Common Evening Primrose): Biennial. 2½ to 4 feet. Erect habit. Night-opening flowers in racemes, pale yellow, to 2 inches across. Variety "*grandiflora*" has larger flowers. A wild garden plant found natively from Canada to Texas.

O. caespitosa (Evening Primrose. Sandlily): Long, narrow, velvety, basal leaves. Flowers open at night and stay open one day. Stemless, four-petaled, white flowers

that gradually turn pink and then red, 2 to 4 inches across. May/July. Native of the western states.

O. flava: Rosette of basal leaves. Yellow flowers fading purple. Indigenous to the West.

O. fremonti: 10 inches. Spreading habit. Yellow day-opening flowers. June/August.

O. fruticosa (syn. *tetragona riparia*): Biennial. 12 to 15 inches. Upright habit. Downy, lance-shaped leaves. Yellow flowers. June/August. Native to eastern states. Var. "Yellow River," 1½ to 2 feet, lemon-yellow; "*youngi*," free-flowering sort with shiny leaves and yellow flowers, requires more moisture.

O. heterantha: Similar to *O. flava*, but the yellow flowers do not change color.

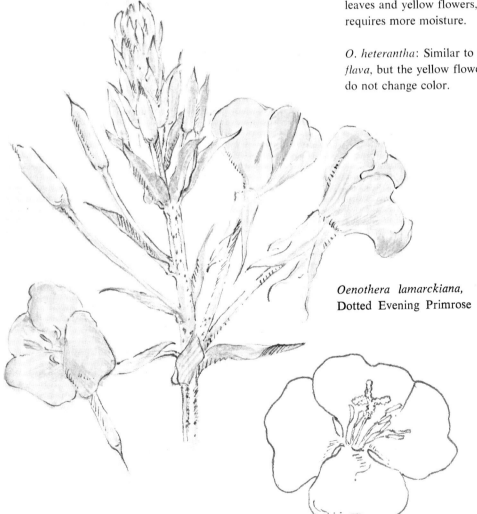

Oenothera lamarckiana,
Dotted Evening Primrose

O. lamarckiana (Dotted Evening Primrose): Biennial 4 feet. Red-dotted stem. Long spikes of large yellow flowers, to 2 inches across, night-opening; not a great amount of bloom at any one time. July/August. A coarse-appearing plant; place at the back of the border.

O. missouriensis (syn. *O. macrocarpa*) Ozark Sundrop. Missouri Primrose or Sundrop: 9 to 10 inches. Trailing habit, stems to 12 inches long. Long-lived. Day-flowering, golden-yellow flowers, to 4 inches across. July to frost. Central to western plains states.

O. rydbergii (syn. *O. strigosa*) Yellow Evening Primrose: 1 to 4 feet. Erect habit. Opens in the evening, pale yellow flowers, 1 inch across. July/August. Rocky Mountains, plains to 8,000 feet.

O. speciosa (Wind Primrose. White Evening Primrose): 1½ to 4 feet. Rosette habit. Spreads by underground runners. White flowers on leafy stems, fade pink, 3 inches across. July/August. Central states.

Onosma

Family: *Boraginaceae* (Borage).

Common name: Golden Drops.

Propagation: Seed sown in spring at 45 degrees.

Cuttings in August, root in sand.

Culture: Sun. Sandy, gravelly soil.

Use: Rock walls. Rock garden.

Species:

O. echioides: 6 inches. Rough leaves. Flowers in pendant, one-sided clusters, pale yellow, corolla tubular or urn-shaped. July/August.

O. stellulatum (syn. *O. helveticum*): 8 inches. Spreading clumps of narrow, rough, dullish green leaves to 2 inches long. Terminal, drooping clusters of fragrant, yellow, tubular flowers, 1 to 1½ inches long. July/August.

Orchis

Family: *Orchidaceae* (Orchid).

Common name: Orchis.

Propagation: Seed (very fine) started in warmth 65 to 70 degrees. Germination is difficult, slow, and erratic.

Division of the tuberous root in fall when the plant is dormant.

Culture: (Also refer to the section on orchid culture in Chapter I.) Open shade. Neutral, woodland soil, rich in leaf mold. Good drainage is necessary. Moist. A good growing mix is:

> 1 part rich loam
> 1 part well-decayed
>   leaf mold
> 1 part sphagnum moss
> ½ part well-rotted
>   manure

Space plants 4 to 6 inches apart, massing in colonies in the company of ferns.

Use: These are hardy terrestrials that adapt well to woodland gardens.

Species:

O. incarnata: 12 inches. Flesh-colored to red flowers.

O. latifolia (Marsh Orchis): 12 inches. Leaves are spotted purple-black. Purple to red flowers in June.

O. maculata: 12 inches. Spikes of variable-colored flowers, may be pale purple or whitish with purple-brown spots. May/August. European.

O. morio: 6 inches. Typically orchid-like flowers, purple helmet, pinkish-purple lip is paler in the mid-section with dark spots.

O. rotundifolia (Small Round-leaved Orchis): 10 to 12 inches. Small round leaves hug the ground. White flowers with purple blotches (smaller than *O. spectabilis*). Soil neutral to limy. A cool, bog plant from Canada and the Rocky Mountains.

O. spectabilis (Showy Orchis): 4 to 12 inches. Two fleshy, oval, shiny green, basal leaves. Loose spikes of small purple, lavender, pinkish, or white flowers having the typical orchid hood and lip. May/July. Native from Canada to Georgia.

Ornith-ogalum

Family: *Liliaceae* (Lily).

Common name: Star of Bethlemen. Summer Snowflake.

Propagation: Seed sown anytime in warmth, 60 to 70 degrees.

Bulb offsets.

Bulbs ordered for spring or fall.

Culture: Sun or light shade. Average soil. Set out bulbs about 3 inches deep, 6 inches apart. Dig and separate every third year. Some of these will self-sow so freely that they will be pesky unless the seed heads are removed.

Use: Border. Long-lasting cut flower. Container.

Species and varieties:

O. narbonense: 1½ to 2 feet. Racemes of white flowers with narrow green keel on outside of petals.

O. nutans: 1 to 2 feet. Grass-like leaves, ½ inch wide and up to 18 inches long. Flowers in nodding clusters; blossoms are white inside, green outside, 2 inches across.

O. pyrenaicum (French Asparagus): 1½ feet. Pale yellow flowers in June. The young shoots may be eaten like asparagus.

O. thyrsoides (Chincherinchee): 1½ feet. Dense spikes bearing 30 to 40 starry flowers, 1 inch across. June/July. Var. "*aureum*" has yellow flowers. This is not hardy. As a garden plant, dig and store as you do all tender bulbs or pot for indoor bloom.

Oxalis

Family: *Oxalidaceae*.

Common name: Wood Sorrel. Cuckoo Bread.

Propagation: Seed sown in spring at 45 degrees.

Division in spring.

Culture: Shade. Sandy to gritty soil.

Use: Rock garden. Woodland. Container.

Species and varieties:

O. acetosella (Shamrock): 3 inches high. Thin creeping rhizome: Leaves trifoliate (3 parted). White flowers with mauve veins. April/May. The viable seeds are produced later in the summer from flowers that do not open (self-pollinated). Native of the British Isles, Europe and Asia. Var. "*rosea*," 3 inches, solitary rose flowers, purple veined; "Dieppe," 8 inches, rose-pink, June/September.

This is the only hardy member of this genus that is not weedy and does not (like *O. montana*) require a very acid soil.

Paeonia

Family: *Ranunculaceae* (Buttercup).

Common name: Peony.

Propagation: Attractive and charming results are obtained when growing the species from seed, although it takes 3 to 5 years for the herbaceous and up to 7 years for the woody types to bloom. The species come true from seed. Seed must be fresh, and even so, germination may take 2 years. Sow in fall, soon after ripening, in cold frame, 1 inch deep and 2 inches apart. There will be little evidence of growth the first year, but the plants will be large enough the second year to transplant to the nursery. Stratification and freezing may help spring-sown seed, but this is not usually the case.

Divide in fall or (weather permitting) very early spring. Cut apart the fleshy root so that each section has 3 to 5 eyes or buds and about 6 inches of root.

Culture: Sun or light shade. Deep, rich, limy soil, well drained. Add peat when planting. Fertilize annually with a fertilizer that is high in phosphorous and low in nitrogen. I have found peonies do better if sited in the open rather than when sheltered by buildings where they start away too early in spring and are consequently hit by every late snow storm. Some support is needed for the heavy blossoms.

If buds shrivel and do not open, it may be due to Botrytis; in which case, spray with a fungicide. I don't allow events to progress to that point anymore——I spray in spring as soon as the shoots appear. Drench the crown and surrounding soil with a Bordeaux mix (4 tablespoons to 1 gallon water), applying about 1 gallon per plant.

Space plants 18 to 20 inches apart, setting the bud 1 to 1½ inches (never over 3 inches) below the soil level.

Use: Border. Cut flower (cut when bud is half open).

Species and varieties:

P. albiflora (syn. *P. lactiflora sinensis*, *P. chinensis*, *P. edulis*) Early White Peony: 3 feet. Single flowers may be white, pink or red. Also a double variety. Siberia to China.

P. anomala: 2½ feet. Deeply divided leaves. Single red flowers, 3 inches across. From Russia and central Asia.

P. arietina: Mediterranean species with rose-pink to red flowers.

P. broteri: Cup-shaped, rose flowers with yellow centers. Spain.

P. cambessedesi: Flowers deep rose, 3 to 4 inches across. From the Mediterranean.

P. clusi: Another Mediterranean species. White, cup-shaped flowers with gold stamens.

P. corallina: 3 feet. European species with rose-red flowers. Prefers shade.

P. coriacea: Rose-red flowers. The parent of many blue hybrids. From Spain.

P. daurica: Deep rose flowers with yellow centers. Caucasus.

P. delavayi: 3 feet. Subshrub. Velvety crimson flowers, 2 inches across.

P. emodi: 2 feet. Fern-like leaves. Yellow tinted, nodding, white flowers, 4 to 5 inches across. Native of India.

P. humilis: Deep red flowers. Spain.

P. japonica: White-flowered species from Japan.

P. lutea: 3 feet. Woody shrub. The woody types will not die down in the winter and are true shrubs. I include them because they are used in the same manner in the flower garden. *P. lutea* has yellow flowers. Var. "*ludlowi*" is the Chinese Tree Paeony.

P. mascula: Flowers, rose-red with purple shading. European.

P. mlokosewitchi: 2 feet. Large, broad, blue-green leaves, paler underneath. Large, single, citron-yellow flowers. Prefers shade. Native to the Caucasus.

P. obvata: White to rose-purple flowers. Siberia to China. Var. "*willmottiae*" is a white form from China.

P. officinalis (Common Peony): 2 to 3 feet. Single flowers, color variable, white to shades of red. May/June. Southern Europe. Var. "*festiva*," white with red center; "*alba*" white; "*rosea*," pink; "*rubra*," red; also a double variety.

P. peregrina: 2 feet. Dull green leaves. Crimson flowers. From the Balkans. Var. "*lobata*," a red dwarf blooming in early June.

131

P. russi: Mediterranean species with rose flowers.

P. suffruticosa (syn. *P. moutan*) Moutan Paeony. Tree Peony: Shrub. 5 to 6 feet. Flowers to 12 inches across, may be white, yellow, rose, or red.

P. veitchii (syn. *P. tenuifolia*) Fernleaf Peony: 1½ feet. Finely divided foliage. Fragrant, deep rose to red flowers, 3 to 4 inches across. May/June. Var. "*flore-pleno*," double; "*woodwardi-ana*," 12-inch-high dwarf with rose-pink flowers.

P. wittmanniana: 1½ to 2 feet. Glaucous leaves. Flowers pale cream to primrose-yellow. June. From southeast Europe. Var. "*macrophylla*," very large, shiny leaves and creamy-white flowers in mid-May.

Papaver

Family: *Papaveraceae* (Poppy).

Common name: Poppy.

Propagation: Sow in fall or spring at 65 degrees; germination should start in 6 days. The alpines require a period of freezing if sown in spring. Transplant seedlings into peat pots for this genus resents handling.

Root cuttings of *P. orientalis* in fall.

Culture: Sun. Light, sandy, well-drained soil. Space dwarfs 4 to 6 inches apart, the taller sorts 18 inches apart. Plants may be moved in early spring or in fall when dormant.
Use: Border. Rock garden. Cut flower (dip the cut end in boiling water for a few seconds or sear with flame).

Species and varieties:

P. alpinum (Alpine Poppy): 4 to 6 inches. Basal rosette of divided, blue-green leaves. Fragrant, typical poppy flower, white, yellow, or orange, 1 to 1½ inches across.

P. atlanticum: 1½ feet. Orange flowers, 2 inches across.

P. bracteatum (Blood Poppy): 3 feet. Blood-red flowers to 4 inches across. Resembles *P. orientalis*, but the petals are a solid color. May/June.

P. nudicaule coonara (Iceland Poppy): 1½ feet. Often biennial in habit, but it self-sows so readily that this is seldom noticed. Flowers in all shades from salmon, pink, rose, white, yellow, or gold. May to frost if the seed pods are removed. The hybrid "Champagne Bubbles" is larger than type. At home in the highlands.

P. orientale (Oriental Poppy): 2 to 2½ feet. Coarse-appearing with hairy leaves and stout stems. Colors vary from white, salmon, pink, rose, red, and bright orange; all have a black blotch in the center. June/July (season of bloom is very short). I put these in an out-of-the-way corner of the garden because they need no care and have a very short period of bloom, and because the leaves are quite unsightly when they die down in August.

P. pilosum (Olympic Poppy): 2 feet. Salmon flowers, 2 inches across.

P. pyrenaicum: 4 to 6 inches. Tufted habit. Yellow or orange flowers to 1 inch across. Related to *P. alpinum*. Var. "*rhaeticum*," 6 inches, white.

P. rupifragrum: 1½ feet. Flowers pale brick-red with greenish centers, 3 inches across.

Paradisea

Family: *Liliaceae*.

Common name: St. Brunos Lily.

Propagation: Seed sown in spring at 45 degrees; germination within 3 weeks.

Division of fleshy rhizome in spring.

Culture: Sun or part shade. Light, sandy soil with humus added. Good drainage absolutely necessary. Moist when in bloom.

Use: Border. Rock garden. Open woodland.

Species:

P. liliastrum: 1 to 2 feet. Fragrant, almost transparent, white, funnel-shaped flowers, 2 inches long, in loose racemes. June/July. Resembles a small lily. Long, narrow, grassy leaves. Native to the Alps at 6,000 feet and above. Although this is often referred to as a tender plant, I have found it to be hardy if protected with a winter mulch.

Pardanthus

(see BELAMCANDA) ....

Parnassia

Family: *Saxifragaceae* (Saxifrage).

Common name: Grass of Parnassus.

Propagation: Seed must be fresh. Sow in fall or spring. Cold is necessary for germination. Spring-sown seed may be stratified and placed in the refrigerator or cold frame in February or March.

Division after flowering.

Culture: Sun (if a wet site) or light shade for drier sites. Limy soil. Naturally wet locations are ideal.

Use: Bog plant. Naturalize at water's edge or in damp meadow.

Species:

P. fimbriata (Rocky Mountain or Fringed Parnassia): 6 to 8 inches. Long-stalked, heart-shaped, basal leaves. The flowering stem has a single leaf at or above the center. Solitary, white flower, ¾ inch across. Conspicuous petals are fringed from midway on the petal to the base. Odd-appearing, gland-tipped, sterile stamens alternate like spokes of a wheel with fertile ones in the flower's center. July/August. Found in the Rockies from 5,000 feet to timberline.

P. palustris (Wideworld Parnassia): 4 to 8 inches. Oval to ovate leaves, palmately, parallel-veined in a basal rosette with the exception of one clasping leaf located below the midway point on the naked stem. Solitary, white, starry flower with petals having distinct green to yellow veins and with the petals much longer than the sepals. The flower has 9 to 15 sterile filaments. July/August. Found throughout most of the northern hemisphere.

Paronychia

Family: *Caryophyllaceae* (Pink).

Common name: Whitlow Wort. Nailwort.

Propagation: Seed sown in spring at 45 degrees.

Division in spring.

Culture: Sun. Light, sandy, well-drained soil. Dry. Use: Rockery. Ground cover.

Species:

P. capitata: 8 to 12 inches. Carpet or matting habit. Foliage covered with silvery, downy hairs. Flattish clusters of small, whitish flowers surrounded by attractive silvery bracts.

Pedicularis

Family: *Scrophulariaceae* (Figwort).

Common name: Lousewort. Wood Betony. Fernleaf.

Propagation: Seed sown when collected in fall. A period of stratification is helpful in germinating spring-sown seed. Seed of some of the species is available from commercial sources.

Division of creeping underground stems.

Culture: Sun or open shade. Sandy to humus-enriched loam. Moist during the growing season, otherwise dry. Some of the species have a mycorrhizal association (see *CASTILLEJA*); when collecting plants from the field, always retain as much of the soil ball and the other kinds of plants growing around your specimen as possible. Never practice bare-earth cultivation around these plants.

Use: Woodland or wild flower garden. Waterside.

Species:

P. bracteosa (Northern Fernleaf): 1 to 2 feet or more. Mostly basal, fern-like leaves. Numerous pale yellow flowers in leafy-bracted, terminal spikes (petals unite into 2, the upper one curved like a hood). July/August. Found in wet meadows to open woods, 6,000 to 9,500 feet in the Rockies.

P. canadensis (Early Fernleaf. Wood Betony): 6 to 18 inches. Prized for its attractive foliage——soft, hairy, ferny leaves. Flowers in short dense spikes of red or yellow, in rather dull hues. An Eastern woodland species that needs a slightly acid soil; add generous quantities of peat when planting.

P. crenulata (Meadow Fernleaf): 4 to 16 inches. Double-toothed, linear leaves have white margins. Dense spikes of white or purple flowers. Mountain meadows from Wyoming to Nevada.

P. densiflora (Indian Warrior): Finely divided leaves and feathery, purplish-red flowers. Easy to grow from seed.

P. groenlandica (Elephanthead): 8 to 24 inches. Ferny-leaved. Purplish-red to pinkish-red flowers in bracted, dense, terminal spikes. The flower resembles an elephant's head with raised, curving trunk (it is impossible to mistake this plant for anything else). June/August. Wet meadow water's edge, 5,500 feet and above, Rocky Mountains from Alaska to California.

P. racemosa (Sickle Top. Parrot's Beak): 8 to 20 inches. Leaves, double-toothed but not divided. Many stems rising from a woody crown. Flowers, loosely arranged, in leafy-bracted spikes, white or pink. The upper corolla curves to suggest a parrot's beak.

Penstemon

Family: *Scrophulariaceae* (Figwort).

Common name: Beardtongue.

Propagation: Seed sown in spring at 65 degrees; germination in 5 days.

Division in eary spring.

Cuttings in spring, use bottom heat.

Stem cuttings in July.

Culture: Sun. Light, sandy to gritty soil, well drained. Dry. Space tall sorts 12 inches apart, dwarfs 6 inches apart. Group for effect.

Use: Border. Rock garden. Cut flower. Dry stone wall. Most are indigenous to the West and are easily naturalized in the wild garden.

Species and varieties:

P. albertinus (Albert's Penstemon): 6 to 12 inches. Small leaves. Flowers bright blue to bluish-purple. A Rocky Mountain native and perhaps the showiest.

P. barbatus (syn. *CHELONE barbata*): 3 feet. Tall upright clumps. Grey-green leaves clasp the stem. Loose spikes of pale pink to scarlet tubular flowers, 1 inch long, hairy bearded. June/August. Western states. Var. "*praecox nana*," a dwarf form.

P. caeruleus: 2 feet. Shiny, dark green leaves. Bright blue flowers in dense spikes. June.

P. cobaea (Cobaea Penstemon): 2 feet. Large, toothed leaves. Flowers to 2 inches across, purple with downy, swollen throats. May/June. Found in midwestern states south to Texas.

P. crandallii: 12 inches. Evergreen matting habit. Narrow leaves. Up-facing flowers, sky blue to lilac and white. June. Rock-garden type from Colorado.

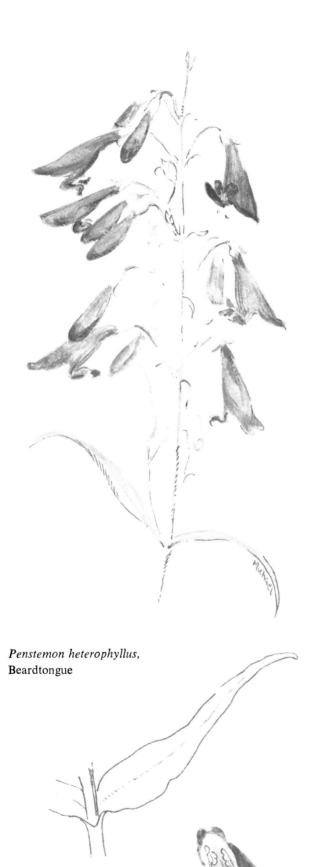

Penstemon heterophyllus,
Beardtongue

P. cyananthus (Wasatch Penstemon): to 3 feet. Bluish-green foliage. Dense clusters of bright blue flowers.

P. digitalis (Smooth White Penstemon): 3 to 4 feet. Flowers white with faint purple lines. June/July. From the eastern half of United States, this requires more moisture and tolerates some shade.

P. erianthus (Crested Beard-tongue): 6 inches. A hairy plant, both flowers and foliage. Large lilac flowers. Common to the Rockies.

P. fruticosus (Bush Pen-stemon): 6 to 24 inches. Woody alpine of the northern Rockies, to 9,000 feet. Toothed leaves. Racemes of rose to lavender-blue flowers to 1½ inches long. May to early July. Give this a rocky site and prune after flowering.

P. glaber (Blue Beardtongue): 1 to 2 feet. Sprawling habit. Glaucous, narrow leaves. Bluish-purple flowers.

P. grandiflorus (Large flowered or Shell leaf Penstemon): 4 to 6 feet. Stout stemmed. Blue-green, glaucous foliage. Flowers pinkish to lavender-blue, rarely white, to 2 inches long. June/July. Often acts as a biennial. From the dry plains of midwestern to western states.

P. hartwegii: 2 to 4 feet. Drooping, red flowers, 2 inches long. Var. "Newberry Gem," 2 feet, deep red; "Scotch Prize Strain," 1½ feet, large flowers, mostly pinks and reds.

P. heterophyllus: 1 to 2 feet. Upright habit. Spikes of lavender to blue. May/July. From California; it may die in an extremely dry and open winter. Var. "True Blue," 1½ feet, brilliant blue, beardless flowers in June. Shiny, dark green leaves.

P. hirsutus (Eastern Pen-stemon): 2 feet. Hairy foliage. Purple flowers with white lip. May/July. Native to eastern states, Canada to Virginia.

P. isophyllus: 5 feet. Flowers bright scarlet and whitish with red lines inside, 2½ inches long.

P. laevigatus digitalis: 4 feet. Very free flowering sort. White, bearded flowers, 1 inch long.

P. menziesii (syn. *P. david-sonii*) Menzies Penstemon: 3 to 12 inches. Woody. Spreading, matting habit. Small, oval leaves to ⅓ inch long. Violet-blue to purple flowers, 1 to 1½ inches long. July/August. Alpine from western mountains. Rocky site. Prune after flowering for neatness.

P. murrayanus: 3 to 4 feet. Bluish foliage. Deep red flowers, 1 inch long. From the southwest, it needs a sunny sheltered spot.

P. newberryi (Mountain Pride): to 20 inches. Woody base. Creeping, matting habit. Round, leathery, thickish leaves, ½ inch long. Rose-red flowers, 1 inch long. June/August. Rocky site.

P. ovatus (Eggleaf Pen-stemon): 2 to 3 feet. Often biennial. West coast species

Penstemon barbata, Beard-tongue

Petrocallis

(see DRABA *pyrenaica*) ......

Phlox

Family: *Polemoniaceae* (Phlox).

Common name: Phlox.

Propagation: Sow in early spring; the seed must be fresh. *P. paniculata* should be sown in fall, and even then you may not meet with any success. To say the least, the seed is difficult to germinate.

Division in spring or after flowering in late summer; use the outer shoots.

Division of rooted runners of *P. stolonifera.*

Cuttings of the trailing sorts after blooming season.

Stem cuttings in spring; use bottom heat.

Root cuttings in late summer to fall of *P. paniculata,* 2 inches long (thicker part of root), set upright or horizontal, cover with ¾ inch of sand, and winter in the cold frame or cold greenhouse. They should flower the following year.

Culture: Sun or open shade. Well-drained, sandy, porous soil, neutral to alkaline. Dry. Easily transplanted. *P. stolonifera, P. suffruticosa,* and *P. paniculata* require a richer, humusy soil, and annual application of superphosphate and well-dried manure.

Plant in masses, spacing dwarf forms 6 to 12 inches apart; *P. paniculata* 1 to 1½ feet apart, and this should be divided every fourth year.

Use: Border. Rockery. Wild garden. Woodland ground cover.

Species and varieties:

P. divaricata (syn. *P. canadensis*) Wild Blue or Blue Phlox. Sweet William Phlox: 6 to 18 inches. Trailing habit. Creeping underground shoots that root at the nodes. Oval leaves, 1 to 2 inches long. Flowers in loose terminal clusters on erect leafy stems, pale blue to lavender, 1½ inches across, deeply notched petals. April/June. Seed germinates easily; flowering the second year. Found in the woodlands of New England to Michigan and southward.

P. hoodii: Mat forming. Wooly leaved. White to blue flowers. May/July. Valleys and foothills of Wyoming and Colorado. Only young plants may be collected in the field, transplanting is difficult because of a long tap root. May also be propagated by seed or cuttings in spring or late summer.

P. longifolia (Long leaved Phlox): to 12 inches. Similar to *P. multiflora* but of upright habit, longer leaves, and large pink flowers. May/July. Rocky Mountain.

P. multiflora (White or Spreading Phlox): Low, mat-forming habit. Prostrate, woody, basal branches to 12 inches long. Leafy herbaceous branches rise from these bearing terminal single flowers, ¾ inch across, white, pink, or lilac. May/July.

with small blue flowers fading to lavender. Freely flowering all summer.

P. palmeri (Palmer Penstemon): 4 feet. Another far west species with bluish leaves and large, fragrant, pink and white flowers. June/July.

P. procerus (Little or Small flowered Penstemon): 4 to 20 inches. Shiny, narrow leaves. Dense terminal clusters of small pale blue to purple flowers, less than ½ inch long. Rocky Mountain native.

P. rupicola: 4 to 6 inches. Shrubby, low trailing; excellent habit of growth for dry stone walls. Round, blue-grey, glaucous leaves. Rose-red to crimson flowers to 1 inch long. June/August. A slow grower. Native to the Cascade Mountains.

P. torreyi: Very much like *P. barbatus,* but the scarlet flowers are larger. Var. "Pink Beauty," shell pink.

Foothill to timberline from Montana to New Mexico.

P. paniculata (syn. *P. decussata*) Garden Phlox: 2 to 4 feet. Upright habit. In its native habitat, eastern United States, the flowers are a magenta shade; now, most of the commercially offered varieties of this are cultivars, and the range of color would satisfy anyone——white, lavender, pink, rose, and red, often with contrasting eyes. Flowers are in large, showy panicles. Unfortunately, they do not reproduce true from seed. July/September.

P. stolonifera (syn. *P. reptans*): Creeping habit (rooting stolons) makes this an admirable ground cover in the woodland garden. Round, hairy, opposite leaves, 3 inches long. Flowers on 6-inch stems in small, flattish clusters, red to bluish-purple. April/June. Moist woods of Pennsylvania and southward. Will not stand very arid conditions. Propagation is simple, merely separate the rooting stolons.

P. subulata (Moss or Creeping Pink or Phlox): 5 inches. Mat-forming with creeping stems. Linear, ½ inch long, prickly, evergreen leaves. Very free blooming, short-stemmed flower clusters. Flowers may be purple, lavender-blue, pink or white, ¾ inch across. May/June. Shear after blooming for neatness. Var. "Blue Hills," lavender-blue, early; "Eventide," pale blue; "Scarlet Flame"; "Emerald Gem," a rose-pink.

P. suffruticosa (syn. *P. carolina*) Thick-leaf or Perennial Phlox: to 2 feet. Resembles *P. paniculata*, and

culture for both is the same. Fragrant flowers in clusters, purple, rose, or white, ¾ inch across. June/July. Var. "Miss Lingard" is a white form.

Physalis

Family: *Solanaceae* (Nightshade).

Common name: Chinese Lantern. Winter Cherry.

Propagation: Seed sown in spring at 65 degrees; germination within 2 to 3 weeks.

Division in spring.

Culture: Sun or part shade. Light soil. Dry. Situate these in an out-of-the-way part of the garden except for "Pygmy." Set plants 12 inches apart, 6 inches apart for the dwarfs.

Use: Container. Winter bouquet (cut when seed pods are brightly colored).

Species and varieties:

P. alkekengi: 1 to 2 feet. Spreads by underground stems; rather invasive and uninteresting plant. Its only redeeming feature being the delightful, bright orange-red, inflated seed pods which do indeed resemble Chinese lanterns. Native from the Caucasus to China.

P. franchetii: 2 to 2½ feet. Japanese species, taller and having much larger lanterns. A variant of this is *P. franchetii pygmaea* or "Pygmy," an 8-inch dwarf that makes an excellent pot plant.

Physostegia

Family: *Labiatae* (Mint).

Common name: Obedient Plant. False Dragonhead.

Propagation: Sow seed in spring at 65 degrees; germination in 9 days.

Division in spring.

Creeping stolons.

Culture: Sun or light shade. Light, sandy soil. Moist. Divide every third year. Space plants 12 inches apart in groups of four or more.

Use: Border. Cut flower (long lasting). Wild garden.

Species and varieties:

P. virginiana: 3 feet. Leaves narrow and toothed. Leafy-stemmed. Dense terminal spikes of snapdragon-like, rose flowers. Native from Minnesota eastward and south to Texas. Var. *"rosea,"* 2 to 3 feet, pink to rose flowers, August; "Summer Snow," 1½ to 2 feet, white flowers freely produced from August on is my favorite; "Vivid," 1½ feet, brilliant rose flowers coming on later than Summer Snow and larger than *rosea;* "Summer Glow," 3 to 4 feet, very long rose-crimson spikes, July/September.

Platycodon

Family: *Campanulaceae* (Bellflower).

Common name: Balloon Flower.

Propagation: Seed sown in spring at 65 to 70 degrees, germination in 8 to 14 days. If sown in April, this will often bloom by August. Seed is the better means of propagation, because this plant has a long fleshy root that makes division or moving difficult. Transplanting has to be done when the plant is very small.

Self-sows.

Root cuttings are sometimes successful.

Culture: Sun or light shade. Well-drained, light soil. Drought tolerant. Taller sorts need staking, as the stem is brittle and easily broken. Slow to start growth in spring so it is well to mark their location. Plant in groups, 10 inches apart except for the dwarfs which are better placed 6 inches apart.

Use: Border. Rock garden. Naturalize under birches and aspen. Cut flower (singe cut end).

Species and varieties:

P. grandiflorum: 1½ to 2 feet. Odd balloon-like buds open into blue or white bells, 2 to 3 inches across. June/July. The season is extended if the faded flowers are removed. Var. *"japonicum,"* star-shaped, double; "Mariesii" (Japanese Bellflower), 1 to 1½ feet, dwarf with violet-blue or white flowers; *"roseum,"* 1½ feet, variable rose-pink flowers, not true to color from seed, although a few will be pink; *"praecox,"* 2 feet, very large, violet-blue, earlier.

Platycodon japonicum, Balloon Flower "Mariesii"

P. species nova: 6 inches. A lovely Japanese dwarf. Waxy blue bells, 3 inches across.

Podophylum

Family: *Berberidaceae* (Barberry).

Common name: May Apple. Mandrake. Mayflower.

Propagation: Seed germinates easily if fresh; remove the pulp first, and sow in fall. Spring sowing requires prechilling treatment in the refrigerator for several weeks. Remove to warmth 50 to 60 degrees. Germination is erratic and will continue throughout the summer. Sow in flats so that the seedlings will not have to be disturbed the first year. Carry over in the frame until large enough to set out or they will not survive.

Division of the creeping rootstock in early spring or summer; treat as a cutting.

Culture: Shade, but tolerates some sun. Neutral woodland soil. Moist. Actually, this is a very tolerant plant. Space 10 to 12 inches apart in colonies.

Use: Wild garden. Ground cover in open woodland.

Species:

P. emodi: 1 to 2 feet. Large, round, marbled leaves, showier than *P. peltatum*. White flowers and large edible scarlet fruits. Himalayan.

P. peltatum: 9 to 12 inches. Pair of terminal, shiny, umbrella-like, deeply lobed leaves. Solitary white flowers, to 2 inches across, rather hidden by the leaves in May. Greenish-yellow, edible fruits in August. Plant is dormant by early fall. Native to eastern and central states.

Polemonium

Family: *Polemoniaceae* (Phlox).

Common name: Jacob's Ladder. Greek Valerian.

Propagation: Sow in fall or spring at 45 degrees; germination in 14 days. Some species are slower, *P. cashmirianum* sprouted at intervals all summer long.

Division in spring or late summer after flowering.

Cuttings in midsummer.

Culture: Light shade. Average well-drained soil. Moist. Space plants 6 to 10 inches apart according to their mature height, setting out in fairly large groups. Self-sows easily so I take the seed pods as they mature and scrunch and scatter their contents where I want new colonies.

Use: Shaded areas under trees or north of buildings. Border. Open woodland garden. The dwarfs are excellent for the rock garden.

Species and varieties:

P. albiflorum: 1 to 2½ feet. Hairy foliage. White to whitish-yellow flowers in terminal clusters, very hairy green calyx (outer part of flower). June/July. Aspen groves in the Rockies.

P. caeruleum: 1½ feet. Ferny pinnate leaves are ornamental all summer. Nodding blue flowers in panicles. May/June. Var. "*album*" or "*lacteum*" are white forms; "Blue Pearl," 1 to 2 feet, clusters of bright blue-lavender flowers to 1 inch across, with yellow eyes.

P. carneum: 15 inches. Flowers cream, apricot, or

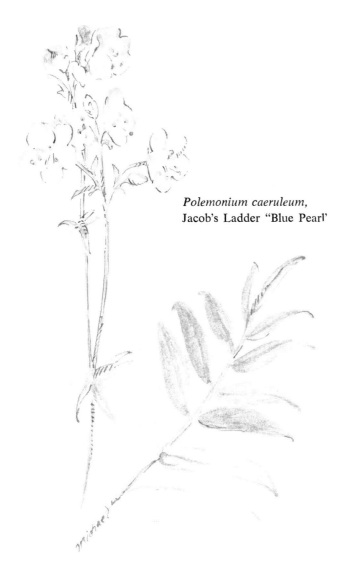

Polemonium caeruleum,
Jacob's Ladder "Blue Pearl'

pink on slender stems. From
the northwestern mountain
ranges of Oregon and
California.

P. cashmirianum: 12 inches.
A blue-flowered species from
Kashmir.

P. flavum: 2½ feet. Yellow
flowers all summer.

P. pauciflorum: 1½ to 2
feet. Drooping, yellow or
yellow-orange flowers. June/
August. Chilean.

P. pulcherrimum (syn. *P.
delicatum*): 6 to 12 inches.
Most of the compound leaves
arranged in a basal rosette.

Color is variable, usually blue
with yellow or white throat
(tube). May/August. Found
at high altitudes in all
western states on gravelly
sites, sun or shade.

P. reptans (Bluebell): 6 to 12
inches. Sprawling plant forms
spreading mats. Nodding,
light blue or white flowers,
to ¾ inch across, white eyes.
May/June. Native to the
eastern and central states.
Var. "Firmament," mound
habit, blue flowers in May.

P. richardsonii: 9 inches.
Creeping habit. Large bright
blue to purple flowers, ½
inch across, in clusters. June.

An arctic species. Var.
"*pulchellum,*" purple or
white flowers are smaller
than type.

P. van-bruntiae: 3 feet.
Darker blue-purple flowers in
terminal panicles. June/July.
Northeastern states.

P. viscosum (Sky Pilot.
Skunkweed): Downy, rather
sticky leaves that have a
skunky odor when crushed.
Broadly funnel-shaped, blue
or purplish flowers, orange
anthers. Found from June to
August, 9,000 feet or above,
in the Rocky Mountains. A
rock-garden plant that prefers a dry gravelly or
rocky site.

Polygonatum

Family: *Liliaceae* (Lily).

Common name: Solomon's
Seal.

Propagation: Seed sown in
fall or early spring. If
gathered, mash and separate
seed from pulp before
sowing. Like some other
members of the lily family,
these often show epicotyl
dormancy; that is, they form
the root the first year, but
no top growth appears until
the second season.

Division after flowering.

Creeping roots or rhizome.

Culture: Shade. Deep, rich or
humusy woodland soil,
neutral to slightly acid.
Moist. Very effective in
masses.

Use: Wild garden. Woodland
ground cover. Shady ground
cover.

Species:

P. biflorum (Small Solomon
Seal): 2 to 3 feet. Alternate,
broadly lance-shaped leaves
clasp arching stems. Small
greenish to white bell-like
flowers hang from slender
peduncles by ones or twos at
the leaf axils. May/June.
Steely blue-black berries in
fall. Woodland plant from
Maine to Michigan south-
ward to Nebraska.

P. commutatum (syn. *P.
canaliculatum*) Great or
Giant Solomon's Seal: Very
like the above specie but
larger——to 4 foot long
arching stems. More and
larger pendant bells hanging
in clusters of 2, 3, or 4. May/
June. Found from New Eng-
land to North Dakota, southward to Texas.

P. multiflorum: 2½ feet.
Stiffly arching, leafy stems,
the leaves 2 to 6 inches long,
turning yellow in fall. Fragrant, greenish-white bells,
½ inch long, hang beneath
the leaves. May. Black or
purple berries in fall. From
Europe and Asia.

Polygonum

Family: *Polygonaceae*
(Buckwheat).

Common name: Knotweed.

Propagation: Seed gathered
and sown in fall or sow in
spring at 65 degrees. Directions for *P. nutans*, see
TYPHA.

Division in spring.

Rooting stems at nodes.

Cuttings in summer.

Culture: Sun. Enriched sandy soil for all except *P. nutans* (for which see below). Prune *P. aubertii* to the ground each year if necessary; the flowering season will only be delayed a bit. *P. nutans* may be easily transplanted from the field by gathering seed or separating the root-stock which is usually rooted all along the stem wherever it lies in the mud.

Use: Large rock garden. Ground cover. Water or bog ornamental (*P. nutans*). Fast-growing vine for screen or arbor (*P. aubertii*).

Species and varieties:

P. affine: 9 to 18 inches. Leaves, nearly evergreen, arranged in mostly basal tufts, 2 to 4 inches long, toothed, deep green, turning bronze in winter. Deep pink to rosy-red flowers in erect, dense spikes. August/October. Var. "Darjeeling Red." Himalayan.

P. aubertii (Silver Lace or China Fleece Vine): Fast-growing, hardy vine, usually to 10 feet a season. Heart-shaped leaves, shiny, wavy-edged, 1½ to 2½ inches long. Fragrant, creamy to greenish-white, tiny flowers in frothy, long clusters. June to frost. Clings to any support but will not injure wooden structures.

P. nutans (syn. *P. amphibium*) Water Lady's Thumb. Water Pepper: Prostrate stems to 3 feet or more long, covered with pointed, oval leaves, 2 to 5 inches long. Erect flowering spike to 1½ inches high, rises from the leaf clusters, forming a dense, cylindrical head of small, pink flowers. June/September. The seeds are good duck food. Found at the water's edge and shallows of streams and ponds of the northern states, including the Rockies, from plains to 8,000 feet.

P. vaccinifolium: Spreading, prostrate, leafy, branching stems, 2 to 4 feet long. Shiny, oval leaves, ½ inch long, turn red in fall. Upright flowering stems, 6 to 9 inches high, bearing spikes of bright rose-pink flowers. August/September. Himalayan.

Potentilla

Family: *Rosaceae* (Rose).

Common name: Cinquefoil. Fivefingers.

Propagation: Sow in fall or spring at 45 degrees; germination in 10 days. Alpine and shrubby species, sow in fall ——or for spring-sown seed, stratification and cold treatment is necessary.

Division in spring.

Cuttings of shrubby types in late summer.

Layering of trailing runners (will root at the nodes).

Culture: Sun. Sandy to average soil (very tolerant and undemanding). Shearing after the main flowering season is over will induce bloom later in the season. Space plants 6 inches apart for dwarfs, 12 to 18 inches apart for the others, except the shrubby species which should be treated as small shrubs.

Use: Border. Cut flower. Rock garden. Low hedge. Wild garden. Ground cover.

Species and varieties:

P. alpestris: 6 to 12 inches. Mound habit. Yellow flowers with darker centers, 1 inch across, in July.

P. argyrophylla: 1½ feet. Silver foliage. Yellow to amber flowers, 1 inch across. Himalayan. Var. "*atrosanguinea*," red or purple flowers.

P. aurea: 6 inches. Free flowering. Yellow flowers, ½ inch across, having dark bases.

P. eriocarpa: 1 to 2 feet. Alpine. Stemless, cup-shaped yellow flowers. June/October.

P. filipes (Slimstem Cinquefoil): Pubescent (hairy) foliage, basal leaves. Flowers in open clusters, yellow or orange, ½ to 1 inch across. Commonest species in the Rockies.

P. fruticosa (Yellow Rose. Shrubby Cinquefoil. Butter-cup Shrub): 2 to 5 feet. Pinnate compound, semi-evergreen leaves. Shredding bark on stems. Golden flowers, solitary or in loose terminal clusters. June/July the main flowering period. Found at moist sites from Alaska to the Dakotas. Var. "Katherine Dykes"; "Snow-flake," semidouble; "Gold Drop"; "Sutter's Gold."

P. glaucophylla (Blueleaf Cinquefoil): 6 to 8 inches. Glaucous, basal leaves. Yellow flowers in loose, open, terminal clusters. Rocky Mountain species found in limy soil, from valley to alpine meadows.

P. hirta pedata: 1¼ feet. Citron-yellow flowers all summer. Very free flowering.

P. hybrida "Mons. Rouil-liard," 1½ feet, crimson-maroon flowers edged with yellow; "Gibson's Scarlet," large red flowers in June/August; "Lady Rolleston," orange flowers, 1½ to 2 inches across, June/September.

P. megalantha: 12 inches high. Yellow-flowered Japanese species.

P. nepalensis (Nepal Cinque-foil): 2 feet. Hairy foliage. Red flowers, 1 inch across. July to frost. Var. "Miss Wilmot" or "*willmottiae*," sprawling habit, 12 inches high by 2½ feet wide, magenta-rose flowers with darker centers, ½ to 1 inch across; "Roxana," 1½ feet, orange-scarlet.

P. nitida: 4 inches. Mat-forming. Silvery leaves. Flowers vary from rose, pink, or white. Give this a rocky site and stone mulch.

P. palustris: The only red-flowering species native to the Rockies. You can't mistake it.

P. rupestris warrenii: 2 feet. Upright habit. Strawberry-like leaves. Bright yellow flowers all summer if the faded blooms are removed. Blossoms do not open til midday.

Potentilla nepalensis will-mottiae, Nepal Cinquefoil

P. tidentata (Wineleaf Cinquefoil): 6 to 12 inches. Woody stemmed alpine creeper with shiny, toothed, evergreen leaves that turn bronze-red in fall. White flowers, ¼ inch across, in flat-topped clusters. June/August. Very tolerant and mat-forming, it is excellent for the rock garden or as a ground cover.

P. verna (Spring Cinquefoil) 6 inches. Dark green, creeping cushions. Flowers in clusters, golden-yellow, ¼ inch across, all summer. Ground cover and rockery.

Poterium

(see SANGUISORBA) ....

Primula

Family: *Primulaceae* (Primrose).

Common name: Primrose. Cowslip.

Propagation: Fresh seed germinates best. Sow as soon as ripe. Spring sowing will require a 3 - or 4-week period of freezing and thawing. Remove to 45 to 55 degrees, germination will follow within 4 weeks, according to species.

Division after flowering.

Creeping rootstocks.

Culture: Shade. Rich, humusy soil, incorporate peat and well-dried manure. Moist, especially when in bloom. Cool. Mulch with pine needles and leaf mold. Alpine species prefer a gritty, limy soil and a stony mulch to keep the roots cool and moist. Space plants according to width of leaf mass instead of height of flowering stem. Most effective in masses.

Use: Border. Rock garden. Cut flower. Naturalize beside water and in woodland.

Species and varieties:

P. alpicola (Moonlight Primrose): 1½ feet. Similar to the candelabra type but only one whorl of flowers on the stem. Flowers, nodding, fragrant, soft cream to sulphur-yellow. Very moist to boggy conditions. Var. *"alba"* white; *"violacea,"* deep velvety violet.

P. auricula (Eyed Primrose): 6 to 8 inches. Alpine. Rosettes of thick, evergreen leaves, often mealy or felted. Umbels of fragrant flowers in various colors, all eyed. Seed slow to germinate, usually not until the second year.

P. beesiana: 1½ to 2 feet. Candelabra type, 5 to 7 whorls of flowers on the stem. Velvety purple to rose-purple flowers with yellow eye. May/June. Asiatic species. Deep-rooted, needs deep watering.

P. bulleyana (Chinese Mountain Primrose): 2 feet. Candelabra. Whorled flowers, deep yellow to apricot-yellow, 1 inch across, open over a long season. May/June. Wet conditions. Dormant by fall.

P. burmanica: 2 feet. Similar to *P. beesiana* but blooms earlier and has larger flowers. Rose-purple to deep purple flowers with golden eye. One of the easiest of candelabra type to grow.

P. capitata: 1 to 1½ feet. Himalayan species with dense heads of blue to purple bells, ½ inch across. Very like *P. denticulata* but blooms in June/July and tolerates drier conditions. Var. "Mooreana."

P. chionantha: 9 to 20 inches. Large leaves dusted underneath with a yellow farina. Umbels of fragrant, white flowers atop mealy stems. April/May.

P. chungensis: 2 feet. Pale orange to yellow flowers in terminal umbels (smaller than *P. bulleyana*). Chinese.

P. cortusoides: 9 inches. Long petioled leaves, deeply scalloped, in an upstanding cluster around hairy flower scapes. Loose umbels of rose flowers with cleft petals. June/July. Hardy alpine from Siberia. Keep moist during the growing season but not boggy.

P. denticulata (Indian Primrose): 12 inches. Small pale violet flowers in dense globular clusters, often appear before the wooly leaves. Blooms very early, but the late snows will not injure the blossoms. Himalayan alpine. Var. *"alba,"* white form; *"casmiriana,"* deep violet to lilac-rose with yellow throat; "ruby," rose, tinged lilac.

P. elatior (Oxlip): 8 inches. Small, tubular, sulphur-yellow flowers, to 1 inch long, in umbels. April/May. Wild gardens. Native from Europe to Iran.

P. farinosa (Bird's Eye Primrose): 12 inches. Mealy-leaved alpine, rosette habit. Leaves about 5 inches long, silvery farinose under. Umbels of lilac-purple flowers with yellow throat, rarely white. From the wet meadows of Europe. Not an easy type to grow.

P. florindae: 2½ to 4 feet. Long-stemmed, broad leaves. Numerous, nodding, bell-shaped flowers in large terminal umbels, vary from cream, apricot, or bright yellow. July/August. Slow to start in spring. Loves very wet sites (will even grow in an inch or so of water). From China.

P. frondosa: 6 inches. Whitish foliage. Flowers rose-lilac to reddish-purple, yellow-eyed.

P. helodoxa: 2 feet. Candelabra form with 5 to 7 tiers of flowers, golden-yellow. April/May. Wet to boggy conditions. A difficult plant to grow. Mulch well over winter.

P. hirsuta (syn. *P. rubra*): 4 inch high alpine. Rosette habit. Rose, lilac with white centers or white flowers, 1 inch across, in umbels. Easiest of alpines to grow. Requires a stony mulch.

P. integrifolia: 2 inches. Rose-lilac flowers, ¾ to 1 inch across in three-flowered umbels. From the Alps. Rocky site.

P. japonica (Japanese Primrose): 2 feet. Candelabra type. Up to 5 tiers of flowers on a stem, may be white, pink, or purple with yellow eyes, 1 inch across. Each whorl opens one tier at a time. May/July. Self-sows, which makes this one of the easiest to establish. Var. "Postford's White"; "Millar's Crimson."

P. juliae: 12 inches. Matting; spreads by creeping rootstocks. Small leaves have red petioles. Solitary, almost stemless, rose, red, or red-purple flowers with yellow eyes, ¾ to 1 inch across. Often blooms before the leaves develop. April/May. From the Caucasus. Tolerant of drier conditions.

P. nutans: 9 inches. Upstanding, narrow, hairy foliage. Large lavender-blue, drooping flowers in dense umbels. Chinese. Blooms the second year from seed.

P. parryi (Alpine Primrose): 6 to 18 inches. Basal rosette of erect, smooth, fleshy,

green leaves to a foot in length. Large, blood-red flowers with yellow eyes, 3 to 12 flowers, in umbels. July/August. Native to the Rocky Mountains. This needs moisture when in bloom, gritty soil and a stone mulch. Dry summers are natural and a winter snow cover imperative.

P. polyneura (syn. *P. veitchii*): 12 inches. Spreading, woodland form. Hairy, geranium-like leaves with wooly petioles. Flowers in 1 or 2 whorls, deep rose, purple, or red with orange or yellow eyes. Easy from seed, needs good drainage, does not require a great deal of moisture, and is slow to appear in spring.

P. pulverulenta: 2 feet. Candelabra type that is easy to grow. Tiered whorls of flowers usually purple but may be red or red-purple with deeper eyes. Asiatic. Requires moist conditions. Var. "Bartley Strain," 3 feet, rose and pink; "Mrs. R. V. Berkley," with orange eyes.

P. sieboldii: 9 inches. Woodland type with underground creeping roots. Long petioled, crinkly, oval leaves. Flowers in umbels, white, rose, or purple with white eyes, 1½ inches across, notched petals. June (dormant by August). Japanese. Hardy and more tolerant of dry conditions than most primroses. Slow to appear in spring. Very easy and probably the most permanent of all; it flowers the second year from seed.

P. sikkimensis: 1½ feet. Fragrant, yellow, drooping flowers. June/July. Bog plant. Mulch to prevent it

from being heaved out of the ground in winter.

P. veris (syn. *P. officinalis*) English Cowslip: 9 inches. Fragrant, drooping, bell-shaped flowers in loose umbels, deep yellow with orange eyes. May. Light shade. For rockery or wild garden. European.

P. vulgaris (syn. *P. acaulis*) Common or English Primrose: 6 inches. Tufts of rough, dark green leaves. Solitary stem with single pale to sulphur-yellow flowers, sometimes blue or purple. April/May. Var. "*hortensis* Mother's Day," extra large flowers to 2 inches across, all colors.

P. vulgaris elatior (Polyanthus Primrose): Hybrid. Clusters of varied-colored flowers, 1½ inches across, on 1-foot stems rising from rosettes of dark green, crinkled leaves. May/June. Often referred to as a separate species *P. polyanthus*. Var. "Gold Laced"; "Festival Strain"; "Giant Bouquet";

"Pacific Strain" and "Munstead Strain."

Pulsatilla

(syn. *ANEMONE pulsatilla*)

Family: *Ranunculaceae* (Buttercup).

Common name: European Pasque Flower.

Propagation: Sow in spring at 65 degrees, removing the feathery tails first. Germination in 3 weeks. Or gather when ripe and sow immediately. The seed must be fresh, as it loses its viability rapidly, which probably has occurred if purchased seed fails to germinate for you.

Root cuttings.

Divide in spring.

Culture: Sun or part shade. Light, sandy to gritty, limy soil. Once established, they do not like to be disturbed.

Pulsatilla vulgaris, European Pasque Flower

Plant in groups, 6 inches apart.

Use: Rock gardens. Naturalize.

Species and varieties:

P. vernalis: 6 inches. Evergreen tufts of deep-cut basal leaves. Flower petals white or tinged violet inside, covered with brownish, silky down on the outside. April/May. An excellent rock-garden plant. Late spring snows will not injure the flowers. Alpine.

P. vulgaris: 9 to 12 inches. Violet, blue or reddish-purple flowers in May. Charming wooly buds open to a 2-inch blossom. The flowers pre-ceed the silky. fern-like leaves. Attractive feathery seed pods. Var. *"alba"* creamy-white; "Budapest." The varieties come fairly true from seed.

Pyrethrum

(syn. *CHRYSANTHEMUM coccineum*) ....

Family: *Compositae* (Daisy).

Propagation: Seed must be fresh. Sow in spring at 65 to 70 degrees. Germination in 7 to 14 days. Seed from double or named varieties not always true to type.

Divide every three of four years in spring.

Culture: Sun. Average garden soil, well drained. Plant in groups or as edging, dwarfs 6 inches apart, the others 12 inches apart.

Use: Border. Rock garden. Edging. Cut flower.

Species and varieties:

P. aureum (Golden Feather): 12 inches. A good edging plant with yellow foliage. Blooms the first year from seed. Var. "Golden Moss," 9 inches, forming a golden-leaved, mossy mound; *"selaginoides,"* 6-inch golden variety, does not bloom the first year.

P. roseum (Painted Daisy. Colored Marguerite): 2 to 3 feet. Bushy habit. Basal, fern-like leaves. Single, long-stemmed flowers in shades of red, pink or white, 3 inches or more across. Blooms from May on through the summer if faded flowers are removed. Native to Persia and southwest Asia. Var. *"album,"* single white; *"atrosanguineum,"* dark crimson; "James Kelway," scarlet hybrid; also double forms.

Ramonda

Family: *Gesneriaceae* (Gesneria).

Common name: Rosette Mullein.

Propagation: Seed sown in fall. Spring-sown seed requires stratification and prechilling treatment. If this is not done, the seed will not germinate until the following spring. Sprouts at cool 45 degrees. Winter the seedlings in a shaded cold frame the first year.

Self-sows.

Division in spring.

Culture: Shade. Peaty loam on the acid side. Perfect drainage is necessary. Moist, but avoid letting water stand in the center of the clump or it may rot. A stone mulch is essential. Hardy but benefits from winter mulch of leaves, snow or evergreen boughs. Rather difficult but worth the trouble.

Use: Rock garden. Rock crevices.

Species:

R. myconi (syn. *R. pyrenaica*): 3- to 6-inch high alpine. Flat rosette. Leaves are conspicuously haired and veined on their upper surfaces, toothed edges. Five-petaled, violet flowers with orange eyes (resembles its relative, the african violet). May/July.

R. nathaliae (Serbian Queen); Flat rosettes of hairy, oval leaves. Clusters of four-petaled, lavendar-blue flowers, yellow eyed. June/July. Balkan.

Ranunculus

Family: *Ranunculaceae* (Crowfoot).

Common name: Buttercup. Crowfoot. Ranunculus.

Propagation: Seed must be fresh. Sow in fall or spring at 45 degrees. *R. asiaticus* requires 65 degrees with germination occuring in 15 days.

Root cuttings.

Division in spring or after flowering.

Culture: Sun or part shade. Well-drained, sandy soil with humus added. Cool. Moist. Space 6 to 8 inches apart in groups of four or more. (I have purposely omitted the weedy and invasive members of this genus, such as *R. repens*.)

R. asiaticus will not withstand our frigid winters, and so the tooth-like, tuberous roots must be dug and stored in a cool, frost-free place during the cold months. Set out in spring when danger of frost is past, 6 to 8 inches apart, 2 inches deep, with teeth pointing down. Due to our shorter growing season, I prefer to start early by planting in flats containing a mix of equal parts perlite, vermiculite, and sphagnum and then transplanting the started plant to the garden bed.

For *R. aquatilis*, which is usually field collected, establish the division or cutting in a pot submerged in a pan of water before setting in its proper position in the shallow water of pond or stream.

Use: Border. Rock garden. Water garden. Excellent cut flower.

Species and varieties:

R. acris flore-pleno (Soldier's Buttons. Butter Rose): 2 to 2½ foot flowering stems topped with bright yellow, double flowers. May/August.

R. adoneus (Alpine or Mountain Buttercup): 4 to 12 inches. Leaves deeply divided into linear lobes. Stems rise in clusters with 1 to 3 bright yellow flowers, ½ to 1 inch across, on a stem. Underside of sepals often purplish. July/August. Found in the Rockies of Wyoming and Colorado only at high altitudes, 9,000 to 11,000 feet. Give it a rocky site and stone chip mulch.

R. asiaticus (Turban or Persian Buttercup): 1½ to 2 feet. Bright green, ferny leaves. Mature bulbs bear up to 70 flowering stems. Flowers are usually double, bright yellow with hairy sepals, 1 to 4 inches across. Var. "*superbissimus*" has larger flowers; "Florentine Strain" large flowers in pastel to brilliant shades; "Palestine Strain," large double flowers resemble double roses, yellow, orange, scarlet, pink, or white. This is a tender perennial and must be handled as you do gladiolus.

R. aquatilis (Water Buttercup): Actually grows in the water, the flowers being the only part of the plant on the surface. Very finely divided leaves. Shiny white flowers, ½ inch across. May/August. Found in the Rockies as well as in most of the northern hemisphere. Easily collected from the field for naturalistic plantings in pond or reservoir; it is excellent duck food in case you would like to entice a wild family or two.

R. glaberrimus (Sagebrush Buttercup): 2 to 6 feet. The only species having both entire and divided leaves on the same plant. One to 3 flowers on a stem, shiny yellow fading white, single. One of the first wild flowers to be seen in spring, blooms from March on, depending

on elevation. Found in the Rocky Mountains from Montana to California. Sunny, rocky site. If happy, it self-sows.

R. glacialis: 4 to 6 inches. Divided grey-green leaves. Large satiny flowers vary from pink to white, often tinted purple or open white and fade to pink and red. Requires wet, rather heavy, stony soil beside stream or pond.

R. gramineus: 9 to 12 inches. Open heads of large pale yellow flowers, to 1 inch across. May/June. Greyish, grassy, basal leaves.

Rodgersia

Family: *Saxifragaceae* (Saxifrage).

Propagation: Seed sown in fall or early spring at 40 to 45 degrees.

Division in spring.

Culture: Shade. Moist, peaty soil. Shelter from wind.

Use: Shaded border. North of buildings. Woodland garden.

Species:

All resemble astilbe and are from China or Japan.

R. pinnata: 3½ feet. Variable seed. Showy terminal clusters of reddish flowers.

R. sambucifolia: 2½ feet. Wide, five-lobed leaves. Small white flowers in terminal clusters.

R. tabularis: 3 feet. Large leaves measure to 20 inches across, turn bronze in fall. Clusters of numerous, small white flowers.

Rudbeckia

Family: *Compositae* (Daisy).

Common name: Cone Flower.

Propagation: Seed sown at 65 degrees, germination in 6 to 20 days. Sown in April, will bloom the first season.

Division in spring.

Cuttings.

Culture: Sunny exposure but will tolerate some shade. Average soil. Space 1 to 1½ feet apart, set out in groups of not less than three. Divide every 3 or 4 years.

Use: Border. Wild garden. Cut flower.

Species and varieties:

R. nitida "Herbstonne": 4 feet. Single flower with primrose-yellow ray florets, greenish disc florets.

R. purpurea (see ECHINACEA).

R. speciosa (syn. *R. newmanni*): 2 feet. Flowers 3 inches across, rays yellow to orange with black disc. August/September.

R. tetra gloriosa (Gloriosa Daisy): Hybrid. Sometimes biennial in habit. 2 to 3 feet. Very large flowers to 7 inches across, may be yellow to mahogany or range in bicolors of golden-orange and gold, mahogany and gold, all having dark discs. June/

Rudbeckia tetra gloriosa, Gloriosa Daisy

August. There is a double
variety, but the flowers are
not as large.

Sagina

Family: *Carophyllaceae*
(Pink).

Common name: Pearlwort.

Propagation: Sow in spring
at 45 degrees.

Division: cut out a section
and plant as you would sod.

Culture: Sun or partial shade.
Good humusy soil. Adequate
moisture. If it humps up (and
it will), beat it down with
the back of your spade or
cut out a section.

Use: Ground cover. Between
paving stones of walk or
patio. Do not allow to enter
the rockery; it is too invasive.

Species:

S. glabra aurea (Scotch
Moss): Creeping habit.
Mossy, golden foliage. White
flowers in August.

S. subulata (Irish Moss):
Forms a dense green mat.
Foliage has the apperance of
moss. White flowers.

Salvia

Family: *Labiatae* (Mint).

Common name: Sage.

Propagation: Sow in spring
at 65 degrees, germination in
5 days.

Self-sows.

Division in spring as soon
as growth appears.

Cuttings in July/August.

Layering.

Culture: Sun. Sandy, limy
soil. Drought resistant. Cut
back after flowering for neatness; they rarely bloom later
on. Space 10 to 12 inches
apart for most species, but
allow at least a 2-foot perimeter around *S. sclarea* and
S. haematodes which take
on the proportions of
medium-sized shrubs.

Use: Border. Cut flower.

Species and varieties:

S. argentea (Silver Salvia):
Biennial. 2 feet. Ornamental
silvery foliage, large downy
leaves to 8 inches long in
basal rosettes. Color variable
in flowers, usually bluish-
white but may also be white,
yellowish, or pale rose.

S. azurea: 3 to 4 feet. Slender
habit (may need staking).
Whorls of pale blue or white
flowers, ½ inch long. July to
frost. From the southeastern
states and not completely
hardy in the highlands in an
open winter. Var. "*grandiflora*," to 5 feet, hairy leaves,
gentian blue flowers.

S. haematodes: Biennial, but
self-sows freely. 3 feet.
Silvery, lilac-blue flowers in
large panicles on branching
stems. May/June. Large,
coarse basal leaves.

S. juriscii: 12-inch-high,
matting clumps of feathery,
hairy leaves. Arching, branching stems carrying long

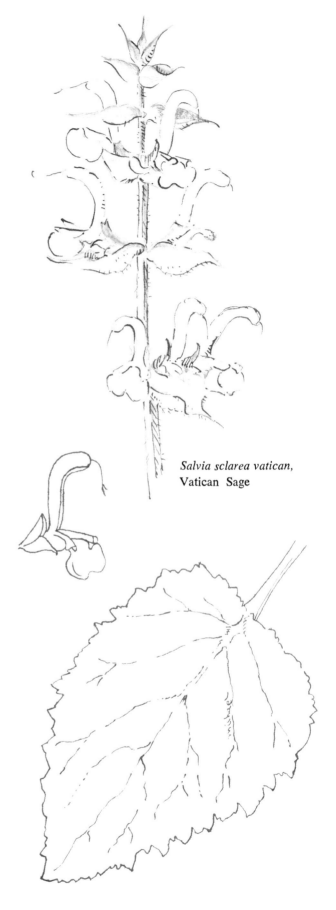

Salvia sclarea vatican,
Vatican Sage

racemes of small mauve to violet flowers. June/August. Not too large for the rock garden. Balkans.

S. officinalis (Garden Sage): 1½ to 2 feet. Spikes of fragrant, violet-blue flowers (sometimes red or white). June/July. Leaves (fresh or dried) are a common seasoning used in cooking.

S. pitcheri: 4 feet. Pale blue flowers, 1 inch across, in spike-like racemes. July/August. May need staking. Native to the dry plains of the midwestern states.

S. pratensis (Meadow Sage): 2½ feet. Mottled leaves. Whorls of flowers, variable in color, usually violet-blue but may also be red to rose-pink or white. May/August. European. Var. "*rosea*," rose flowers; "*tenorii*," deep blue, free flowering.

S. sclarea (Clary): Biennial. 3 feet. Large wooly leaves. Blue and white flowers. July/August. A very dramatic accent to the border, but be warned——give it enough room. Var. "*vatican*" (Vatican Sage), lavender or white flowers dominated by pinkish leaf bracts, June/July; "*turkestanica*" (Pink Turkestanica) bright bluish-pink and white flowers with large pink bracts. They all self-sow abundantly; even though short-lived, there are always new plants coming along. Transplant where you want them. (See illustration, p. 28.)

Sanguinaria

Family: *Papaveraceae* (Poppy).

Common name: Bloodroot.

Propagation: Fresh seed germinates readily; if possible, sow as soon as seeds ripen, and they should germinate the following spring. Spring-sown seeds require stratification and a period of cold (and even that may not help).

Self-sows.

Root cuttings should be taken in fall or earliest spring before top growth starts. You will need to mark the location beforehand, because the plant will be dormant and impossible to find, otherwise.

Division is late summer or fall when the plant becomes dormant.

Culture: Sun in spring and shade in summer. Light, neutral to limy soil with generous amounts of peat and leaf mold added. Moist in spring, dry in summer. Pine needle mulch. Space 6 inches apart, setting out in colonies.

Use: Shaded rock garden. Woodland garden. Beneath trees and shrubs.

Species and varieties:

S. canadensis: 9 inches high. Mat forming. Blue-green, deep lobed, basal leaves, as wide as the plant is high. Solitary, white flowers (often having a pinkish tint) with a golden center. April/May. Blooms often before the leaves have unfolded. Eastern and Great Lakes states.

Var. "*Multiplex*," double-flowered form, sterile and must be propagated by division.

Sanguisorba

(syn. *POTERIUM*) ....

Family: *Rosaceae* (Rose).

Common name: Burnet.

Propagation: Seed gathered and sown in fall, or may be sown in spring at 45 to 65 degrees (temperatures, cool or warm, do not seem to be a factor). Sow thickly, as the viability of any one lot of seed appears to be quite low. The freshness of the seed may also be important in that it does not remain viable for very long.

Division after flowering.

Culture: Sun or light to heavy shade. Light, sandy soil with peat added, well drained. Moist. Remove the spent blossoms, as this self-sows a bit too readily.

Use: Border. Woodland. Water's edge ornamental. Container.

Species:

S. canadensis: 1 -to 5-foot flowering stems with terminal, 6-inch-long, cylindrical heads of small white flowers. July/September. Mostly basal, pinnate leaves made up of 13 to 21 leaflets (resembles the mountain ash). An ornamental for the water garden, this needs soil on the acid side, damp to boggy. Manitoba to eastern Canada.

S. minor (syn. *POTERIUM sanguisorba*) Small or Salad Burnet. Pimpinelle: 8 to 12 inches. Rosettes of deeply toothed, compound leaves. Leaves are used in salads and for seasoning cream cheese, as you would use chives. Long-stemmed, thimble-like, pinkish-white flowers.

S. officinalis (Garden Burnet): 2 - to 5-foot flowering stalks with terminal, 12 inch long flowering spikes of deep purple to reddish-brown flowers. European.

Santolina

Family: *Compositae* (Daisy).

Common name: Lavender Cotton.

Propagation: Sow in spring at 45 degrees, germination in 9 days.

Cuttings taken with a heel in July after new growth has firmed.

Culture: Sun. Light, average soil. Dry. Requires pruning every so often to keep it within bounds (unless you've placed it in an area where it doesn't matter). Space plants 18 inches apart enmass or for hedging at 2 feet apart. The woody stems sprawl along the ground. (See illustration p. 30.)

Use: Low hedge. Border.

Species:

S. chamaecyparissus: 1½ to 2 feet. Spreading, woody-stemmed subshrub. Distinctively fragrant, frosty-appearing foliage; the fern-like leaves have a felty texture. Sweet-scented, small, button-like, yellow flowers. July/August. Although this is originally from the Mediterranean, I have found it to be completely hardy.

Saponaria

Family: *Caryophyllaceae* (Pink).

Common name: Soapwort.

Propagation: Seed sown in fall or spring, 45 to 60 degrees; germination in 10 days.

Culture: Sun. Light, sandy to average garden loam. Very tolerant plant. Tap rooted; should be moved while it is young.

Use: Border. Rock garden. Rock crevice. Ground cover.

Species and varieties:

S. officinalis (Common Soapwort. Bouncing Bet): 1 to 2 feet. Spreads by underground stems but is not weedy. Fragrant, pink or white flowers, 1 inch across, in dense clusters. May/September. European. A double pink variety is an improvement over the type.

S. ocymoides (Creeping Soapwort): 6 to 12 inches. Trailing stems will cover a perimeter of up to 3 feet. Hairy foliage, dark green, oval leaves. Small phlox-like flowers, rose-purple with purple calyx, in loose flat clusters. May/June. Var.

"*splendens*," larger, bright pink flowers; "*alba*," white. Prune after flowering to retain a neat outline.

Saxifraga

Family: *Saxifragaceae* (Saxifrage).

Common name: Saxifrage. Rockfoil.

Propagation: Sow in fall. Spring sowing requires a prechilling period in the refrigerator for several weeks, remove to 45 degrees; germination will begin within 18 days. They are all very slow growing, and so I leave the seedlings in a flat for a year and do not put into the garden until the second spring.

Offsets rooted like cuttings.

Division of tufts in spring or after flowering.

Culture: Encrusted types prefer sun and stony, limy soils. Mossy forms need a richer soil and shade with adequate moisture all summer. Give all mountain moraine conditions; gritty, stony, alkaline soils and moisture are their natural habitat. Most are quite small but spreading, plant 4 to 8 inches apart in groups.

Use: Rock garden. Wild garden. House, greenhouse or outdoor pot culture (good drainage an absolute necessity).

Species and varieties:

S. aizoides (Arctic Rockfoil): Trailing, matting habit. Narrow, green, succulent

leaves. Tiny starry flowers, orange or yellow, dotted red, solitary or a few on 7-inch branching stems. June/July. Shady, rocky, moist site beside stream or pond.

S. aizoon: 6 inches. Rosettes of encrusted, white-edged, narrow, spatulate, evergreen leaves. Sprays of small, white, often spotted red or purple, flowers, ½ inch across in June. Var. "*minor*," densely silvered rosettes, creamy-white flowers; "*rosea*," rose-pink flowers fading paler.

S. aquatica: Leaves to 2 feet long. White flowers, ¾ inch across. July/August.

S. arguta (Brook Saxifrage): Basal leaves, large, round, and coarsely toothed. White flowers with a few yellow dots, 1½ inch across, in open panicles on long stems. July/August. Rocky Mountains.

S. bronchillis (Yellowdot Saxifrage): 6 inches. Trailing, matting habit. Spiny-tipped, linear leaves. Starry, white flowers, spotted red-purple. July/August. Shaded streamside in the Rockies.

S. burseriana: 1 to 2 inches high. Mat forming. Hummocks of prickly, narrow, blue-grey leaves. Numerous, solitary, white flowers, 1 to 1½ inches wide, on 1 to 2 inch high reddish stems. April/June. Rock-loving type, likes to cling to porous rocks. Var. "*sulphurea*," yellow flowers.

S. cochlearis (Alpine Rockfoil): Tufts of encrusted, spoon-shaped leaves. Starry, white flowers, ¾ inch across, in loose, onesided panicles

atop stems 6 to 9 inches high, in May.

S. cotyledon: 1½ to 2 feet. Large rosettes of broad, white-encrusted leaves. Large panicles of fragrant, white flowers (often tinted or veined pink) in June. As with sempervirens, the flowering rosette dies after blooming.

S. cunefolia: 4 inches. Spreading, dark green rosettes. Profuse small white flowers.

S. decipiens (syn. *S. rosacea*): Mossy type, 5 to 6 inches high. Jewel-like, white or pink flowers, ½ to 1 inch across, rise from bright green rosettes in June. Prefers high shade. Var. "Purple Mantle," 12 inches, deep purple flowers.

S. granulata (Meadow Saxifrage): 20 inches. White, nodding flowers, 1 inch wide, in May. Stems are bulbous at their bases.

S. hostii (Silver Rockfoil): 1 to 2 feet. Encrusted, strap-shaped, toothed leaves. Flattish panicles of creamy-white flowers (rarely dotted purple or red), ½ inch across.

S. lingulata: 9 inches. Encrusted, linear, rather erect leaves. Erect, white panicles on leafy stems. June

S. x macnabiana (Spotted Rockfoil): 12 inches. Large rosettes of long stiff leaves having encrustations of lime on their edges. Solitary flower spike is covered with white flowers, often spotted or tinted pink. May/June. This is a hybrid (*S. cotyledon* x *S. lingulata*).

S. muscoides: 4 inches. Mossy type. Spreading tufts of

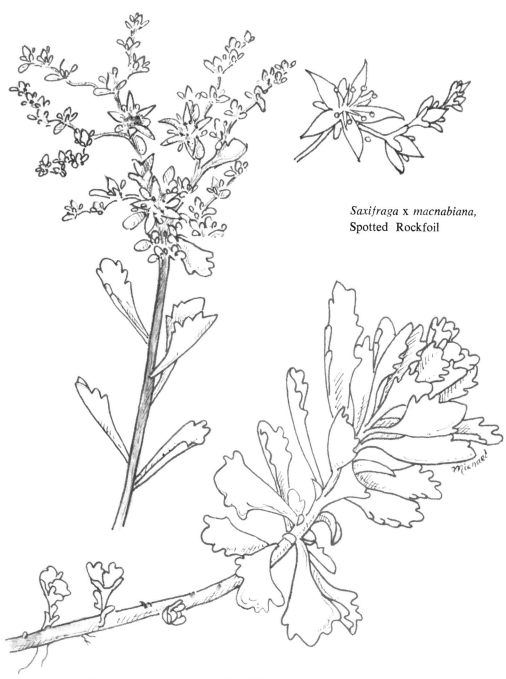

propagated. Prefers shade and woodland soil.

S. virginiensis: 12 inches. Mossy type with round, scallop-edged, dark green leaves that turn red in fall. Very tiny white flowers in dense heads on thick hairy stems. May/June. Native to the eastern states. Sun or shade. Easily transplanted anytime.

Saxifraga x *macnabiana*,
Spotted Rockfoil

Scabiosa

Family: *Dipsaceae* (Teasel).

Common name: Pincushion Flower. Blue Scabious. Blue Bonnet. Mourning Bride.

Propagation: Seed sown when ripe in fall. Spring sowing at 65 degrees; germination in 9 days. From a late March sowing, there is some bloom in August.

Division in spring. Save the outer portions of the clump and discard the woody center.

Culture: Sun. Sandy, limy, well-drained soil. Moist and cool. Set out in groups, spacing plants 8 to 12 inches apart.

Use: Border. Rock garden for the dwarfs. Cut flower.

Species and varieties:

S. caucasica: 2 feet. Mostly basal leaves, 6 to 8 inches long and narrow; leaves on the stems are finely divided. Pale blue flowers in flat heads, 3 inches across, atop stiff stems. June/September. Native to the Caucasus. Many of the garden varieties originate from this species; a few

minute leaves. Tiny spring flowers, ¼ inch across, may be white, yellow or red.

S. oppositifolia (Purple or Twinleaf Saxifrage): 2 inches high and mat forming. Tiny, ¼ inch long, hairy-edged, round, fleshy leaves (exactly opposite each other) form tiny rosettes along a rather woody stem. Single, cup-like flower to a stem, pinkish-purple to wine-colored,

rarely white. July/August. Alpine species indigenous to both the Rocky Mountains and the European Alps. Rather difficult to domesticate. Requires humusy yet stony soil and must have adequate moisture, at least in spring.

S. rhomboidea (Diamondleaf Saxifrage): White flowers clustered head-like, atop leafless stems, 2 to 12 inches high,

rising out of rather large basal clump of leaves. July/August. Common to the Rockies.

S. umbrosa (London Pride): 1¼ feet. Spreading rosettes of thick, shiny, dark green leaves, 2½ inches long, reddish undersides. Profuse pink or white flowers, to ⅓ inch across, in loose umbels. June/July. Easily

147

Scabiosa caucasica, Pincushion Flower "House's Novelty Mixture"

are "House's Novelty Mixture," a definite improvement, colors vary from blue and lavender to white, some fringed and ruffled, June to frost; "*alba,*" white form; "*goldingensis,*" deep lavender flowers; "*magnifica,*" bluish-lavender; "Clive Greaves," 2½ feet, large, rich mauve shade; "Miss Wilmott," white; "Blue Lady"; "Constancy," violet.

S. columbaria: 1½ feet. Branching habit. Grey-green, finely cut leaves. Flowers are more globular than flat, lilac or purple-blue, 1½ inches wide (also a pink form). July/August.

S. graminifolia (Grassleaf Scabiosa): 9 to 12 inches. Downy, silver-grey, grass-like foliage. Flowers appear in July, variable in color, pale mauve to violet-pink, rose or pale blue. Rock garden.

S. japonica: 2 feet. Finely cut leaves. Large, dark purple-blue flowers.

S. lucida: 6 to 12 inches. Rock plant that blooms all summer, rose-lilac or lilac-blue pincushion flowers.

S. ochroleuca: 2 feet. Greyish foliage. Primrose-yellow flowers like tiny 1 inch globes. June/September. Var. "Webbiana," cream-colored flowers.

S. rumelica: 2½ feet. Bushy habit. Profuse, globular, crimson flower.

Schizostylis

Family: *Iridaceae* (Iris).

Common name: Kaffir Lily. Crimson Flag.

Propagation: Seed sown warm, 65 to 70 degrees.

Division of rhizomatous clumps, 5 shoots to a division.

Culture: Sun or filtered shade. Sandy loam with peat added. Moist while actively growing. Set out when the soil has warmed. A tender sort that must be dug up and stored in fall or pot and it will bloom again during the winter in the house.

Use: Border. Long-lasting cut flower. Pot plant.

Species and varieties:

S. coccinea: 1½ to 3 feet. Gladiola-like leaves to 2 feet long. Spikes of tubular, scarlet flowers in autumn. Var. "*viscountess byng,*" satiny pink; "Mrs. Hegarty," rose-pink.

Scilla

Family: *Liliaceae* (Lily).

Common name: Squill. Wild Hyacinth.

Propagation: Seed sown when ripe or in very early spring; even so, spring seeding seldom germinates until very early the following year, often in February. Grow on undisturbed in the flat and winter in the cold frame the first year.

Bulb offsets, separate when foliage has matured.

Bulbs purchased for fall planting.

Culture: Sun or light shade. Light, sandy soil, Mix in a small quantity of bone meal and superphosphate before planting, if possible. Top dress in fall or spring with well-rotted manure. Set bulbs 2 to 3 inches deep in fall (as early as possible), 4 to 6 inches apart, in groups of at least a dozen or more. If not disturbed, colonies will form in about three years; once established, they require little or no additional care.

For winter forcing indoors, prepare as you would Narcissus (see above), in this case using 5 to 6 bulbs per 5-inch pot.

Use: Naturalize in woodland or wild garden. Rock garden. Cut flower. Ground cover under trees. Winter indoor pot plant.

Species and varieties:

S. bifolia (Two-leaved Squill): 6 to 8 inches. Gentian-blue, starry flowers, 1 inch across, in racemes of up to 8 flowers on a stem. March/April. Variations of this may also be white, violet-blue, or pale lavender-pink.

S. hispanica (syn. *S. campanulata*) Scotch Blue Bells. Spanish Blue Bell. Woods Hyacinth: 12 to 20 inches. Racemes of 12 or more flowers on a stem, nodding, ¾ inch long, usually dark blue but may also be white or rosy-pink. May. Vigorous, robust plant, most commonly grown of the genus. Var. "Excelsior," deep blue; "Rose Beauty"; "*Alba Maxima*," white.

S. nutans (syn. *S. nonscripta*) Common or English Blue

Bell. English Wood or Wild Hyacinth: 12 to 18 inches. Racemes of nodding bells, color varies from purplish-blue, violet-pink, or white. The bells are small and narrower than *S. hispanica*. May/June.

S. siberica (Forest Hyacinth. Siberian Squill): 3 to 9 inches. Pendulous bells in loose spikes, white, violet-pink, or violet-blue, 1 to 3 per stem. Var. "Spring Beauty" has dark blue stripes and is larger and more vigorous than the type; "*alba*," white form. Must have sun to bloom.

S. tubergiana: 9 inches. Pale blue flowers with a dark stripe, 4 or more bells to a stem, 3 or more stems to a bulb.

Scutellaria

Family: *Labiatae* (Mint).

Common name: Skullcap.

Propagation: Seed sown fall or spring, germination is slow and erratic. Alpine species require a period of pre-chilling if spring sown.

All self-sow but are not weedy.

Division in early spring.

Cuttings in June/July.

Culture: Sun or light shade. Humusy soil. Moist. Set out in colonies, spacing plants 6 inches apart except for *S. serrata* which needs about 10 to 12 inches of room.

Use: Border. Rock garden. Open woodland. Beside pool or stream.

Species:

S. alpina: 9 inches. Creeping habit. Violet and white flowers, 1 inch long, in dense terminal racemes. Also rare pink and white forms. Alpine.

S. augustifolia: 6 inches. Narrow leaves. Large, solitary, bright blue flowers, 1 inch long, in leaf axils. June/August. Bog plant of the Rocky Mountains.

S. baicalensis coelestina: 12 inches. Flowers, lavender-blue, 1 inch long, tube dilated upward and hood incurved. Late August/September.

S. galericulata (March Skullcap): 1 to 3 feet. Lance-shaped, toothed leaves on slender, square stems. Solitary, dull blue flowers in upper axils, ¾ inch long (rarely pink or white). June/August. Found throughout the Rockies in very wet sites, even shallow water.

S. indica japonica: 9 inches high. Neat shrubby habit. Grey-green leaves. Spikes of blue or lilac flowers.

S. integrifolia (Hyssop Skullcap): 6 to 18 inches. Narrow leaves. Solitary, violet-blue flowers, 1 inch long, one in each upper leaf axil, forming attractive terminal clusters. June/July. Native to eastern and central states.

S. orientalis: 6 inches. Spreading habit. Grey-green leaves. Spikes of yellow flowers, the lower lip purple or brown.

S. serrata (Showy Skullcap): 2 feet. Ovate leaves. Large purple-blue flowers in pairs at the branch tips. June. Found in open woodland in eastern and central states.

Sedum

Family: *Crassulaceae* (Orpine).

Common name: Stonecrop.

Propagation: Seed sown in late summer or spring at 65 degrees.

Division of crown in spring.

Cuttings root very easily at any time. Indeed, when pruning or thinning, care must be taken to pick up every portion cut off or it will root where it falls. Cuttings taken in spring are rooted with bottom heat.

Culture: Sun. Dry. Rocky, sandy, gritty soils. Space 4 to 8 inches apart for those of neat habit, allow to 10 inches for the trailers. Native species are easily collected in the field at any time.

Use: Rock garden or wall crevice. Ground cover. Wild garden.

Species and varieties:

S. acre (Goldmoss Sedum. Wall-pepper. Mossy Stonecrop): 2 to 4 inches. Spreading, mat-forming habit. Trailing, rooting stems having tiny, evergreen, pale green leaves, ¼ inch long. Tiny, bright golden-yellow flowers in terminal clusters in June. Be quite ruthless in pruning this for it will stray out-of-bounds. Var. "*aureum*" has bright yellow leaves in spring; "*minus*" is small and not as spreading.

S. albopilosum: 1½ feet. Pale, glaucous green leaves. Greenish-white flowers.

S. album (White Stonecrop): 6 inches. Creeping habit. Dense clumps of fleshy leaves (often reddish hue), ¼ to ½ inch long. White to pinkish-white flowers in flat heads in July. European.

S. aizoon (syn. *S. maximow-iczii*): 12 to 18 inches. Profuse yellow to orange flowers, ½ inch across, in August.

S. cauticola: 3 inches high. Trailing stems to 8 inches long. Round leaves. Rose-red flower heads on tip of each branch. July/August.

S. ewersii: 4 to 12 inches. Fleshy, blue-grey leaves on trailing stems. Pink to red flowers. August/October.

S. kamtschaticum: 6 to 9 inches. Erect habit. Toothed, dark green leaves, sometimes edged white. Orange-yellow flowers. July/August.

S. middendorfianum: 6 to 10 inches. Dense clumps of narrow, toothed leaves, to 2 inches long. Neat habit of growth. Siberian species with yellow flowers. July/August.

S. reflexum (Yellow Stonecrop. Stone Orpine): 6 to 12 inches high flower stems. Trailing, matting habit. Evergreen, linear leaves. Yellow flowers in July. Var. "*chameleon*," variegated leaves; "*elegant*," 8 inches,

upright habit, neat, grey cushion with yellow flowers in June/August.

S. rhodanthum (Red Orpine. Rosecrown): Erect habit. 6 to 15 inches high unbranching stems, topped with dense terminal cluster of rose flowers. June/August. Oblong, fleshy leaves, ½ to 1 inch long. Moist sites at high elevations, near timberline or above, in the Rocky Mountains from Montana to New Mexico.

S. selskianum (syn. *ella-combianum*): 4 to 9 inches. Cushion type with yellow flowers, ½ inch across, in August. Japanese.

S. sexangulace: 2 inches. An evergreen mat similar to *S. acre*. Bronze-green leaves. Yellow flowers in July.

S. sieboldi: Trailing stems to 9 inches long. Fleshy, round leaves, glaucous, grey-blue, edged in red. Flat clusters of pink flowers. August/October. Japanese.

S. spathulifolium: 4 inches. Rosettes of glaucous, blue-green to reddish-purple foliage; spoon-shaped, fleshy leaves. (Rather variable in foliage and form) Large heads of yellow flowers. June/August. Native to the Pacific coast from British Columbia to California, it is not absolutely hardy in this area and needs protection. Var. "Capa Blanca," 3 inches, leaves coated with a white farina, yellow flowers in May/June; "*purpureum*," purple leaves.

S. spectabile: 1 to 2 feet. Upright habit (will not spread). Large and showy

enough to hold its own in the border. Glaucous, light to greyish-green leaves, 3 inches long, obvate. Small, rose-pink flowers in flat cymes, 3 to 4 inches across. August/September. Japanese. Requires more humus in the soil. Var. "Brilliant," 18 inches, rose-red flowers, 1½ inches across; "Carmen," rose; "Meteor," wine red.

S. spurium (Running Rock Cress): 6 inches. Semi-evergreen. Creeping, matting habit. (Very like *S. acre*, use in the same manner.) Roundish, wavy-edged, 1-inch leaves. Flowers white or pink appear August/September. Var. "coccineum," crimson to deep pink; "Bronze Carpet," bronze-red foliage; "Dragon's Blood," bright red flowers and leaves.

S. stenopetalum (Yellow Stonecrop): 4 to 8 inches. Tufts of fleshy, green to bronze leaves, narrow, and ¼ to ½ inch long. Yellow flowers in dense terminal clusters, ¼ to ½ inch across. June/August. Rocky Mountains, up to 9,000 feet.

S. telephium: 15 inches. Reddish-purple flowers. August/September. Var. "Indian Chief," upright habit, grey-green foliage, red flowers in August.

Semi-aquilegia

(syn. *AQUILEGIA* .... *ecalcarata*) ....

Family: *Ranunculaceae* (Buttercup).

Propagation: Sow in spring at 45 degrees, germination in 19 days.

Division in spring.

Culture: Sun. Average soil. More decorative when planted in masses; set plants 6 inches apart.

Use: A delicate, charming rock garden plant.

Species:

S. ecalcarata: 15 inches high. Chinese species with small, nodding, spurless, crimson or reddish-brown flowers in June. Closely resembles columbine and is often classified as such.

Semper-vivum

Family: *Crassulaceae* (Orpine).

Common name: Hen and Chickens. Houseleek.

Propagation: Sow in spring at 45 degrees; germination in 6 days.

Separation of the small outer rosettes (offsets) from the parent plant. If they haven't developed roots, place in rooting medium and treat as a cutting.

Culture: Sun. Light, sandy soil with good drainage. Does best with adequate moisture during the summer. Set plants about 8 to 10 inches apart, as they all spread to some extent.

Sempervivum tectorum, Hen and Chickens

Use: Rock garden. Front of border. Container on patio. Rock walls or rock crevices.

Species:

S. arachnoideum (Cobweb Houseleek): Small, grey-green rosettes, ¾ inch wide, covered and connected with lacy, cobweb hairs. Slow spreading. This seldom blooms; but if it does, there are bright red flowers on 3- to 4-inch high stems, along about June.

S. arenarium: Globe-like rosettes of bright green leaves. Pale yellow flowers, often tinged red, on 9 inch stems.

S. atlanticum: Pale red, 1 inch flowers on stems to 12 inches high. Rosettes of pale green leaves, tipped reddish brown.

S. fimbriatum: Hybrid with bright red flowers 8 to 10 inch high flowering stalks rising from rosettes of reddish leaves, tipped with hairs. July.

S. flagelliforme: 4 inches high. Tiny wooly rosettes. Red flowers, 1 inch across, close to the leaves.

S. globiferum: Flowering stems 12 inches high, yellow flowers, purple inside, 1 inch across.

S. montanum: Rosettes, 2 inches wide, composed of dark green, hairy leaves. Hairy panicle of bright purple to reddish-purple flowers, 1 inch across, on 6-inch stems. June. From the Alps.

S. soboliferum: Rosettes, 1½ inches wide with the outer leaves tinged brown, form dense mats. Pale yellow flowers on 9 inch stems.

S. tectorum: The species most commonly offered. Rosettes to 6 inches across, thick, succulent leaves vary from green to purplish brown in color, usually with red tips. Sturdy, hairy, branching flower stalk rises from the center to 12 inches high, covered with clusters of 1-inch, reddish-pink flowers in July. The flowering plant dies, but its place is filled by the many offsets it has produced in the meantime. (See illustration p. 28.)

Sidalcea

Family: *Malvaceae* (Mallow).

Common name: Prairie Mallow.

Propagation: Sow in spring at 65 degrees; germination in 9 days.

Division in spring, usually necessary every third or fourth year.

Culture: Sun. Humus-enriched, sandy soil. Dry. Space plants 12 to 15 inches apart, in groups of at least 3.

Use: Border. Cut flower. Wild garden.

Species and varieties:

S. malvaeflora (Checker-bloom): 3 feet. Resembles the hollyhock but is not so large or coarse appearing. Racemes of rose-pink flowers. July/September. Native to the western states. Var. "*atropurpurea*," purple

151

flowers; "*listeri*," pink. Named varieties also to be found in shades of rose, red, salmon, and lilac.

Silene

Family: *Caryophyllaceae* (Pink).

Common name: Campion. Catchfly.

Propagation: Seed sown when ripe in fall or in spring at 45 degrees.

Division in spring or fall.

Cuttings in July or August.

Root cuttings.

Culture: Sun or part shade. Sandy to gravely, limy soil. Perfect drainage is imperative. Moist. A stone mulch will help keep the roots cool. Transplanting is possible anytime. Space 10 to 12 inches apart, all spread to some extent.

Use: Rock garden. Border.

Species and varieties:

S. acaulis (Cushion Pink. Moss Campion or Catchfly): 2 inches. Cushion habit of growth forms mound a foot or more across. Tiny, bright green, needle-like leaves, narrow, ½ to 1 inch long. Numerous, solitary, stemless, bright rose flowers, ¼ to ½ inch across. June/August. Var. "*alba*" is a rare white form. A plant of the high country, found natively from 9,000 to 12,000 feet in the Rockies, it also occurs in similar areas in other parts of the world.

S. alpestris (Alpine Catchfly): 6 inch dwarf of creeping habit. Sticky foliaged, dense, narrow-leaved clumps. Shiny white flowers, ½ inch across, in loose clusters. June/August.

S. armeria (Sweet William Catchfly): Biennial. 1 to 2 feet. Clusters of flowers, ½ inch across, purple, rose, or white. July/September.

S. californica (California Indian Pink): 6 to 18 inches. Flowers, 1½ inches across, bright pink to red, with fringed, notched petals, in May. Open branching, sticky stems, light green leaves to 3 inches long. Native from Oregon to California. Prefers shade and a more acid soil. Dry in summer. Mulch for winter protection.

S. compacta (syn. *S. orientalis*): Biennial. 1 to 2 feet. Glaucous foliage. Pink flowers in heads to 3 inches across, enclosed in the upper leaves. Var. "Red Dawn," 2½ feet, deep rose.

S. maritima (Sea Campion): 12 inches. Tufts of shiny, glaucous foliage. Distinctive balloon-like calyxes. White flowers, to ¾ inch across, on arching stems, in June. Var. "Robin Whitebreast," 6 inches, mound of silvery foliage, numerous small double white flowers, June/August; "*rosea*" pink flowers in May.

S. saxifraga: 6 inches. Bushy, tufted habit. White flowers throughout the summer. From Asia Minor.

S. schafta (Moss Campion. Rosetuft Catchfly): 6 inches. Spreading tufts. Small, narrow, soft, hairy leaves on

Silene maritima, Sea Campion "Robin White Breast"

wiry, trailing and branching stems. Flowers terminal and in axils, rose-purple with notched petals, 1 or 2 on a stem. August/September. Var. "*alba*," white.

S. virginica (Indian Pink. Fire Pink): 10 inches. Evergreen rosette of long sticky leaves. Loppy, weak stems, sticky and hairy with a few narrow leaves. Flowers, 1 inch across, bright red with deeply clefted petals, 1 to 4 to a cluster. June/August. Dry, shady site. Found from Minnesota to Oklahoma and eastward.

Sisyrinchium

Family: *Iridaceae* (Iris).

Common name: Blue-eyed Grass.

Propagation: Seed sown in fall or early spring. Cool temperatures are necessary for germination, which even at best is slow. *S. douglasii* takes 2 years.

Self-sows.

Division (fibrous rooted).

In field collection, dig as clumps, carefully maintaining the soil around the roots. Easily established.

Culture: Sun. Tolerant of all naturally moist soils, light to heavy types, but prefers the former. Not difficult to transplant, even when in bloom. (In fact, it is quite difficult to recognize this plant except when it is in flower.) Space 4 to 6 inches apart, in colonies.

Use: Ground cover in wild garden. Moist site beside pool or stream.

Species:

S. augustifolium: 4 to 14 inches. Tussocks of stiff, narrow, grass-like, blue-green leaves. Loose clusters of small flowers, ½ inch across, deep violet-blue to lavender; they (like flax) last but a day. May/July. Pennsylvania to Minnesota.

S. bellum: 4 to 16 inches. Purple to purple-blue flowers, ½ inch across. April/May.

S. californicum (Golden or Yellow-eyed Grass): 12 inches. Dull green, grass-like leaves, rather broader than type. Bright yellow flowers, ½ inch across. May/June. Moist site. Oregon to California.

S. douglasii (syn. *S. grandiflorum*) Spring Bell: 6 inches. Rush-like, blue-green leaves. Large, nodding, satiny purple flowers. A West Coast species that should have a rocky, peaty soil that is somewhat

acid. Moist in spring and
dry in summer.

S. graminoides (syn. *S.
graminea*): 1½ feet. Pale
green leaves. Blue flowers,
¾ inch across.

S. inflatum (Grass Widows.
Purple-eyed Grass): 6 to 24
inches. Grass-like leaves,
both basal and on the stems.
Flowers in umbels of 1 to 4,
pinkish-purple, 1 inch across.
April/May. Rocky Mountain
species of open woodland and
wet meadow.

S. sarmentosum (syn. *S.
halophyllum, S. idahoense*):
5 to 12 inches. Tufts of grass-
like leaves. Flat, sharp-edged
stems, 1 to 5 flowers on a
stem, purplish-blue to pale
blue, usually with yellow
centers. May/July. Found in
the Rockies up to 8,000 feet.

Smilacina

Family: *Liliaceae* (Lily).

Common name: Wild Lily-of-
the-Valley. False or Solomon's
Seal. False or Wild Spikenard.

Propagation: Separate seed
from pulp and sow in fall.
The seed is doubly dormant;
that is, it has an impermeable
seed coat and an immature
embryo. A planned sequence
of stratification (3 months
at 80 degrees or room
temperature and then 3
months at 41 degrees or
refrigeration) will be of some
aid. Regardless of treatment,
this usually takes 2 years
to germinate.

Division of the creeping
rootstock after flowering.

Culture: Sun or open shade.
Humus enriched, well-drained
soil. Moist. (Very tolerant
plant.) Space 18 to 20 inches
apart, in colonies. All spread
by underground stems but
are not weedy.

Use: Woodland garden. Pool
or streamside. Shady
ground cover.

Species:

S. amplexicaulis: to 3 feet.
Ribbed leaves clasp the stem
at the base of the plant.
Large, terminal panicles to 6
inches long of small white
flowers, followed by red
berries spotted purple.
Native to the Rockies.

S. racemosa (False Spikenard): 2 to 3 feet. Ovate
leaves to 3 inches wide,
hairy-edged, sessile. Arching
leafy stems, unbranching.
Dense, conical terminal
clusters of fragrant, tiny,
creamy-white flowers like
feathery plumes. May/July.
Whitish berries turn red in
fall. Found natively over
much of North America.
Tolerates sun and dry
conditions.

S. stellata (Star Flowered
Lily-of-the-Valley): 12 to 20
inches. Unbranching, leafy
stems. Long, lance-like leaves
fold on the midrib, pale
bluish-green, downy undersides. Starry, white flowers
are larger than *S. racemosa*
and form a more open,
sparsely flowered, terminal
raceme. May/July. Shiny
green berries with black
stripes. Found over much of
North America as well as in
the Rockies up to 9,000 feet.

Soldanella

Family: *Primulaceae*
(Primrose).

Propagation: Seed must be
fresh for success. Sow when
ripe in late summer; if sown
in spring, see directions for
Primula. Not easy.

Division of underground
stems after flowering.

Culture: Shade. Rich, sandy
yet humusy soil, add stone
chips. Cool with stone or
mulch of some kind. Moist;
these cannot endure drought.
Mulch in winter if you live
where a snow cover is not
constant. They are all natives
of the European Alps.

Use: Shady rock garden.
Woodland garden. Beside
rock-strewn stream or pool.

Species:

S. alpina: 4 to 6 inches.
Roundish leaves form a
rosette. Umbels of 1 to 3,
bell-shaped, pale blue flowers,
often with red markings.
May/June.

S. minima: 4 inches. Tiny
round leaves. Solitary flowers,
funnel-shaped, pale blue or
white with violet streaks.

S. montana: 4 to 15 inches.
Clumps of round, leathery
leaves, to 2½ inches across.
Pendant, funnel-shaped
flowers in umbels, color varies
from mauve, light lavender,
blue-lilac to clear blue.
May/July. Easiest and showiest of the species.

S. pusilla: 4 to 6 inches.
Usually solitary flowers of
pale violet to deep blue.

Solidago

Family: *Compositae* (Daisy).

Common name: Golden Rod.

Propagation: Seed sown in
spring at 65 degrees; germination in 14 days.

Division in spring.

Attractive selections easily
collected in the field anytime.

Culture: Sun. Sandy, porous
soil. Well behaved, it never
needs dividing. It is host to
a pine tree rust; therefore,
care should be taken as to
its placing in relation to any
pines nearby. Golden rod is
also supposed to be a villain
for hay fever sufferers, and
this is true to a certain extent,
but there are many other
plants that have that effect on
humans, including sagebrush.
Space plants 10 to 12
inches apart.

Use: Border. Wild flower
garden.

Species and varieties:

S. caesia (Bluestemmed or
Wreath Goldenrod): 2 feet.
Slender purple-blue stems
bearing light golden-yellow
flowers in leaf axils and
terminal clusters. September.
Prefers partial shade.
From Canada to Texas.

S. canadensis: The commonest
species usually associated
with this genus. I prefer the
named variety "Golden
Baby," 2 feet high, plume-
like flower sprays of golden-
yellow, July/September. Some
of the other varieties are
"Cloth of Gold," "Golden

Moss," "Golden Shower," and "Peter Pan."

S. bicolor (Silver-rod. White Goldenrod): 1 to 2 feet. Downy leaves. Slender spike-like heads of small creamy-white flowers. August/September. Native from Canada to Missouri.

S. elongata (Creek Goldenrod. Yellowweed): 1 to 6 feet. Numerous hairy leaves that are 2 to 5 inches long. Large clusters of myriads of small yellow flower heads on one side only of arching stems. July/September. Most common woodland form in the Rockies, to 8,000 feet from British Columbia to Colorado.

S. occidentalis: The leaves have tiny resinous dots. Yellow flowers in terminal, open panicles on stout leafy stems. Native to the same area as *S. elongata*.

S. sempervirens (Seaside or Beach Goldenrod): 2 to 6 feet. Blue-green leaves. Large, flattish panicles of deep yellow flowers. A very desirable form that is neither a spreader or biennial. East coast from St. Lawrence to Florida.

S. squarrosa (Stout Goldenrod): 1 to 3 feet. Basal leaves form large rosettes. The showest of the woodland. types having long, dense, terminal racemes of brilliant yellow. Erect habit. August/September. Northeastern states.

Sparaxis

Family: *Iridaceae* (Iris).

Common name: Wand Flower. Harlequin Flower.

Propagation: Sow seeds at 45 degrees. Spring-sown seeds will not germinate well until October; it would appear there may be an immature embryo to contend with here.

Corm offsets.

Culture: Outdoors: Sun. Well-drained, sandy loam. A half-hardy plant. Set out in spring, 3 inches deep, massing for effect (the flower is not large). Even though intended largely for winter forcing, they will benefit by being set outdoors. Allow the foliage to ripen before digging and storing.

Indoors: Put 5 to 6 corms, 1 inch deep, in a 6-inch pot. These require cool (not freezing) temperatures for roots to form, so place in cold frame or cellar for several weeks. After bringing indoors, night temperatures should not be over 55 degrees, and after blooming allow the foliage to ripen before storing.

Use: Border. Rock garden. Container. Long-lasting cut flower.

Species:

S. hybrida: 12 inches. Narrow, grass-like, basal leaves. Spike-like clusters of funnel-shaped flowers, purple, blue, red, rose, or yellow and usually marked with contrasting colors. June. From South Africa.

Sphaeralcea

(see ILIAMNA) ....

Spiraea

(see FILIPENDULA ....

Spiranthes

Family: *Orchidaceae* (Orchid).

Common name: Ladies' Tresses.

Propagation: Sow in fall or early spring. Cool temperatures are necessary for germination. It will take 3 years for a plant to bloom from seed.

Self-sows.

Division in spring.

Culture: Sun or part shade. Neutral to slightly acid, rich soil. Moist. Easily transplanted. Scatter in colonies in the same manner that you would naturalize bulbs. Cut plugs from the sod where you wish to insert the plant ball.

Use: Wild garden. Moist, open woodland and wet meadow.

Species:

S. cerna (Nodding Ladies' Tresses): 1 to 2 feet. Narrow, slender outline. Flowering spikes having small, fragrant, tubular, whitish flowers. August/September. A marsh plant found from South Dakota to Texas.

S. gracilis (Slender Ladies' Tresses): Spikes of very small green-lipped, white flowers that spiral up the stem. July/August. Found in quite dry sites from Manitoba to Texas

S. ramanzoffiana (Hooded Ladies' Tresses): 4 to 20 inches. Fleshy, narrow, lance-shaped leaves, mostly on the lower portion of the stem. Dense, terminal spike of small, tubular, creamy-white flowers that distinctly spiral up the stem in three rows. Along about August, look for it in the wet meadows and open woods of the Rockies; it is also found in similar environment as far east as Newfoundland.

Sprekelia

(syn. *AMARYLLIS*) ....

Family: *Amaryllidaceae* (Amaryllis).

Common name: Jacobean Lily. St. James Lily. Aztec Lily. Mexican Fire Lily.

Propagation: Seeds sown at anytime of the year at 70 degrees. Germination usually follows within a month.

Offsets.

Bulbs purchased for spring planting.

Culture: Sun. Enriched, light, sandy, well-drained soil. Moist.

Outdoors: Sheltered, sunny spot, well watered. After the soil has warmed, set bulbs 3 to 4 inches deep, 6 inches apart. They will bloom 6 to 8 weeks after planting. Lift in the fall as you do the gladiolus when the leaves have turned yellow but do not remove the dried top growth. Store at 50 to 55 degrees.

Indoors: As a potted plant, the bulb requires a cool outdoor rooting period (not freezing) before bringing into warmth. For a potting mix, use equal parts of rich loam, sand, and peat. Pot with upper third of bulb showing. This requires extra humidity until growth is well advanced; a covering of a plastic tent will do.

Use: Border. Container. Winter forcing.

Species:

S. formosissima: 1 to 1½ feet. Leaves like narcissus. Solitary, terminal flowers of deep red, 3 to 4 inches across the narrow petals give a spidery effect (there are 3 erect upper petals and 3 lower, drooping or curled). Tender bulb originating in Mexico.

Stachys

Family: *Labiatae* (Mint).

Common name: Woundwort. Betony. Lamb's Ears.

Propagation: Sow in spring at 65 degrees; germination in 5 days.

Division in spring. Roots form along trailing stems.

Culture: Sun or light shade. Sandy to avearge soil. Very adaptable plants. Space 12 to 18 inches apart. Trailing

stems spread and root; severe pruning is required every spring to keep these in bounds.

Use: Border. Rock garden. Dry bank.

Species and varieties:

S. grandiflora (Betony): 1½ to 3 feet. Hairy leaves. Purple-violet flowers to 1 inch long. June/July. Tolerates part shade. Var. "*superba*," purple; "*superba alba*," white; "*robusta*," rose-pink flowers.

S. lanata (syn. *S. olympica*) Lamb's Ears. Bunnies Ears. Wooly Woundwort: Foliage is like nothing else; the silky-wooly leaf actually resembles a lamb's ear. Small, purple-red flowers in whorls on sturdy stalks about 1 foot high attract bees for miles around. July/September. If this is a foreground plant, it is preferable to cut off the flower stalks. Prune the elongating leafy stems at anytime to keep within bounds. Allow enough room for these plants. (See illustration, p-27.)

S. officinalis (syn. *S. betonica*) Horse Mint. Woundwort. Bishop's Wort. Wood Betony: 9 to 30 inches high. Terminal flower spikes of purple-red, purple, lilac, or white. June/July.

Statice

(see ARMERIA .... or LIMONIUM) ....

Stylophorum

Family: *Papaveraceae* (Poppy).

Common name: Celandine Poppy.

Propagation: Seeds sown in fall or early spring at 45 degrees.

Division after flowering.

Self-sows.

Culture: Open, filtered shade. Neutral, light, humus rich, woodland soil. Easily transplanted.

Use: Woodland garden.

Species:

Symphyandra hofmannii

S. diphyllum: 1 to 1½ feet. Bushy habit. Grey-green leaves, divided into 5 to 7, wavy, deeply cut lobes, whitish undersides. Sparsely flowered clusters of deep yellow flowers, 1 to 2 inches across. May/June. Native to the central and Great Lakes states.

Symphyandra

Family: *Campanulaceae* (Bellflower).

Propagation: Seed sown at 65 degrees, germination in 15 days.

Division in spring at the first appearance of growth.

Culture: Sun or light shade. Rich, well-drained soil. Moist. Very attractive in fairly large groups, space 8 inches apart.

Use: Border. Rock garden.

Species:

S. hofmannii: 12 inches. Upright habit, bushy. Drooping, white, 1½ inches long, bell-shaped flowers in leafy panicles. Resembles a dainty canterbury bell. Hardy, but so short-lived as to appear biennial.

S. wanneri: 6 inches. Nodding, purple-blue, bell-shaped flowers, to 1½ inches long, on branching stems. August/September. A fine well-behaved dwarf for the rockery.

Tellima

Family: *Saxifragaceae* (Saxifrage).

Common name: False Alum Root. Fringe Cups.

Propagation: Seed germinates readily when fresh; gather and sow as soon as ripe. Purchased seed sown in fall or in very early spring at 45 to 50 degrees; cool temperatures are needed.

Division in early spring.

Softwood cuttings in summer.

Culture: Shade. Neutral, humusy, woodland soil. Moist.

Use: Woodland garden. Shaded rockery.

Species and varieties:

T. grandiflora: 2 feet. Attractive tufts of broadly round, toothed leaves. Flowers similar to lily-of-the-valley borne in racemes, greenish-pink in bud, opening red, fringed petals. May/June. Related to the eastern *MITELLA*, this is native to the northwestern states. Var. "*purpureum*," reddish leaves, yellow flowers.

Teucrium

Family: *Labiatae* (Mint).

Common name: Germander.

Propagation: Sow in spring at 45 to 65 degrees; germination in 11 days.

Divide in early spring.

Tellima grandifolia, Fringe Cups

Cuttings in summer.

Culture: Sun. Light, well-drained soil. Rocky sites. Space 8 to 10 inches apart, setting the crown slightly below soil level. *T. canadense* should be planted 12 to 18 inches apart.

Use: Low hedging border. Rock garden. Wild garden.

Species and varieties:

T. canadense (American Germander. Wood Sage): Grows to 3 feet. Erect, bushy plant with narrow, thick leaves, whitish underneath. Spikes of flowers arranged in whorls, pink, purple, or white. July/September. Needs more moisture than the others. Found along the east coast from Maine to Florida. For the wild garden.

T. chamaedrys (Wall Germander): 6 to 12 inches high. Woody stems spread to twice the height. Shrubby

habit of growth. Covered with small dark green, toothed leaves. Small spikes of rose flowers, lower lip often spotted white and red. May be pruned for a neat formal effect. It is completely hardy here. Var. "*prostratum*," 4 to 6 inches high, spreading to 3 feet.

T. montanum: Asian species with tiny, narrow, rolled,

Teucrium chamaedrys, Wall Germander

silvery leaves. Six-inch prostrate, trailing stems. Cream to pale yellow flower heads. July/August.

T. polium: Procumbent habit. Semi-evergreen. White, yellow, or purple flowers.

Thalictrum

Family: *Ranunculaceae* (Buttercup).

Common name: Meadow Rue.

Propagation: Seed sown in fall while fresh (fresh seed germinates best). Spring sown seed benefits by a period of prechilling in the refrigerator for several weeks. Germination temperature is 45 degrees. Without treatment, sprouting is slow, 4 weeks or more.

Division every fourth year in spring.

Cuttings of side shoots in summer.

Culture: Sun or light shade. Rich humusy soil, peat added. Moist. Space plants 12 to 18 inches apart. Taller sorts may need staking.

Use: Border. Cut flower. Wild or woodland garden.

Species and varieties:

T. aquilegifolium (Feathered Columbine. Columbine Meadow Rue): 3½ feet. Foliage resembles that of columbine but is often grey-green in color. Creamy-white, light purple, or rose-purple flowers in clusters. June/

July. Native to Europe and Asia. Var. "Dwarf Purple," 2½ feet, purple flowers; "*purpureum*," 3 feet, yellowish flowers.

T. chelidonii: 2 feet. Bisexual flowers, mauve with yellow anthers. Himalayan.

T. delavayi: 3 feet. Arching purplish stems having nodding lavender or purple flowers. Resembles *T. dipterocarpum* but not as tall.

T. diffusiflorum: 3 feet. Tibetan species with cup-shaped, lavender, mauve, or blue flowers. Blooms in July.

T. dioicum (Early Meadow Rue. Silverweed): 2 feet. Usually grown for its attractive thick clumps of feathery foliage. Purple to greenish flowers. May/June. Useful as ground cover under tall trees. Native to dry woodlands from Canada to Alabama and west to Kansas. Sow seeds in summer.

T. dipterocarpum (Chinese Meadow Rue): 3 to 4 feet. Large pyramidal panicles of rose-mauve to purple flowers, yellow anthers. August/September. From China. Var. "*album*," a white form.

T. flavum (False Rhubarb): 4 feet. Creamy-yellow flowers, yellow stamens, in panicles resembling rhubarb.

T. kiusianum: 3 feet. Spreading habit. Japanese species with fern-like, divided, purple leaves. Flowers, pink-lilac or lavender with blue stamens. Prefers shade. Slow to start growth in spring. Alpine.

T. minus adiantifolium (syn. *T. adiantifolium*, *T. major*): 1 to 3 feet. Low robust plant with very attractive ferny foliage (wonderful in bouquets). Greenish-yellow flowers in June are not very noticeable. Asiatic.

T. polygamum: 8 to 10 feet. Large clusters of feathery white flowers. Found in sunny wet meadows of the northeastern states.

T. rocquebrunianum (Lavender Mist): 3 to 4½ feet. Showy terminal clusters of lilac-mauve flowers, lemon-yellow stamens. July to frost. Native to northern Japan.

T. speciosissimum (syn. *T. glaucum*, *T. rugosum*) Dusty Meadow Rue: 3 to 5 feet. Blue-grey leaves. Plumy panicles of pale yellow. flowers. July/August. From south Europe.

Thymus

Family: *Labiatae* (Mint).

Comon name: Thyme.

Propagation: Seeds sown in fall or early spring at 45 degrees. Germination will follow in 6 days. Does not always reproduce true to type from seed.

Division in spring.

Rooting stems (creeping types).

Cuttings in July.

Culture: Sun. Well-drained, light, sandy, gritty soil with some humus added. Dry. For

carpeting, plant 6 inches apart.

Use: Rock garden. Rock crevices. Stone walks and edging. Ground cover. Containers. Herb garden.

Species and varieties:

T. langinosus (Wooly leaved or Mountain Thyme): 2 to 3 inches. Matting, prostrate habit. Stems covered with small, wooly, grey-green leaves. Masses of bright pink flowers. May/June. Northern Europe.

T. nitidus: 9 inches. Aromatic subshrub. Compact habit. Shiny, silvery-grey leaves. Small lilac-rose flowers. June/July. From Sicily.

T. serpyllum (Mother of Thyme. Wild Thyme): 2 to 6 inches. Subshrub of trailing, creeping habit (rooting stems). Carpet forming, it is quite tolerant of being trod on, even mowed. Evergreen, scented foliage— roundish, small, hairy, dark green leaves. Masses of flowers in small, erect racemes, purple to reddish-purple hues. June/September. Leaves may be used for seasoning. European origins. Var. "*albus*," a white form; "*coccineus*" is taller and has bright red flowers; "*vulgaris*," lemon-scented; "*argenteus*," silver, mottled leaves; "*splendens*," rose-red flowers.

T. vulgaris (Common Garden Thyme): 6 to 12 inches. Erect subshrub. Can be invasive——be careful where you place this. Fragrant, grey-green leaves to ¼ inch long. Tiny lilac or purple flowers in dense whorls. May/July. A kitchen herb; use dried leaves for seasoning meat, gravy, dressings, and soups; for salads, use fresh leaves.

Tiarella

Family: *Saxifragaceae* (Saxifrage).

Common name: False Miterwort. Foamflower.

Propagation: Seed sown when ripe in late summer or subject to a period of prechilling and sow in spring at 45 degrees.

Division in spring after flowering.

Runners or stolons (*T. cordifolia*).

Culture: Light shade. Humusy soil enriched with leaf mold, neutral to slightly acid.

Use: Woodland garden. Shaded rock garden.

Species:

T. cordifolia: 6 to 12 inches. Rosette habit, looks much like a small heuchera. Leaves more likely to remain evergreen. Produces runners like those of the strawberry . Small, feathery, white flowers (rarely pink or red). May/ June. Native to the eastern states.

T. polyphylla: 15 inches. Wavy, toothed leaves. Racemes of delicate, small, white to reddish flowers in spring. Asiatic origin.

Tigridia

Family: *Iridaceae* (Iris).

Common name: Mexican Tiger Flower. Shellflower.

Propagation: Sow in spring at 65 degrees, germination within 4 weeks. Winter seedlings in cool greenhouse or cold frame to lengthen the growing season as long as possible. Protect from extreme cold with a vermiculite mulch.

Bulbs purchased in spring.

Culture: Sun or light shade. Sandy, well-drained soil. Moist. Stems are rather weak and require staking. Culture is the same as for gladiolus. Dig and store in vermiculite in frost-free place for the winter. Set bulbs 4 inches deep, in groups 4 to 8 inches apart when the soil is warm (which in our area is the first week in June). I prefer to begin early in the season and start these in pots in the greenhouse the first week of April.

Use: Border. Potted plant for terrace or greenhouse.

Species:

T. pavonia: 1 to 2 feet. Basal, strap-like leaves. Upfacing flowers, 4 to 6 inches across, in shades of orange, yellow or red with spotted centers. Flowers last but a day; however, there is a constant succession of bloom. Late July/September. Native of Mexico.

Townsendia

Family: *Compositae* (Daisy).

Common name: Giant Aster. Easter Daisy.

Propagation: Seed collected and sown as soon as ripe in summer. Field collection would be necessary, I do not know of a commercial source.

Culture: Sun. Sandy, gravelly, well-drained soil, Dry summers are normal. Transplanting may be successful with quite small plants.

Use: Wild flower garden. Excellent rock garden plant.

Species:

T. incana: Rosette habit of growth. Flowers pink to white. June/September. Entire plant, foliage and flower, covered with downy white hairs. Rocky Mountains.

T. parryi (Parry Townsendia): Leaves in basal rosette, spatulate, 1 to 2 inches long. Daisy-like flowers on unbranching stems 2 to 12 inches high, solitary, 1 to 2 inches across, lavender-blue rays and yellow discs. June/September. Rockies, up to timberline.

T. sericea (syn. *T. escapa*) Easter Daisy: Very like *T. parryi* but leaves are very narrow and the flowers almost stemless. June/October. Found throughout the Rockies, timberline and above.

Tradescantia

Family: *Commelinaceae* (Spiderwort).

Common name: Spiderwort. Snake Grass.

Propagation: Seeds collected and sown in August—— freshness of seed is vital. Sow in early spring at 45 degrees, germination in 15 days.

Self-sows.

Cuttings in July.

Division in early spring, usually every third year.

Culture: Sun or light shade. Average soil. Moist. Space plants 8 inches apart, setting out in groups of at least three.

Use: Border. Woodland garden.

Species and varieties:

T. reflexa: 3 feet. Blue or white flowers. Found in the central states.

T. pilosa: 3 feet. Lilac-blue flowered species found natively from Pennsylvania to Missouri.

T. virginiana: 1½ feet. Blue to purple flowers in terminal clusters, last but a day. Blooms off and on from July to frost. Clumps of grass-like leaves. Spreads by underground stolons but is not weedy. Native to the eastern half of the United States. Var. "*alba*," *white*; "*coccinea*," red flowers.

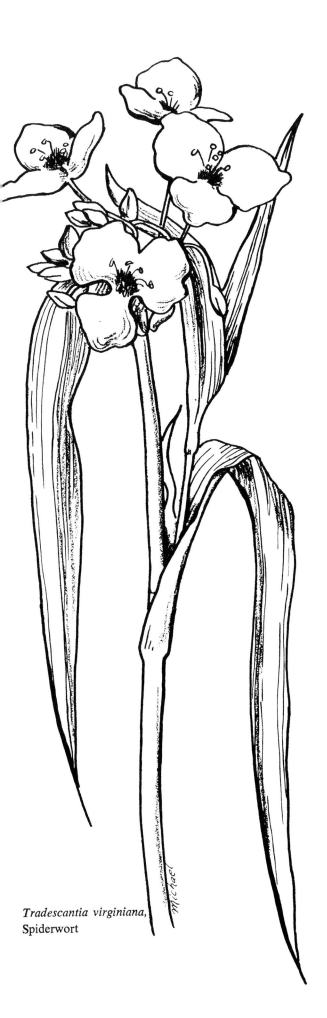

Tradescantia virginiana,
Spiderwort

Trientalis

Family: *Primulaceae* (Primrose).

Common name: Star Flower.

Propagation: Seed must be fresh. Sow when collected, or stratify and sow in spring at 45 degrees. A period of cold is needed for germination.

Division of stolons at any time.

Culture: Shade. Light, rich soil, add peat and leaf mold. Average moisture to boggy. Transplanting from the field is possible if the plant is moved with a large clump of soil.

Use: Woodland or rock garden. Edge of stream or pond. Shady ground cover.

Species:

T. borealis: 9 inches. Thin, creeping rhizome. Slender stems atop which are borne a whorl of narrow, pointed, 4-inch leaves like the spokes of a wheel. Held above the leaves on thread-like stalks are 1 or 2 starry, white flowers. May/June. Native to northeastern North America and European woodlands.

Trillium

Family: *Liliaceae* (Lily).

Common name: Trillium.

Propagation: Seeds sown in fall; remove pulp and sow

immediately. Seeds may also be treated as follows: sow in flat and expose to 41 degrees for 3 months (this is to remove the block in root growth), then 65 degrees for 3 months (to start root to growing), return again to 41 degrees for 5 months to remove the shoot block. Now bring the flat into warmth again, and there should be evidence of shoot growth. If seed is not fresh, it may not germinate until the second year or later. Using simple winter stratification, it may take 2 years anyway——do not despair and toss it all out.

Root is a tuber-like rhizome. Division may be attempted in summer before the plant goes dormant but is not always successful.

Culture: Light shade. Woodland soil. Yearly mulch of rotted pine needles and very old manure. Cool. Plants are easily transplanted even when in bloom. Set tubers 2 to 6 inches deep in late summer, planting in groups, 6 to 8 inches apart. They form colonies under favorable conditions.

Use: Woodland garden. Beneath deciduous trees and shrubs. Warning! Never pick the flowers or the plant is likely to die, for it is impossible to take the bloom without its foliage and thereby leaving the root without sustenance.

Species and varieties:

T. cernuum (Nodding Trillium): 6 to 18 inches. Very small or no rhizome. Three broad leaves. Nodding, small, white flowers. May/June. Moderately acid soil. Northeastern states, Maine to Minnesota.

T. erectum (Birth Root. Lamb's Quarter. Purple trillium): 12 inches. Flowers are held erect above the leaves, red to dark purple, rarely white or yellow, 1 inch long and ill-scented. May/June. Var. *"album,"* Wax Trillium, is a white form with dark centers. Easily grown in neutral soil. Northeastern states.

T. flexipes (syn. *T. declinatum*): Fragrant, white to maroon flowers. Native from New York to Minnesota.

T. grandiflorum: Wake Robin. White or Great Trillium. Snow Trillium): 15 inches. Nodding, stalked flowers, 3 inches across, held well above the leaves, petals white gradually turning pink. May. (Many variations possible) It takes 5 to 10 years to flower from seed. Neutral soil. Easily cultivated species found natively from Maine to Minnesota.

T. luteum (Yellow Trillium): Mottled leaves. Fragrant, pale yellow to greenish-yellow flowers. Native to the southern states but hardy north.

T. nivale (Snow or Dwarf White Trillium): 4 to 6 inches. Small, often drooping, white flowers, 1 inch across. Very early, usually April. Neutral soil and drier conditions. Good for the shady rock garden. Found from Pennsylvania to Nebraska.

T. ovatum (Western Trillium): 9 to 18 inches. Fragrant, white flowers fading deep rose. Resembles *T. grandiflorum*, but the

flower is held erect and is smaller. April/May or on to June, according to elevation and as the snow disappears. Easy to grow in the garden even though its native habitat is a cool peaty bog. Rocky Mountains from Montana to California.

T. petiolatum: Another Rocky Mountain species, this one is characterized by stemless flowers, dark purple, to 2 inches across, and not very noticeable. It is more curious than attractive.

T. recurvatum (Prairie Trillium): 1½ feet. Mottled leaves. Flowers are brownish-red to purple with recurved petals. Native from Ohio to Arkansas.

T. rivale (Western Snow Trillium): 8 inches. Resembles *T. nivale,* but flowers are smaller, erect, and shading from pink to white, often with purple markings. Give this a rocky site. Found from California to Oregon.

T. sessile rubrum (Toad or Stemless Trillium): 9 inches. Leaves mottled with brown shadings. Erect flowers are variable, may be dark red, reddish-purple, purplish-green, yellow or white. April/May. Found in moist, neutral soil from Pennsylvania to Missouri. Var. *"californicum"* (syn. *T. chloropetalum*) has spotted leaves, purple, rose, or white flowers to 4 inches across, and is a native westerner.

T. stylosum (Rose Trillium): 1½ feet. Similar to *T. grandiflorum*, this has rose-pink flowers 2½ inches across. From the southern mountains.

T. undulatum (Painted Trillium): 12 inches. White flowers with purple or crimson basal markings and stripes, wavy-edged petals. May/June. This is difficult as it requires an acid, peaty, boggy soil. Locate beside that woodland stream or pond. From Maine to Pennsylvania.

Tritonia

(syn. *MONTBRETIA*) . . .

Family: *Iridaceae* (Iris).

Common name: Montbretia.

Propagation: Seed sown in spring at 65 to 70 degrees.

Offsets.

Corms purchased for spring planting.

Culture: Sun, tolerates some light shade. Well-drained, rich, light sandy soil. Adequate moisture. Profits from well-rotted manure worked into the bed before planting. Rather weak stems, usually requires staking. Set out corms in spring when danger of frost is past, 4 inches deep and 5 inches apart. Of borderline hardiness, place in a sheltered site and mulch, and its possible to winter these in the garden. Mine have thrived for years in a planting bed between house and patio. Otherwise, lift and store as you would a gladiolus, but store in vermiculite or sand to prevent them from drying out. Must be planted in masses for effect.

Indoor winter flower: Pot up and expose to cool tempera-

tures before bringing into the house.

Use: Long-lasting cut flower. Border. Container. Winter forcing.

Species and varieties:

T. crocata: 1 to 3 feet. Long, narrow, sword-like, deeply grooved leaves. Slender, arching, branching stems carry spikes of funnel-shaped flowers, 2 inches across, in shades of red, orange, or yellow (smaller by far than the ordinary gladiolus blossom). July/September. Native of South Africa. Commercial sources usually offer only named horticultural varieties, a few are "Aurora," orange-gold with lemon-yellow eye; "Lady Oxford," pale yellow; "Vesuvius," red; "Earlham hybrid" is quite an improvement, having larger flowers, 3 to 4 inches across, and greater range of colors, both clear and bicolored.

Trollius

Family: *Ranunculaceae* (Buttercup).

Common name: Globeflower.

Propagation: Sow in fall. Fresh seed germinates well; old seed may take up to 2 years. Spring sowing will require a period of cold; stratify for several weeks, remove to 45 degrees; germination follows within 6 weeks.

Divide into sections with one or two crowns in spring.

Culture: Shade, tolerates sun

Tritona crocata, Montbretia

if given a moist site. Rich, peaty soil. Moist. Space 6 inches apart for dwarfs, 8 inches apart otherwise, planting in groups.

Use: Shaded border. Cut flower (cut when buds just open). Naturalistic planting beside water.

Species and varieties:

T. acaulis: 6 inches. Rock-garden type from northern India. Solitary, lemon-yellow flowers, 2 inches across.

T. asiaticus (Asiatic Globe Flower): 1½ to 3 feet. Leaves bronze-green. Ball-shaped, orange-yellow flowers with bright orange-red anthers. June. Siberian.

T. chinensis: 2 feet. Very large leaves, to 7 inches long. Golden-yellow, cup-shaped flowers. May/June. Bog plant.

T. europaeus (Mountain Globeflower. European Globeflower. Butterballs): 1½ to 2 feet. Pale yellow to lemon-yellow, globe-shaped flowers, 1 to 2 inches across. May/July. Many named varieties of this.

T. laxus (syn. *T. albiflorus*): 1 to 1½ feet. Creamy-white to yellow, cup-like flowers, 1½ inches across, conspicuous stamens. May/July. Bog plant found from 6,000 feet to timberline in the Rocky Mountains from British Columbia to Colorado. There is a difference of opinion by some authorities as to the correct classification of this species. *T. laxus* is sometimes referred to as an eastern species and *T. albiflorus* as western.

T. ledebouri (Siberian Globeflower) var. "Golden Queen": 1 to 1½ feet. Shiny, cup-like, golden flowers with unusually long, prominent stamens. July. Siberian. (See illustration, p. 29.)

T. pumilus: 8 inches. Rock-garden plant from the Himalayas. Bright yellow flowers, 1 to 2 inches across.

Tulbaghia

Family: *Liliaceae* (Lily).

Propagation: Seed sown in warmth, 65 to 70 degrees, anytime.

Offsets.

Corms purchased for spring planting (usually the only time they are offered).

Culture: Sun. Light, sandy soil, peat added. Well drained. Keep on the dry side if potted, as the roots are easily damaged by overwatering. These are half-hardy and will not withstand temperatures of less than 25 degrees. If used in the garden, lift and store over winter as a pot plant, for it does not really have a dormant period. (It is nearly everblooming as an indoor plant.) Handle much as you would an Agapanthus (see above).

Use: Border. Cut flower. Container. House plant (winter blooming).

Species:

T. fragrans: 18 inches. Long, narrow, grey-green leaves. Fragrant, urn-shaped, pink to lavender-pink flowers in terminal clusters, 20 to 30 blooms per stem.

T. pulchella: 12 inches. Evergreen linear leaves. Flowers, small, pale mauve-white stars in clusters.

Tulipa

Family: *Liliaceae* (Lily).

Common name: Tulip.

Propagation: Seeds are usually sown when gathered

161

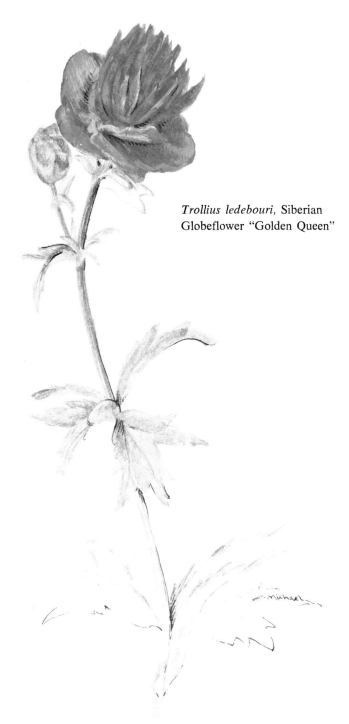

Trollius ledebouri, Siberian Globeflower "Golden Queen"

Culture: Sun. Well-drained, rich, sandy loam. The species prefer drier conditions than the horticultural varieties. Fertilize in spring, choosing a fertilizer high in phosphate but low in nitrogen. Plant in fall, 6 to 8 inches deep (better too deep than too shallow), 5 to 8 inches apart, always in groups of at least 10 to 12. Cut off seed pods unless you are trying to save seed of any particular specimen. Allow the leaves to die down naturally (they are building the bulbs for next year).

Winter forcing: Most homes are really too warm for tulips, but if you want to try, this is the way to go about it. Pot up bulbs in October, place in trench or cold frame and leave out until December (freezing temperatures are required). Bring into cool (about 45 degrees), dark place to root. When the pot is pretty well filled with roots, expose gradually to more light and warmer temperatures, finally to sunniest window.

Use: Cut flower. Winter forcing. Border or special bed for the large horticultural varieties. Rock garden or naturalize the species.

Species and varieties:

T. acuminata (Spider Tulip): 10 inches. Flowers are yellow, streaked with red, the long narrow petals tapering to very fine points. April.

T. australis: 9 inches. Clear yellow, fragrant flowers. The urn-shaped buds open to a star.

T. batalinii: 4 to 10 inches. Very narrow leaves. Single flowers of soft buff-yellow with pale olive blotch and deeper yellow centers. April.

T. clusiana (Candlestick, Lady or Candy Tulip): 12 inches. Slender, pointed, small to medium-sized blooms. Petals red on outside, white inside with dark blue base. April/May.

T. eichleri: 10 inches. Rather large red flowers with yellow and black centers.

T. kaufmanniana (Water Lily Tulip): 9 inches. Variable from seed. Medium to large, broad, flattish flowers in primrose, yellow or white. Many hybrids from this. Var. "Scarlet Elegance," numerous small red flowers; "Vivaldi," creamy-yellow outside, red blotch and distinct ring inside, brownish dots on the leaves.

T. montana: 6 inches. Flowers a deep red with a small black blotch.

T. praestans: 6 to 10 inches. Two to 4 cup-shaped flowers to a stem, red with pointed petals. Var. "Fusilier" has 4 to 6 red flowers per stem.

T. sprengeri: 1½ feet. Flowers brilliant orange-scarlet, shading to buff and orange.

T. sylvestris: 12 inches. Fragrant, yellow flowers with red and green markings on the backs.

T. tarda (syn. *T. dasystemon*): 3 to 5 inches. Star-shaped, up-facing flowers, 3 to 5 on a stem, yellow and white, green shadings on the outside.

T. turkestanica: 9 to 12 inches. Open, starry flowers,

in late summer. Sown in very early spring, they often do not germinate until the following spring. Stratification of seed for spring sowing and exposure to freezing temperatures will sometimes hasten the process.

Bulblets: Lift clumps when leaves are dried and separate bulbs. All 1 inch or more in

diameter may be replanted immediately as ornamentals. The smaller bulblets should be planted in rows in the garden (much as you would peas). They will take another year or two to be large enough to flower.

Bulbs purchased for fall planting.

often up to 8 on a stem, ivory-white with orange centers and greenish shadings on outside of petals. March/April.

Horticultural varieties below are arranged more or less in sequence of bloom, starting with the earliest.

Single Early: 10 to 14 inches. Single cup, colors of red, yellow, or white.

Double Early: 10 to 12 inches. Longer lasting cut flower. Double cups, self-colored or bicolored, in reds, yellows, or white.

Triumphs and Mendels (Early Single x Darwin): 16 to 20 inches. Large single cup, self-colored or edged in contrasting color. "Fuga," a good red; "Dreaming Maid," violet, edged in white; "Blizzard," huge creamy-white; "Red Giant."

Peony (really a double Triumph): I have never had any great success with these. The late spring snows (which you can always count on) mash them to the ground and, unlike other types, these do not recover. "Eros," long-lasting rose; "Nizza," red and yellow, feathery petals; "Palette," red-violet; "Uncle Tom," deep maroon color.

Cottage: 20 to 30 inches. Oval or egg-shaped with long, pointed petals. Colors predominantly yellow and orange, pastels and light hues, never any purples.

Darwin: 4 to 30 inches. Very sturdy. Huge squarish cups in a great range of colors, from white to almost black, often with contrasting centers.

Breeder: 2 to 3 feet. Long oval, single cups on stiff, stout stems, bicolored in Rembrandt colors, especially orange, bronze and purple shades (never white).

Parrot: 20 to 26 inches. Petals are frilled, lacinated, or twisted, every hue, cups often having green markings on their outsides. "Fantasy," rose, green on outside.

Lily Flowered: 20 to 24 inches. Urn-shaped cups with long, pointed, recurving petal tips. Long-lasting flowers in shades of red, violet, and yellow.

Rembrandt: 22 to 26 inches. Large, single, squarish cups, colors striped and streaked as though an artist had cleaned his brush on them.

Tunic

Family: *Caryophyllaceae* (Pink).

Common name: Tunic Flower. Coatflower. Saxifrage Pink.

Propagation: Sow in spring, and it will bloom the first year. Germination in 4 days at 65 degrees.

Division in spring. If grass has invaded the clumps, this is the only means of getting rid of it.

Cuttings form close to the taproot.

Culture: Sun. Average soil. Set out in large groups, 6 inches apart, for this not an imposing plant by itself.

Use: Rock garden. Edging. Sunny, hot, gravelly bare spaces where nothing (it seems) will grow.

Species and varieties:

T. saxifraga: 6 inches. Sprawling, sparsely leaved, wiry stems. Tiny pale pink flowers; "*alba*," white form. Mediterranean.

Typha

Family: *Typhaceae* (Cattail).

Common name: Cattail. Reed mace.

Propagation: Sow seed in pots set in a pan of water; the soil must be constantly wet. Air temperature, 50 to 60 degrees. Germination within 5 weeks or less.

Division of creeping rootstock, spring and summer.

Culture: Sun or shade. Bog soil at margins of ponds, prefers a depth of 6 inches of water. Space plants 12 to 18 inches apart; they soon form a colony.

Use: Water garden, edge of pond or quiet stream. Dried bouquet.

Species:

T. augustifolia (Small Reed Mace): 4 to 10 feet. Very narrow, basal, sword-like leaves, ½ inch wide, 3 to 5 feet long. Dense, blunt flower spikes; the upper (male) portion is separated about an inch from the lower or female portion of the flower spike. The flowers are petal-

less. May/July. Felty, brown seeds. Rather rare, but preferable for the small pool, as it is not invasive. Found in the same environment as *T. latifolia*.

T. latifolia (Common Cattail. Reed Mace): 6 to 8 feet. Very like *T. augustifolia*, but the leaves are broader, to 1 inch wide, the flowers are dark brown in color, and there is no distinct separation midway between the male and female sections of the flower spike. This is also common to the Rocky Mountain area but does not grow above 7,000 feet.

Valeriana

Family: *Valerianaceae* (Valerian).

Common name: Valerian. Garden Heliotrope. All Heal. Cat's Valerian. St. George's Herb.

Propagation: Seed must be fresh. Sow in late fall or spring at 45 degrees. Germination in 8 days.

Self-sows.

Division in spring or after flowering.

Culture: Sun or light shade. Light loam on the limy side. Moist. Tall sorts may need staking. Space 12 inches apart, dwarfs 6 to 8 inches apart.

Use: Border. Cut flower. Rock garden. Wild garden.

Species and varieties:

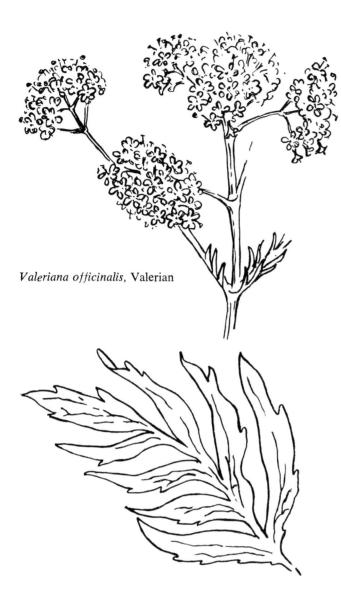

Valeriana officinalis, Valerian

V. arizonica: 6 inches. Creeping carpet. Round leaves. Pale pink or white flowers. Western states.

V. dioica (syn. *V. acutiloba*, *V. occidentalis*) Western Valerian. Tobacco root. Wild Heliotrope: 10 to 18 inches. Small, white flowers in terminal clusters (rarely pink). May/July. Native to the Rocky Mountains from Canada to Arizona.

V. officinalis: 3 feet. Fragrant, white, pink, red or lavender flowers in dense clusters. July/August. Var. "alba," white; "rubra," a red

form. Most commonly grown of all, this is native from Europe to Asia.

V. phu aurea: 3 feet. New growth in spring is a bright gold color. White flowers. Native from south Europe to western Asia.

V. sitchensis (Sitka Valerian): 1 to 3 feet. This species with fragrant, white or lavender flowers comes from Alaska.

V. supina: 6-inch rock-garden type. Oval, hairy-edged leaves form dense clumps. Large heads of pink flowers. June/July. Austrian.

Veratrum

Family: *Liliaceae* (Lily).

Common name: False Hellebore.

Propagation: Seeds sown when ripe in fall or in early spring. Cool temperatures are needed.

Division in spring.

Culture: Shade. Average soil. Moist to wet. Not easily transplanted when mature.

Use: Woodland and wild garden. Foliage accent plant. Waterside.

Species:

V. album (European White Hellebore): 3½ to 4 feet. Large, clasping (in the manner of corn), ribbed leaves. Greenish-white flowers in large terminal panicles. July/September.

V. nigrum: 3 feet. Rare species with purple-black flowers.

V. viride (Green Hellebore. Indian Poke): 3½ to 5 feet. Broad, ribbed, clasping leaves. Terminal panicles of yellowish-green flowers. June/July. Found in swamps and woodland from Oregon to Ontario.

Verbascum

Family: *Scrophulariaceae* (Figwort).

Common name: Mullein.

Propagation: Sow in spring at 45 degrees; germination in 8 to 14 days. Long tap root; it must be transplanted to permanent position when small.

Root cuttings in early spring.

Self-sows readily.

Culture: Sun or light shade. Light sandy soil. Drought resistant but does much better with adequate moisture. Plant in groups of at least 4, spacing 10 inches apart.

Use: Border. Wild garden.

Species and varieties:

V. blattaria (Moth Mullein): Biennial. 3 to 6 feet. Smooth, dark green, toothed leaves in basal clumps. Flowers yellow with lilac throat and purple stamens, loosely spaced on the stalk. Var. "alba," white. Originally from Europe but now escaped and found all over North America.

V. bombyciferum (syn. *V. broussa* "Silver Spire") Arctic Summer: Often biennial or short-lived. 4 feet. Grey, downy foliage. Yellow flowers.

V. chaixii: Biennial. 4 feet. White wooly leaves. Free flowering. Tall spikes of bright yellow flowers, purple stamens.

V. hybrida: "Harkness Hybrids," biennial, 10 feet, vigorous, huge spikes of yellow flowers; "Miss Willmot," biennial, 6 feet, large white flowers; "Pink Domino," 3 feet, branching, rose flowers, June/September; "Cotswold Gem," 4 feet, reddish-amber flowers with purple centers.

Verbascum phoeniceum,
Mullein

V. longifolium (Italian Mullein): Biennial. 4 feet. Spikes of yellow flowers. Felt-like lower leaves.

V. nigrum (Dark Mullein): 3 to 5 feet. Smooth leaves, downy undersides. Small yellow flowers, lilac throat, and wooly, purple stamens.

V. olympicum (Greek Mullein): 5 to 6 feet. Short-lived, so that it seems biennial. Very large whitish, wooly leaves to 2 feet long, in basal rosette. Clusters of deep yellow flowers, 1 inch across, with prominent white stamens. Greece.

V. phoeniceum (Purple Mullein): 3 to 5 feet. Leaves smooth above and downy under. Usually has purple flowers with prominent purple stamens. June/August. Parent of pastel hybrids. Prefers semi-shade.

V. plicatum: Long, ribbed leaves. 5-foot-high spikes of sulphur-yellow flowers.

V. thapsus (Wooly or Common Mullein. Aaron's Rod): Biennial. Up to 3 feet high. Very wooly rosette of foliage. Yellow flowers. July/August. Native to Europe, now scattered all over North America, including the Rocky Mountain area.

V. weidednannianum: 3 feet. Flower spikes of indigo blue, fading purplish-lilac. June/September. From southern Europe.

Verbena

Family: *Verbenaceae* (Vervain).

Common name: Verbena. Vervain.

Propagation: Seed sown at 65 degrees; germination in 10 days. Seed sown in April will bloom by August the first year.

Division in spring.

Cuttings in July or August.

Culture: Sun. Average soil. Drought resistant. Space plants 10 to 12 inches apart in fairly large groups.

Use: Border. Cut flower. Wild garden.

Species and varieties:

V. bipinnafida (Fern Verbena): 12 inches high. Sprawling stems to 18 inches long. Fern-like foliage. Showy clusters of lavender-blue flowers, very free flowering. July until finally buried under the snow (late fall cold snaps do not faze this plant). Very attractive and hardy in spite of its short-lived habit (it will often live to 4 years and so cannot be classed as a biennial. (See illustration, p. 28.)

V. bonaraiensis: 3 to 4 feet. Very slender, upright habit. Terminal heads of bright lavender flowers. June to frost. Flowers the first year from seed. Treat as an annual, as it will not live over the winter.

V. canadensis (Clump Vervain. Rose Verbena): 12 inches. Low spreading plant for the wild garden. Self-rooting stems. Elongated, terminal heads of rose-purple flowers. June/August. Neutral soil. Illinois to Colorado.

V. hasata (Blue Vervain):
to 7 feet. Many long terminal
spikes of tiny purple or dark
blue flowers. July/September.
Moderately acid soil. For
the moist, boggy area in the
wild garden. Canada to
Nebraska.

V. venosa (syn. *V. rigida*):
1½ feet. Erect habit. Tuber-
like root. Flowers in short,
dense spikes of reddish or
violet-purple. Long season
of bloom.

Verbena bipinnafida, Fern
Verbena

Verbena venosa

Veronica

Family: *Scrophulariaceae*
(Figwort).

Common name: Speedwell.

Propagation: Sow in spring
at 65 degrees; germination
in 5 to 15 days.

Cuttings in summer.

Division in spring.

Culture: Sun. Average soil.
Usually quite drought resistant. Set out plants 6 to 8
inches apart in colonies. It
takes at least a dozen in one
location to be effective.
V. spicata "Blue Peter" is
very susceptible to the
parasite, dodder. Remove
every single portion of the
strangler and cut back the
plant; if it all looks hopeless,
yank out and burn the
affected plants. There are no
chemical means of controlling this pest; fortunately, for
some reason, it prefers this
particular species and variety,
ignoring all others even when
growing in the immediate
proximity.

Use: Border. Cut flower.
Rockery. Ground cover.

Species and varieties:

V. chamaedrys (Angel Eyes.
Germander): 1½ feet.
Racemes of small blue
flowers. May/June.

V. colensoi: 12 inches. Evergreen. White-flowering
species for the rock garden.

V. fruticulosa: 6 inches.
Evergreen rock plant with
short spikes of pink flowers.

V. gentianoides (Gentian Speedwell): 15 inches. Glossy green leaves. Dainty flower spikes of light blue or pale lavender, veined blue. May/June. Var. *"pallida,"* wedgewood-blue.

V. holophylla: 1 to 2 feet. Japanese species with shiny, leathery, dark green leaves and deep blue flowers in August.

V. hookeriana: Trailing type for the rockery. Stiff, leathery leaves. Purplish or white flowers often streaked pink.

V. hybrida: (Most are crosses of *V. spicata x V. longifolia*) "Blue Champion," 2½ feet, medium-blue flowers in July; "Icicle," 1½ to 2 feet, grey-green leaves, white flowers, June/September; "Sunny Border Blue," to 2 feet, navy blue flowers, July/September; "Blue Spires," 1½ feet, deep blue, July/September; "Barcarolle," to 10 inches. rose-pink flowers; "Minuet," light pink.

V. incana (Wooly Speedwell. Hoary Speedwell): 9 to 12 inches. Silvery, downy, basal foliage. Violet to deep blue flowers in short, dense spikes. June/July. Var. *"rosea,"* rose-pink flowers. (See illustration, p. 28.)

V. longiflorum: 3 feet. Long, dense racemes of lilac flowers.

V. longifolia (syn. *V. maritima*) Slender Speedwell: 2 feet. Long racemes of deep blue to deep lavender-blue shades. July/September. Parent of most hybrids. Var. *"subsessilis,"* 2 feet, deep royal blue flowers. Shade tolerant. Japan.

Veronica incana, Wooly Speedwell

V. pectinata (Comb Speedwell): 5 inches. Matting habit; creeping stems root at the joints. Evergreen. Small, round, ½-inch-long, wooly, silver leaves. Short racemes of blue flowers, white eyes. Free flowering. May/June. Var. *"rosea."* a pink form A good rockery plant from Asia Minor.

V. peduncularis: 5-inch-high mounds of bronze-green foliage. Small white flowers, pink veined.

V. prostrata (syn. *V. rupestris*): 6 to 8 inches. Tufted habit. Many creeping, prostrate shoots. Small, dark green leaves, ½ to ¾ inch long. Flowers in terminal clusters, pale blue, pink, or white. June/July. Var. "Shirley Blue" has brilliant blue flowers; "Hav-a-look," blue and white flowers on the same plant.

V. repens: 2 inches. Mossy creeper with shiny, oval, ½-inch-long leaves. Almost stemless flowers may be pale to bright blue, white, or rose. May/June. From Spain. Shade tolerant. Ground cover or rock garden.

Veronica spicata, Cat-tail Speedwell "Blue Peter"

167

V. spicata (Cattail or Rattail Speedwell. Spiked Speedwell): 1½ to 2½ feet. Spikes of blue flowers, usually shorter than *V. longifolia*. June/August. Var. "Blue Peter," 15 inches, bushy, blue racemes; "*alba*," white; "*rosea*," rose-pink; "*erica*," pink heather-like flowers; "*nana*," 6-inch dwarf with small, dense spikes of violet-blue flowers, June/July.

V. teucrium (syn. *V. latifolia*) Hungarian Speedwell: 2 feet. Rather weak stemmed. Blue flowers, rarely pink or white. Shade tolerant. Var. "*prostrata*," low rock-garden type with rich blue flowers; "Crater Lake Blue."

V. traversii (syn. *V. brachysiphon*): 6 feet. Woody subshrub with numerous white flowers.

V. virginica (syn. *VERONICASTRUM virginicum*) Culver's Root. Blackroot: 1 to 6 feet. Dark green leaves in whorls around the stem. Erect, branching spikes of small white flowers. July/September. Tolerates shade. Var. "*alba*," white flowers with yellow anthers. Found in moderately acid soils from New England to Manitoba.

Vinca

Family: *Apocynaceae* (Dogbane).

Common name: Periwinkle. Trailing Myrtle.

Propagation: Seed sown at 65 degrees. Difficult to find a commercial source of seed, but many nurseries offer plants.

Layering.

Culture: Light shade preferred but tolerates sun. Humusy soil. Adequate moisture. Fertilize in spring. Prune to induce neater growth habit. Space plants 6 to 8 inches apart; they may be moved anytime during the growing season.

Use: Excellent ground cover (aggressive enough to combat weeds). Erosion control on sloping sites. I would not recommend this for the rock garden, as it is quite a strong grower.

Species and varieties:

V. minor (Dwarf Periwinkle): Evergreen, shiny leaves. Violet-blue flowers in May. This is the only vinca that is hardy in the highlands. Native to Europe. Var. "*bowlei*" has deeper blue flowers.

Viola

Family: *Violaceae* (Violet).

Common name: Violet. Pansy.

Propagation: Seed collected in summer, sown in late summer; maintain cool, moist conditions; winter seedlings in the cold frame and transplant to permanent locations in spring.
Seed may be sown in early spring. *V. cornuta* at 65 to 70 degrees, germinates in 14 to 20 days; *V. canadensis* should be stratified at cold temperatures over winter; *V. tricolor* needs cool nights to germinate (this is usually treated as an annual, for even if it lives

through the winter, the flowers are smaller and scanty).

Note that when collecting seeds in the field, for many of the species, the showy flowers are sterile and the flowers that bear the seeds are hidden under the leaves at the base of the plant. They are an inconspicuous green color and never open.

Cuttings of basal shoots after flowering.

Underground stolons.

Division in early spring or late summer after flowering. Plants may be collected in the field if the soil is moist and cool and they are dug with a ball of soil.

Culture: Sun or open shade (seedlings require shade). Well-drained, neutral, humusy soil. They love a very rich soil and benefit from having well-rotted manure worked into the bed. Space pansies 6 inches apart, violas 4 inches apart. Cut off faded flowers to prolong the season.

The western species, except *V. pedunculata*, will probably have to be collected in the field; I do not know of a commercial source. All the other species mentioned are available from American or English seedsmen or nurseries.

Use: Rock garden. Border. Woodland garden. Shady ground cover. Cut flower.

Species and varieties:

V. adunca (syn. *V. subvestita*) Purple, Blue or Hook Violet: Variable species. Flowering

stem to 8 inches high. Ovate leaves to 1½ inches long, slightly toothed. Flowers blue-violet, ½ inch long; the lower petal is spur-like. May/July. Meadow and woodland of the Rocky Mountains.

V. blanda (Sweet White Violet): 3 to 5 inches. Stoloniferous. Pubescent, heart-shaped leaves. Short-stemmed, solitary, fragrant, tiny, white, purple-veined flowers. April/May. A good shady ground cover. Found in wet meadow and moist woods from Quebec to Minnesota and southward.

V. canadensis (Canadian or Yellow-eye Violet): 12 inches. Heart-shaped leaves with pointed tips. White flowers, veined and often tinged with violet on undersides, yellow centers. Blooms on and off through summer and fall. Easy to grow in average soil and shade. Canadian woodlands and southward into the northern states.

V. cornuta (Tufted Pansy. Horned Violet): 6 to 8 inches. Spreads by underground stolons. Violet flowers, to 1½ inches across, with distinctive spur. May/July. Originally from the Pyrenees. Many named varieties; "*alba*," white; "Bambini"; "Blue Gem" (syn. "Jersey Gem"); "Papillo."

V. cucullata (Blue Marsh Violet): 6 inches. Tufted habit. Heart-shaped leaves. Long-stemmed, fragrant, blue-violet flowers. April/June. A vigorous plant, any good soil will do even though it is natively a marsh plant found from Canada to as far south as Georgia.

Viola cornuta papillo, Tufted Pansy

V. gracilis: 6 inches. Spreads by creeping runners. Starry, purple-violet flowers. Native to eastern Europe. Var. "Lord Nelson," deep blue flowers; "*lutea splendens.*" yellow.

V. hybrida: "Arkwright's Ruby," 6 to 10 inches, ruby-crimson; "Mrs. Dutton," primrose to pale yellow shades; grandiflora hybrids or Tufted Pansy include "Blue Heaven," "Clear Crystals," solid color (no patches), and "Perfection Blue."

V. nephrophylla: Leaves and flowers rise directly from the crown. Purple, lilac, or blue, stemless flowers. May/July. This plant does not produce runners. Found in the open forests of the Rockies.

V. nuttallii (Yellow Violet): Lance-shaped leaves. Bright yellow flowers. May/July. Rocky Mountains.

V. odorata (Sweet or Garden Violet. Florists or English Violet): 6 inches. Spreads by runners, rooting at the nodes. Broad, heart-shaped leaves. Very fragrant, single or double flowers, short-spurred and usually in violet shades, rarely rose or white. Many varieties: *semperflorens,*" pinkish-lavender; "*sulphurea,*" yellow: "Princess of Wales," blue; "*rosina,*" pink to rose, blooms in spring and again in fall; "The Czar," 9 inches, blue; "Double Russian," small, double, purple flowers in June; "Royal Robe," 8 inches, dark violet-blue.

V. papilionacea (Common Blue Violet): Vigorous blue violet; do not plant too near the shyer types, for these are spreaders. Resembles *V. cucullata* but the leaves are larger and the flowers a deeper shade. Found from Maine to Wyoming and southward. Var. "*priceana*" (or Confederate Violet), flowers pale grey-blue with blue veins.

V. pedata (Pansy Violet. Bird's Foot Violet): 4 to 6 inches. Tufted habit. Deeply divided leaves somewhat resemble a bird's foot. Flattish pansy-like flower, 1 inch across, usually bicolored, the two upper petals deep violet, the lower petals pale laven-der. April/May and again in fall. Must have sun and a gravelly, slightly acid soil. Found from Maine to Minnesota and south to Texas.

V. pedunculata (Yellow Pansy. Johnny-Jump-Up): A Californian native with golden flowers, veined in brown.

V. praemorsa: Long-stemmed, oval leaves. Yellow flowers, often shading to bronze on the outer edges of the petals. The whole plant is covered with downy hairs. May/July. Rocky Mountains.

V. pubescens (Downy Yellow): 8 to 12 inches. Long-stemmed, small, bright yellow flowers, brown veined, in terminal clusters. April/May. Broad, downy leaves. Prefers a sandy soil and light shade. Found from Maine to South Dakota and south.

V. rotundifolia (Round Leaf Violet): Large, round leaves lie close to the ground. Yellow flowers. Blooms very early, soon after the snow melts. April/May. Native to the coniferous forests from Maine to Ontario and south as far as Pennsylvania. Requires a cool, moist, acid soil. Difficult to propagate except by seed. Makes an excellent shady ground cover if conditions are met.

V. rugulosa: Resembles *V. canadensis* but is a larger, more vigorous plant, and the underside of the leaf is hairy. Spreads by stolons as well as by seed. Western American.

V. sagittata (Arrowleaf Violet): Arrow-shaped leaves. Flowers deep blue to violet shades with white centers. Maine to Minnesota and south to Texas.

V. tricolor (Viola. Johnny-Jump-Up): 6 to 9 inches. Tufted habit. Flowers in purple, blue, yellow, or white combinations. May/July. Short-lived but self-sows readily. Var. "*maxima* Cardinal Giant"; "Chantreyland," apricot; "Englmann's Giant"; "Felix Strain," large, cat's whiskered on yellow centers; "Feltham Triumph"; "Westland Giants" largest flowered strain; "Swiss Giants" and the "Roggli Strains."

V. tricolor hortensis (syn. *major*) Pansy. Heart's Ease: Biennial or short-lived perennial. Flowers, 2 to 4 inches across, plain or bicolored, striped or blotched, short spurred.

Viscaria

(syn. *LYCHNIS*) . ...

Family: *Caryophyllaceae* (Pink).

Common name: German Catchfly.

Propagation: Sow in spring at 45 degrees; germination in 12 days.

Culture: Sun. Light soil. Set out plants in groups of 4 to 6, spacing 8 inches apart.

Use: Border. Rock garden. Wild garden.

Species and varieties:

V. vulgaris splendens (syn. *V. viscosa*): Clumps of grass-

Viscaria vulgaris splendens,
German Catchfly

like foliage. Hollow flower stems, 18 inches high; the brownish portion of the stem beneath the flowers is as sticky as fly paper. Clusters of reddish-purple or white flowers in May; a rather short blooming season, but as it is one of the first flowers to appear in spring, it is very appreciated. Var. "*flore-pleno,*" 20 or more flowering spikes to a plant, 12 to 18 inches high, topped by double rose-red flowers.

Wahlenbergia

(syn.*EDRAIANTHUS*) ......

Family: *Campanulaceae* (Bellflower).

Common name: Wheel Bell.

Propagation: Seed sown at 65 degrees; germination in 11 days.

Division in spring.

Culture: Sun. Open, well-drained site. Gravelly, limy soil. Limestone scree. The "wheel" is about 12 to 18 inches in diameter——space plants accordingly.

Use: Rock garden.

Species:

W. pumilo: Greyish, linear leaves, ½ inch long. Mound habit. Single to few up-facing, blue-purple bells. May/June. Dalmatian.

W. tenuifolia: 3 inches. Quite different from *W. pumilo*. The procumbent, leafy branches form whorls extending out from tht crown like spokes on a wheel. Erect, up-facing, blue bells in clusters on the branch tips. Mediterranean.

Watsonia

Family: *Iridaceae* (Iris).

Common name: Bugle Lily.

Propagation: Sow in spring at 65 degrees; germination is slow, to 8 weeks. Winter the seedlings in cool greenhouse to develop as much foliage as possible. Raising plants from seed offers a great deal of variation.

Offsets of corms.

Culture: Sun. Sandy loam with peat added. Set corms 3 to 6 inches deep. Water well to force growth as with galtonia; they need a long growing season; start early in frame or greenhouse. Lift before freezing and store in cool, dry, frost-free place. These usually require staking. Dormancy period is short; spot check bulbs often. If growth has started, pot up and grow cool.

Use: Border. Cool greenhouse. Cut flower.

Species and varieties:

W. ardernei: 3½ feet. White flowers.

W. beatricis: 3 feet. Evergreen. Yellow-red flowers, 3 inches long. July/August.

W. brevifolia: 1½ feet. Rose-red flowers.

W. bulbillifera: Rose-flowered species; bulbils form in the upper leaf axils.

W. coccinea: Scarlet-flowered species.

W. fourcadei: 3½ feet high with salmon-pink flowers.

W. hybrida: 3½ to 5 feet. Branching stems. Flowers resemble those of gladiolus but are smaller and more tubular in shape. They come in shades of orange, pink, and red. August to frost.

W. iridifolia: 4 feet. Pink flowers. Variety *"obrieni"* is white.

W. longifolia: 5 feet. Flowers may be white, pink, or rose.

W. marginata: 5 feet high. Fragrant, rose-red flowers.

W. meriana: 4 feet. Rose flowers.

W. pillansi: 6 feet tall with red flowers.

W. rosea: 4 to 6 feet. Deciduous. Spike-like clusters of rose flowers on branching stems.

W. vanderspuyae: 5 feet high. Purple-flowered species.

Wyethia

Family: *Compositae* (Daisy).

Common name: Mule's Ears.

Propagation: Seed collected and sown in fall (sometimes offered by seed houses). Sow in spring at 65 degrees.

Culture: Sun or open shade. Porous, gravelly, well-drained soils (I have noted this also growing in rather heavy clay soils). Dry or moist. When collecting plants in the field, it is wiser to choose the smallest specimens in the patch, as they have a rather long tap root. Dormant by late summer.

Use: Wild flower garden. Your rancher friend (or husband) may consider this a weed, but it is easily controlled by removing the seed heads (it spreads only by seed). The artist in you will enjoy the bright patches of color.

Species:

W. amplexicaulis: 1 to 2 feet. Leaves are shiny green, mostly basal, oblong lance shaped, erect, and often taller than the flower stem. One to 5 flower heads to a stem, bright yellow-orange rays and discs, 2 to 3 inches across. May/July. Northern Rocky Mountains, up to 7,500 feet.

W. helianthoides (White Mule's Ears): 8 to 20 inches. Very like the above species, but the rays are white or creamy colored, 2 to 5 inches across, and the flower stems are hairy. May/July. Found in rather wet sites from the foothills to 8,000 feet in the northern Rockies.

Xerophyllum

Family: *Liliaceae* (Lily).

Common name: Beargrass. Turkey Beard.

Propagation: Seed collected and sown in fall. Seed sown in spring needs a period of one or two months of freezing temperatures, or it will not germinate until the second spring. (Plants are obtainable from commerical sources.)

Division: As with yucca, only the small perimeter plants can be moved successfully. Be very careful not to injure the roots' thin outer layers.

Culture: Sun or part shade. Well-drained, sandy loam with a good quantity of peat added. Space 2 feet apart, planting in groups of three or more. Difficult to cultivate but well worth the effort.

Use: Border. Wild garden.

Species:

X. asphodeloides: 5 feet. Long, narrow leaves in basal clump. Flower stem rises from the center of the leaves. Fragrant, small, yellowish-white flowers in raceme 6 inches long. May/July. Eastern species, found in slightly acid, dry, sandy pine woods from New Jersey to Georgia.

X. tenax: Flowering stalk 2 to 6 feet high. Evergreen, stiff, grass-like leaves to 3 feet long, in basal clumps. Numerous, tiny, white flowers with violet stamens form a dense, pyramid-shaped raceme. June/September (depending on elevation). Does not bloom every year. Prefers a rocky soil with excellent drainage. Found in alpine meadows or open woods of the Rockies, 3,000 to 8,000 feet.

Yucca

Family: *Liliaceae* (Lily).

Common name: Small Soap-weed. Soapweed Yucca. Small Spanish Bayonet. Dwarf Blue Yucca.

Propagation: Seed collected and sown immediately, sprouts readily; otherwise, store and sow in spring at 45 degrees; germination in 3 weeks. It takes 3 or more years to bloom from seed. These have long tap roots; transplanting must be done while the plant is small.

Division is not easy, but you may have some success by removing the small new plants which form around the perimeter of the old clump.

Culture: Sun. Sandy, well-drained soil. Dry, Space 12 to 15 inches apart in groups of 3 or 4.

Use: Border accent. Strategic-ally placed, they will divert dogs and children from cutting corners through lawn or garden.

Species:

Y. filamentosa (Adam's Needle): Resembles *Y. flaccida*, but leaves and flower clusters are narrower. Native to southeastern states.

Y. flaccida: Stemless. Leaves to 2½ feet long with loose fibers on the edges. Flowers in branching clusters. Flower-ing stalk 4 to 7 feet high. Also found in the south-eastern states.

Y. glauca: 2 - to 3-foot-high erect flowering stalk with white to greenish-white, drooping flowers. July/August. Although the flowers are perfect (contain both male and female parts), they depend on a small moth for pollinization. Stemless. Sharp-pointed, stiff, ever-green leaves, 1 to 2½ feet long, form a basal clump. Native throughout the western states from Montana to Texas.

172

Bibliography

Aiken, George D. *Pioneering With Wildflowers*. Englewood Cliffs, New Jersey: Prentice-Hall, 1968.

Brooklyn Botanic Garden *Plants and Gardens,* Vol. 18. (A booklet published quarterly by the Brooklyn Botanic Garden, Brooklyn, New York and well worth becoming acquainted with by gardeners everywhere. This issue is devoted to wild flowers of America, all regions, and their propagation.) Spring, 1962.

Calkins, Carroll, *Gardening with water, Plantings and Stone*. New York: Walker & Co., 1974.

Craighead, John J., Craighead, Frank C., and Davis, Ray J., *A Field Guide to Rocky Mountain Wildflowers*. Boston: Houghton Mifflin, 1963.

Cumming, Robert W. and Lee, Robert E. *Contemporary Perennials*. New York: Macmillan, 1960.

Emery, D. *Seed Propagation of Native California Plants*. *Leaflet,* vol. 1, no. 10. Santa Barbara, California: Santa Barbara Botanic Garden, 1964.

Free, Montague. *All About the Perennial Garden*. New York: Doubleday, 1955.

——————————.
Plant Propagation in Pictures. New York: Doubleday, 1957.

Foster, H. L. *Rock Gardening*. Boston: Houghton Mifflin, 1968.

Heritage, Bill. *The Lotus Book of Water Gardening*. London: Hamlyn, 1973.

Hull, H. S. *Wild Flowers for Your Garden*. New York. Gramercy, 1951.

Johnson, M. P. *The Concise Encyclopedia of Favorite Flowers*. New York: Doubleday, 1953.

Kelly, George. *Rocky Mountain Horticulture*. Boulder, Colorado: Pruett Press, 1967.

McDougall, W. B. and Baggley, Herma A. *Plants of Yellowstone National Park*. Yellowstone Library and Museum Assoc., 1956.

Nehrling, Arno, and Nehrling, Irene. *Easy Gardening With Drought-Resistant Plants*. New York: Hearthside, 1968.

——————————.
The Picture Book of Perennials. New York: Hearthside, 1964.

Novak, F. A. *The Pictorial Encyclopedia of Plants and Flowers*. New York: Crown, and London: Hamlyn, 1966.

Nuese, J. *The Country Garden*. New York: Scribners, 1970.

Ortloff, H. S. and Raymore, H. B. *A Book About Soils for the Home Gardener*. New York: Barrows, 1962.

Rockwell, F. F. and Grayson, Esther C. *The Complete Book of Bulbs.* New York: Doubleday, 1953.

Steffek, E. F. *Wild Flowers and How to Grow Them*. New York: Crown, 1963.

Sunset Western Garden Book, edited by Sunset Magazine and Sunset Books. Menlo Park, California: Lane Magazine and Book Company, 1967.

Taylor, K. S. and Hamblin, S. F. *Handbook of Wild Flower Cultivation*. New York: Macmillan, 1963.

The University of California System of Producing Healthy Container-Grown Plants. Manual 23. Berkeley 4, California: Agricultural Publications, University of California, 1957.

United States Department of Agriculture. *Seeds—The 1961 Yearbook of Agriculture*. Washington, D.C.: Government Printing Office, 1961.

United States Forest Service. *Range Plant Handbook*. Washington, D. C.: Government Printing Office, 1937.

——————————.
Woody-Plant Seed Manual. Miscellaneous Publication No. 654. Washington, D. C.: Government Printing Office, 1948.

Wells, J. S. *Plant Propagation Practices*. New York: Macmillan, 1963.

Wilson, Helen Van Pelt. *Helen Van Pelt Wilson's Own Garden and Landscape Book*. Garden City, New York: Doubleday, 1973.

Table of Equivalents

1 teaspoon equals ⅓ tablespoon or 80 drops
1 tablespoon equals 3 teaspoons or ½ ounce
2 tablespoons equal ⅛ cup or 1 ounce
1 cup equals 16 tablespoons or 8 ounces or ½ pint
2 cups equal 16 ounces or 1 pint or ½ quart
2 pints equal 32 ounces or 1 quart
4 quarts equal 128 ounces or 1 gallon

Dilutions for garden chemicals in liquid form (always use a level measure) are as follows:
If concentration in bottle is stated to be 1-10 and you want to make a quart, use 3 ounces of concentrate per quart; use 12 ounces for 1 gallon and to make 2 gallons use 1½ pints concentrate.

1-50 use 4 teaspoons concentrate per quart; 5 tablespoons per 1 gallon; 5 ounces for 2 gallons.

1-80 use 1 tablespoon concentrate for 1 quart; 2 ounces for 1 gallon; 4 ounces per 2 gallons water.

1-100 use 2 teaspoons concentrate per quart of water; 2½ tablespoons per 1 gallon; 2½ ounces per 2 gallons.

1 cubic foot of soil equals 8 one gallon containers.

Sources of Supplies

Burgess Seed and Plant Co., P.O. Box 218, Galesburg, MI. 49053. Seeds, plants, and bulbs.

Burnett Brothers, Inc., 92 Chambers St., New York, NY 10007. Seeds, bulbs, and plants.

W. Atlee Burpee Co., Clinton, IA. 52732. Plants, bulbs, seeds, and garden supplies.

Clyde Robin, P.O. 2091, Castro Valley, CA. 94546. Wild flower seeds, plants, bulbs, also tree seeds and nursery stock. Plants are very well packed and arrive in excellent condition.

Farmer Seed and Nursery Co., Fairbault, MN. 55201. Seeds and plants.

Gardens of the Blue Ridge, Ashford, McDowell Co., N.C. 28603. Wild flowers, ferns, and bog plants.

Gurney Seed and Nursery Co., Yankton, SD 57078. Seeds and plants.

Joseph Harris Co., Inc., Moreton Farm, 3670 Buffalo Road, Rochester, NY 14624. Seeds.

A. H. Hummert Seed Co., 2746 Chouteau Ave., St. Louis, MO 63103. Seeds, bulbs, and garden equipment. Wide range of fertilizers, insecticides, plant containers, greenhouse supplies, etc.; equipment which would be difficult to find locally.

J. W. Jung Seed Co., Randolph, WI 53956. Seeds, bulbs and plants.

Hollands Glory, Inc., 1360 Stony Brook Road, Stony Brook, Long Island, NY 11790. U.S. representative of a Dutch firm. Bulbs.

Horta-Craft Corp., 1100 Industrial Park Blvd., Albion, MI 49224. Plant markers and tags.

Jamieson Valley Gardens, Jamieson Road, Rt. 3, Spokane, WA 99203. Wild flowers.

Lamb Nurseries, E. 101 Sharp Ave., Spokane, WA 99202. Include many of the perennials.

Earl May Seed and Nursery Co., Shenandoah, IA 51601. Seeds and plants.

Mellinger's Inc., 2310 West South Range Rd., North Lima, OH 44452. Excellent source of garden equipment at almost wholesale prices. Perennials and nursery stock, and although we are concerned in this volume with perennials, you may be interested to know they have an inclusive list of shrub and tree seeds as well.

Musser Forests, Inc., Indiana, PA 15701. Perennials as well as nursery stock.

Geo. W. Park Seed Co., Inc., Greenwood, SC 29646. Seeds, plants, bulbs, and garden supplies. Probably the largest listing of perennial seeds offered by an American seedsman.

Putney Nursery, Inc., Putney, VT 05346. Perennials and wild flowers.

John Scheepers, Inc., 63 Wall Street, New York, NY 10005. Bulbs, ferns, and wild flowers.

Sperka's Woodland Acres Nursery, Crivitz, WI 54114. Perennials, wild flowers, and ferns.

Sterns Nurseries, Inc., Geneva, NY 14456. Plants and bulbs. Catalog 50¢.

Thompson & Morgan P. O. Box 24, 401 Kentucky Blvd., Somerdale, NJ 08083. (American outlet for English firm) This English seedhouse is the source of most of my perennials (including wild flowers), for they probably have the most comprehensive list of seeds to be found anywhere.

Thon's Garden Mums, 4815 Oak Street, Crystal Lake IL. 60014.

The Tree Laurels, Madison County, Marshall, NC 28753. Wild flowers.

Three Springs Fisheries, Lilypons, MD 21717. Water plants. Catalog 50¢.

Van Bourgondien Bros., Dept. 4, P.O. Box A, Babylon, NY 11702. Bulbs and plants.

The Wayside Gardens Co., Mentor, OH 44060. Catalog $2.00.

White Flower Farm, Litchfield, CT 06759. Catalog $2.50.

Gilbert H. Wild & Son, Inc., Sarcoxie, MO 64862. Peonies, iris, and day lilies. Catalogue 50¢.

Plant Index